LITURGICAL
SPIRITUALITY

WEIL SERIES IN LITURGICS

LITURGICAL SPIRITUALITY

Anglican Reflections on the Church's Prayer

EDITED BY STEPHEN BURNS

Seabury Books
NEW YORK

Unless otherwise noted, the Scripture quotations contained herein are from the New Revised Standard Version Bible, copyright © 1989 by the Division of Christian Education of the National Council of Churches of Christ in the U.S.A. Used by permission. All rights reserved.

Library of Congress Cataloging-in-Publication Data

Liturgical spirituality : Anglican reflections on the church's prayer / edited by Stephen Burns.
    pages cm. -- (Weil studies in liturgics series)
  Includes bibliographical references.
  ISBN 978-1-59627-254-5 (pbk.) -- ISBN 978-1-59627-255-2 (ebook)
1. Anglican Communion--Liturgy. 2. Church year. 3. Prayer--Anglican Communion. I. Burns, Stephen, 1970– editor of compilation.
  BX5141.L58 2013
  264'.03--dc23
                        2013029525

Seabury Books
19 East 34th Street
New York, New York 10016

www.churchpublishing.org
An imprint of Church Publishing Incorporated

Printed in the United States of America

Contents

Introduction
to the Series

LOUIS WEIL'S ACADEMIC LIFE HAS paralleled the liturgical renewal that led up to—and grew out of—Vatican II. It has been a rich time of liturgical scholarship from the new discoveries regarding the Apostolic era to the latest research in neuropsychology and ritual studies. Louis Weil has been a pioneer in the scholarship of a generation.

In a teaching ministry of over fifty years, Weil has taught liturgical and sacramental studies at three Episcopal seminaries, in Puerto Rico, in Wisconsin, and in California. He has given programs for laity and clergy on five continents, and has written, either in books or articles, about the major aspects of liturgical renewal in the United States and abroad. In 2012, the North American Academy of Liturgy presented him with its *Berakah Award* for his work as a teacher of liturgy both ecumenically and in the Anglican Communion.

It is in recognition of his work in and on behalf of the Church he so loves that Church Publishing is proud to introduce the Weil Series in Liturgics, an occasional series dedicated to the sort of liturgical and academic scholarship that has been the hallmark of Weil's professional life.

Nancy Bryan
Editorial Director for Books and Music
Church Publishing, Inc.

Introduction

DON SALIERS' *WORSHIP AND SPIRITUALITY* includes a luminous sequence in which he correlates the practices of sacramental celebration and meanings of sacramental living. Saliers suggests, "The pattern [of Christ's actions at table: taking, blessing, breaking, and giving] gives us the very shape of the life God calls us to live responsibly in this world. . . ." Firstly, mirroring Jesus' taking of bread at table, in our own celebration of the eucharist we are to "offer ourselves . . . giving ourselves over to the mercy and to the compassion of the One who created all things and called them good." Secondly, mirroring Jesus' thanksgiving at table, we are to pattern our lives on the eucharistic prayer, for:

> The act of the great thanksgiving is what our lives are meant to be . . . We may follow in our lives the structure of the ancient eucharistic prayers: acknowledge God in praise for who God is, a mystery of being yet a furnace of compassion, our creator hidden in glory yet revealed in the whole created order . . . Then we acknowledge God's holiness . . . And, as the prayer of thanksgiving develops, so do our lives.[1]

For the eucharistic prayer illumines not only the faithfulness of God, but remembering events on "the night in which [Jesus] was betrayed" also illumines "our alienation, our turning aside." Thirdly, as Jesus broke bread at table, so too "our lives must be broken in order to be shared"; and fourthly, just as Jesus gave bread at table, "so we must be prepared to

---

1. Don E. Saliers, *Worship and Spirituality*, 2nd ed. (Akron, OH: OSL Publications, 1996), 68.

be given for others." For Saliers, eucharistic prayer links with life, embracing human hopes and fears, and giving shape to the life of Christian people:

> And this is the most terrifying and beautiful matter—through this form of life we receive back our own lives . . . Grace is given in the eucharist, but this is the grace we also encounter in offering, blessing, breaking open, and sharing our lives with all in this needy world. This is our lost identity; this is the secret hidden from the eyes of the detached and self-possessed world.[2]

These are demanding ideas for the practice of a liturgical spirituality. In his sequence of reflection, Saliers illumines the heart of such a spirituality for Christians in sacramental traditions, but the self-giving of God in the eucharist, and our response in return, is itself surrounded by a larger repertoire of liturgical action, including the various "moods" of prayer into which the liturgy beckons worshipers, as well as the seasons that envelop each particular celebration, each with their own distinctive timbre and tone. Each of these features and foci shapes liturgical spirituality, and so *Liturgical Spirituality* explores them in juxtaposition, placing the sacramental actions at the center of its reflections, and moving to and from them across wider terrain that relates liturgy and the fullness of life.

The essays that follow combine in different and related ways history, theology, reflection on practice, and personal testimony. They offer sometimes different perspectives, different "slants" on things—and occasionally on the same thing. They also commend some different approaches, emphases, and practices. For example, some begin to show the contours of key issues in recent liturgical revision in the Anglican Communion, highlighting some distinctions in ongoing liturgical reform between the Episcopal Church and others within the Anglican Communion—one notable instance being around

---

2. Saliers, *Worship and Spirituality* (1996), 68.

alternatives to the so-called "manual acts," which the 1979 Book of Common Prayer prescribes in the ritual action of the eucharist.[3] In all sorts of ways, the essays are an invitation to further exploration, opening up a conversation in which readers may place themselves, find their own voice, and perhaps encounter both affirmation and questions from the writers here. No doubt part of the difference that emerges across the essays is because the authors quite literally come from different places, but also because they represent appreciation of different traditions all characteristic of Anglicanism. Together, they are an invitation to "real presence" in worship—they call readers to participation that is sensitive, non-defensive, animated.

---

3. On this point, the present volume offers further vantage points around a key concern in its predecessor in the Weil Series on Liturgics, Louis Weil's own *Liturgical Sense: The Logic of Rite* (New York: Church Publishing, 2012).

Contributors

Alan Bartlett is Vicar of St. Giles, Durham and Visiting Fellow in Anglicanism at Cranmer Hall, St. John's College, Durham. His publications include *Humane Christianity* (2004) and *A Passionate Balance: The Anglican Tradition* (2007).

Stephen Burns is Associate Professor of Liturgical Theology and the Study of Anglicanism at Episcopal Divinity School, Cambridge. His publications include *Liturgy* (2006), *Worship in Context* (2006), *Exchanges of Grace* (co-editor, 2008), *The Edge of God* (co-editor, 2008), *Christian Worship in Australia* (co-editor, 2009), *Presiding Like a Woman* (co-editor, 2010), *Christian Worship: Postcolonial Perspectives* (co-author, 2011), *The Art of Tentmaking* (editor, 2012), *Pilgrim People* (2012), *Worship and Ministry* (2012), and *Home and Away* (co-editor, 2013).

Ellen Clark-King is Archdeacon of Vancouver. Her publications include *Theology by Heart* (2004) and *A Path to Your Door* (2011).

Mark Earey is Tutor in Liturgy at the Queen's Foundation for Ecumenical Theological Education, Birmingham. His publications include *Producing Your Own Orders of Service* (2000), *Common Worship Today* (co-editor, 2001), *Liturgical Worship* (2002), *Connecting with Baptism* (co-editor, 2007), *Finding Your Way Around Common Worship* (2011), *Worship that Cares* (2012), and *Beyond Common Worship* (2013).

Harriet Harris is Chaplain at the University of Edinburgh. Her publications include *Faith Without Hostages* (2003), *The Call for Women Bishops* (co-editor, 2004), *Faith and Philosophical Analysis* (co-editor, 2005), *Fundamentalism and Evangelicals* (2008), and *God, Goodness and Philosophy* (editor, 2011).

Lizette Larson-Miller is Nancy and Michael Kaehr Professor of Liturgical Leadership at Church Divinity School of the Pacific, Berkeley. Her publications include *The Sacrament of Anointing of the Sick* (2005) and *Drenched in Grace* (co-editor, 2013).

Ruth A. Meyers is Hodges-Haynes Professor of Liturgics at Church Divinity School of the Pacific, Berkeley and Chair of the Episcopal Church's Standing Committee on Liturgy and Music. Her publications include *Worship-Shaped Life* (co-editor, 2010).

Stephen Platten is Bishop of Wakefield and Chair of the Church of England's Liturgical Commission. His publications include *Ink and Spirit* (editor, 2000), *Runcie: On Reflection* (editor, 2002), *Anglicanism and the Western Catholic Tradition* (co-editor, 2003), *Dreaming Spires?* (co-editor, 2006), *Rebuilding Jerusalem* (2007), *Vocation* (2007), *Reinhold Niebuhr and Contemporary Politics* (co-editor, 2010), and *Comfortable Words* (co-editor, 2012).

John Pritchard is Bishop of Oxford. His publications include *Leading Intercessions* (2004), *Beginning Again* (2005), *Practical Theology in Action* (co-author, 2006), *The Life and Work of a Priest* (2007), *How to Explain Your Faith* (2006), *Living Jesus* (2010), *Going to Church* (2010), *How to Pray* (2011), *The Intercessions Handbook* (2011), *God Lost and Found* (2011), and *Living Faithfully* (2013).

Mark Pryce is Bishop's Advisor in the Diocese of Birmingham. His publications include *Literary Companion to the Lectionary* (2001), *Literary Companion to Festivals* (2003), and *Journeying with Luke* (co-author, 2012).

David Runcorn is a "free range priest" who was formerly Tutor in Spirituality at St. John's College, Nottingham. His publications include *Choice, Desire and the Will of God* (2003),

Rumours of Life (2006), *A Spirituality Workbook* (2007), and *Fear and Trust* (2011).

David Stancliffe is retired and was Bishop of Salisbury and former Chair of the Church of England's Liturgical Commission. His publications include *God's Pattern* (2003), *The Pilgrim Prayerbook* (2007), and *Church Architecture* (2009).

John B. Thomson is Director of Ministry in the Diocese of Sheffield. His publications include *The Ecclesiology of Stanley Hauerwas* (2003), *Church on Edge?* (2004), *DOXA* (editor, 2007), and *Living Holiness* (2010).

Part One

Moods of Prayer

T FIRST LOOK, PRAYER MIGHT seem easy. After all, the Latin *precai*, from which we get the word "prayer," simply means to beg. When we draw in some of the basic meanings carried by the words translated as "pray/er" in the Hebrew Bible, we then find at least: ask, bend, and bow. Each of these might be part of begging. From the Greek of the New Testament, we have vow, wish, and call for. So the range of meanings expands again slightly. Prayer is a word or gesture that combines honor and beseeching.

Yet these simple words pale alongside the manifold, complex elaborations that the Christian tradition, over time, has nurtured in relation to prayer. To begin to do its richness justice, we need to consider prayer in its public and private modes (the former linking back at least to memories of Jesus in the synagogue and temple, the latter linking back to Jesus' talk of "secret" prayer in Matthew 6:6)—that is, expressions of both devotional and communal prayer (though with both in relation to the prayers of the saints and the "whole company of heaven"). We need to consider creative and extempore[1] forms (including *glossalalia*, that is, "speaking in tongues") alongside disciplined forms of silence, song,[2] music, and other arts (e.g., of icons being painted as acts of prayer). Alongside spontaneous and sensory experiences of prayer, we then need to remember particular texts and patterns of prayer we inherit from our forebears, some of which draw, in a wide variety of ways, from the scriptures—leaning

---

1. Ruth Duck, *Finding Words for Worship: A Guide for Leaders* (Louisville, KY: Westminster John Knox Press, 1995); Laurence Hull Stookey, *Let the Whole Church Say Amen! A Guide for Those Who Pray in Public* (Nashville, TN: Abingdon Press, 2002).

2. See Brian Wren, *Praying Twice: The Music and Words of Congregational Song* (Louisville, KY: Westminster John Knox Press, 2000).

into the Prayer That Jesus Taught and the Lucan songs that shape daily offices[3] are just two of the most obvious examples. And all this is before we start to name different traditions, schools, and styles of prayer that have developed in different times and places, all of which leave a lively legacy and offer orientation to present-day pray-ers: the early desert abbas and ammas, Benedict and Francis and their heirs, Julian of Norwich[4] and her mystic revelations—these as a handful of examples among a massive host of others. Towering figures in the Christian spiritual tradition—Julian, Francis, Benedict, et al.—take their place in a company that encircles the spiritual companionship available through the pages of the writings of more recent seekers: Evelyn Underhill, Henri Nouwen, and Dorothee Soelle, for example, apart from contemporary spiritual classics and introductions to the fertile realms of "spirituality" that will fascinate and beckon those willing to be open to them. All of this means that there is plenty of help available to encourage the contemporary person who desires to pray, if they can learn where to look and are willing to live with a measure of strangeness inevitably involved in an attempt to attend to others' particular experiences across time and space. These rich seams of prayer take us beyond "techniques" and in many various ways can teach pray-ers to ally their prayer to action, perhaps even to consider their intent to live a life of love and share caring acts as itself a kind of prayer, or indeed, to come to see themselves as a "living prayer." So, on action as a kind of prayer, Ann Loades writes of child-rearing like this:

> For Christians at any rate, having children is now
> a vocation, a witness to our faith in God as well as
> a kind of living prayer for the future of the world in
> which they live. Having children can be seen as a

---

3. These with other scriptural and ancient texts form the "prayers we have in common," ecumenically, across many Christian traditions.

4. Benedict: July 11; Francis: October 4; Julian: May 8 in the *sanctorale* of the Uniting Church in Australia. *Uniting in Worship 2* (Sydney: Uniting Church Press, 2005), 566–71.

kind of ministry, in which adults receive from children as much as vice versa . . .[5]

And the idea of actually becoming a prayer comes to dazzling focus in the hagiographies of St. Francis, of whom it is said: "More than someone who prayed, he had become a prayer."[6]

Part One of this book attends to particular modes and moods of prayer in the liturgy: thanksgiving, praise, confession, and intercession. These forms of prayer are present in the liturgy in different ways—surfacing, as it were, in hymns and songs; in "prayers we have in common" like the *kyrie eleison, Gloria in excelsis*, and so on—themselves often sung—apart from the thanksgiving of the eucharistic prayer; or the intercessions that shape the Prayers of the People. The Prayers of the People themselves invite a blending of thanksgiving and intercession. And the collect is a distinct, succinct style of prayer that honors and asks things of God in a single terse, graceful sentence.

Stephen Platten writes about giving thanks. He begins and continually returns to the much-loved story of Gerald Durrell, *My Family and Other Animals*, tracing connections between thanksgiving, happiness, gift, and grace. As his chapter unfolds, he draws not only on the magic of Durrell's narratives, but amongst other things on writing that emerged in the awful context of Nazi concentration camps, where— remarkably—some persons forced into such hideous places found it somehow possible to find cause to give thanks to God. Platten turns to other pieces of literature, between the charms of Durrell and the horror of the Holocaust, to explore "the ambiguity of Christian thanksgiving." So a diverse range of reference shapes his evocative speech of "profitable wonders," of being "un-selfed" by God, and other dynamics involved in becoming "a eucharistic person." While his explorations do indeed make special reference to eucharistic prayer (as well

---

5. Ann Loades, "Death and Disvalue: Some Reflections on 'Sick' Children," *Hospital Chaplain* 93 (1985): 11.

6. William Short, OFM, *Poverty and Joy: The Franciscan Tradition* (London: DLT, 1999), 31.

as the "general thanksgiving"), in fact he offers not simply an understanding of liturgical modes of thanksgiving, but a vision of grace-filled life in a world of both beauty and terror, and beloved by God.

Mark Earey focuses on praise, an activity he describes as "resulting from something wonderful." Like Platten, he places the mode of prayer that is his particular focus within an understanding of other modes of prayer in and beyond the setting of eucharistic worship, and especially suggests how praise is an outward and communal expression of adoration. It is embodied— possibly resulting in persons who give praise "looking funny"— and this is one dimension of it being public, "political" even, possibly putting the ones giving praise at odds with all that might contest or distract from the center of the wonderful "something" of God to whom praise is offered. As such, praise is much more than joyful singing; it is a way of life within which every action of the worshipers may come to express.

Harriet Harris writes on confession. She finds orientation for her reflections in Luke 15, the parable of the forgiving father/prodigal son. Harris sets this parable at the center of a rich tapestry of biblical references, into which she also draws extracts from spiritual writings, liturgical texts, and narrative testimony from Poland and Kenya. Likewise, she sets the penitential rite of Holy Communion within a wider frame of "multiple opportunity to confess throughout the service." She argues that the eucharist "schools" us in repentance, and throughout she places emphasis on God's mercy, which is "God's perfection."

Unlike Harris' essay, the final chapter includes no direct reference to biblical texts; rather John Pritchard provides a vivid reflection on experience, beginning from his sense of something "amiss" with the way the prayers of the people can be offered. As well as clearly pointing to problems with how intercession is sometimes approached, he also asserts the opportunity for them to be lively, engaging, and helpful, giving us a stream of ideas and directly discussing a number of possible practices. In doing so, he helps us to "stretch the possibilities" of our common prayer so that we might "get hold of God."

CHAPTER 1

Thanksgiving

Stephen Platten

In Newness of Life: Eucharistic Living

"CHAIRETE," HE CALLED IN HIS deep voice, the beautiful Greek greeting, *"chairete, kyrioi"* . . . be happy.

The goats poured among the olives, uttering stammering cries to each other, the leader's bell clonking rhythmically. The chaffinches tinkled excitedly. A robin puffed out his chest like a tangerine among the myrtles and gave a trickle of song. The island was drenched with dew, radiant with early morning sun, full of stirring life. Be happy. How could one be anything else in such a season?[1]

Gerald Durrell's *My Family and Other Animals* has been a popular favorite since its first publication in 1956. Transformed into television programs, it continues to weave its magic spell. That brief opening quotation suggests why the book touches peoples' hearts. For alongside the humor and

---

1. Gerald Durrell, *My Family and Other Animals* (London: Puffin Books, 2006), 109.

Durrell's perceptive reflections about his family, it is ultimately a celebration of life. The humor itself is part of that celebration, but the focus is broader still. In that paragraph above, the animal and plant life of Corfu sing the song of happiness. There are countless other extracts in the book which pick up a similar resonant note. Durrell's youthful life on Corfu was formative, indeed seminal. Page by page his book celebrates the beauty of nature and the rich tapestry of human life. The characters, not only from within his own family but all who are caught up in his experience, are drawn with humor and generosity. It is not an overtly religious book, but much of the narrative, and certainly the description of the celebrations for St. Spyridon, the island's patron, in Corfu Town, capture the same sense of excitement and celebration.

That extract above begins with a Greek word *chairete*. Durrell translates it as: "Be happy." These same words are encountered in the New Testament. In Philippians 4:4, Paul exhorts his readers in almost precisely the same words: "Chairete, en kyrio," he writes. Here he means "rejoice in the Lord" and he refers us to Jesus, the incarnate Lord. Durrell's exhortation, from the lips of Yani, the Greek shepherd, are less portentous. He simply means "rejoice," or "be happy, sir!" *Kyrios* in modern Greek has come to have a less exalted feel; it has become a term of politeness, almost a part of social etiquette. But the resonances are still strong. Anyone knowing the New Testament could hardly fail to respond to these echoes. Durrell clearly intends a profound sense of happiness and thanksgiving to sound out from the lips of that Corfot shepherd. It says something about an attitude to life and indeed an attitude to the whole of creation.

Ironically, the echoes between modernity and antiquity, between contemporary Mediterranean culture and that of New Testament times, between Yani the shepherd and the life of Jesus do not end here. For, along with *kalimera* (good day) and *yasas* (hello), perhaps the most frequently used word in modern Greece, and so in Corfu, is the word *eucharisto*. It simply means "thanks," and although it is pronounced quite differently from our word *eucharist*, it is precisely the same word. So, it would not be pressing the meaning too far to say that Greek people (whether they consciously realize it or not) live "a eucharistic life." That same resonant word, which stands at the very heart of the Christian community, is on the lips of Greek men, women, and children, morning, noon, and night. It is one of the keynotes of their culture. Who would have thought that we could have found ourselves so profoundly caught up in elements of the Christian life starting from *My Family and Other Animals*?

Echoes and Resonances: "In Newness of Life"

Of course, we have only just got started. These are but echoes and resonances. It would be unfair to Durrell to turn his magical book, by sleight of hand, into a Christian classic. Nonetheless, it has set us out on our way. For these Greek words take us into the very center of Christian life down the ages and into the present day. What might this mean for Christian people? In the general confession, we are called to acknowledge our sins and to repent:

> Ye who do truly and earnestly repent you of your sins, and are in love and charity with your neighbors, and intend to lead a new life, following the commandments of God, and walking from henceforth in his holy ways: Draw near with faith, and make your humble confession to Almighty God . . .[2]

Repentance means a radical turning again, and the confession very positively moves on to make us say: "And grant that we may hereafter serve and please thee *in newness of life*, to the honor and glory of thy name; through Jesus Christ our Lord." Newness of life means a pattern of living fashioned after the manner of our sovereign and savior. It is a life rooted in the revolutionary teaching and ministry of Jesus.

---

2. Book of Common Prayer (New York: Church Publishing, 1979), 330.

The challenge of Jesus' teaching to his own age lay in his radical acceptance of all whom he met and his similarly refreshing acceptance of the whole of life as "gift." Again and again Jesus turns upside down the values and attitudes of the world. This is clear in his response to people. Sinners and outcasts are welcomed unconditionally. Jesus eats with Zacchaeus the tax collector (Luke 19:1–10); he refuses to condemn an adulterous woman (John 8:1–11): "Let anyone among you who is without sin be the first to throw a stone" (v. 7). In his healings he often begins with an unconditional forgiveness of sins. Not only does Jesus proclaim these values, which describe the divine reign through his responses and action; it is made clear, too, in his teaching and most obviously in his parables. Luke captures this most vividly in his gospel. The Good Samaritan acts compassionately almost by instinct (Luke 10:25–37); the tax collector beats his breast in penitence whereas the Pharisee seems to claim righteousness as his own (Luke 18:9–14). The father in the parable of the prodigal son embraces his returning wayward child; he remembers his son as "gift" and receives him back in the same manner (Luke 15:11–33). Matthew's account of the laborer in the vineyard indicates that justice and reward are just the beginning (Matthew 20:1–16). In the reign of God, all that we receive is gift and calls out of us our gratitude.

This essence of Jesus' teaching and ministry was captured well by Professor James Mackey when he was reflecting upon the nature of Christianity and Jesus' witness. The parables, Mackey argues, encapsulate this life of acceptance, giving, and ultimately sacrifice. In these unique stories Jesus describes what he also lives. Prayer and the eucharist, Mackey believes, are the ritual and service that stand at the heart of the way of Jesus, and the parables offer a pattern of living. So Mackey writes:

> Is there a shorter way of conveying an understanding of this experience, at once so complex to the analyst and apparently so singular to the one who enjoys it. Probably not . . . but if the experience

itself could find words to summarize its impact in a short space, it would say something like this:

The treasure we can at any moment discover, the banquet to which we are all equally invited.

That delay must not mar this discovery, nor decline the invitation, for such ingratitude instantly un-graces us; it means too that life is more than bread, more than accumulated possessions; that to realise the true value of someone or something and to discover treasure are one and the same imperative act.

That the true value of all that exists is discovered in the unique way in which one values a gift; that we should therefore not crush by grasping, or tear by trying to pull away. The gift has its roots in the giver; like a flower with roots hidden that breaks ground to brighten the common day . . .[3]

In these few sentences Mackey captures something of what is meant in the New Testament by the reign of God. It is a way of living, uniquely revealed in the life, ministry, and teaching, and in the passion, death, and resurrection of Jesus Christ. It is a way of living that is nothing less than participation with Christ and the Holy Spirit in the life of God. We set out something of this above from the New Testament in Jesus' life, witness, and ministry. It is what Paul describes elsewhere in the New Testament as the "new creation" (2 Corinthians 5:16–17). The reign of God with the set of responses seen in Jesus thus has its own patterning power for all humanity in all ages. This takes us to the very heart of the gospel as lived in Jesus. Indeed it has been claimed that "It is this patterning power of the kingdom that gives the Church its distinctive character."[4]

This pattern, then, is encapsulated in a way of living which receives life and indeed all experience as *gift*. Unexpectedly,

---

3. James Mackey, *Jesus the Man and the Myth* (London: SCM Press, 1979), 159.

4. ARCIC II, *Life in Christ: Morals, Communion and the Church* (London: SPCK/CTS, 1994), 8 (para. 20).

perhaps, we find ourselves back almost where we began. Yani, the shepherd, called out: *"chairete, kyrioi . . ."*—be happy, sir! *Chairete* is itself derived from the word *chara*, which means joy, and this word is closely related to *charis*, which is the word we translate as *grace*. The word *charis* is rich in resonances; it means graciousness, attractiveness, gracious care, or simply gift. Although he may not have realized it then, the attitude to life captured in much of Durrell's book exemplifies the essence of the Christian way. In doing so, it helps us to understand still more vividly what this might mean for us in our own contemporary world. For the Christian this is what life means within the "patterning power of the kingdom." It is the pattern established in Christ, but it is recognizable in Christian lives in every age. Durrell's recapturing of his youthful innocence focuses it perfectly. At root, it is a pattern fashioned by both *chara* (*joy*) and by *charis* (*grace* or *gift*). All this triggers within the human spirit one instinct and one only, the spirit of thanksgiving, of eucharist. That spirit can itself transform lives. The rite that above all manifests this is, of course, the eucharist itself. So, before we go any further, let us pause for a moment to reflect upon the eucharist, the sacrament of life and of thanksgiving.

A Rich Tapestry

One of the most vivid pictures of the celebration of the eucharist springs from Taizé in Burgundy in southeastern France. The community there witnesses to the life of God's reign in its commitment to peace and justice. The eucharist issues from that same commitment and also nourishes it. The scene there is still more remarkable because of the ecumenical nature of the religious community at Taizé. From across the world, Orthodox and Reformed Christians, Roman Catholics and Anglicans, Lutherans and Mennonites from all nations and countless ethnic groups receive communion together. The predominance of young people also enriches the picture of the nature of Christian community. The action of the eucharist both makes God's *Church* present through our gathering around the altar and assures all of God's presence there in

Jesus Christ. Fifty years ago, the Anglican Benedictine monk, Gregory Dix, helped us better understand the nature of the eucharist. Although understandings of the eucharist are now more sophisticated, it was Dix who showed the importance of the shape of the sacramental action. This has helped all to see that the eucharist is not a static rite, but rather that the unfolding drama of the sacrament itself establishes God's *presence*, which thus brings us into intimate communion with each other and with God. The proclamation of God's word, the different actions within the "liturgy of the eucharist" itself and the sending out—all form one integrated whole. At the center of this stands the great *prayer of thanksgiving*.

Thanksgiving is thus not only a synonym for eucharist, it is also there in the solemn central prayer said or sung by the presider of the rite. This prayer is variously known as the *prayer of consecration*, the *anaphora*, or the *canon* of the eucharist. Each of these independently is inadequate as a title for the prayer. *Prayer of consecration* can be confusing since now, within Christian theology, the entire sacrament is seen as one integrated piece of "eucharistic time"; time is transfigured as we experience *"communion in sacris,"* as it is technically known. Thus to look for a specific moment of consecration is misleading. *Canon*, too, can be misleading; it effectively means measuring rod or measuring line. It is an identifier of authenticity. Once again it can point too sharply to a specific moment when the bread and wine are believed to be consecrated. *Anaphora*, a Greek term, came from the root verb meaning "to offer." Frequently it was also used to refer to the whole liturgy and so is richer in its resonances, but even here the strict emphasis on offering focuses on just one element within a far richer whole. To speak of the great *prayer of thanksgiving*, however, weaves all of these strands into its rich tapestry. It reminds us too of the meaning of the entire liturgy, and of the way in which the eucharist encapsulates a life patterned by the reign of God. Eucharistic living transforms lives such that all our experience may then be received as *gift*, as *graced* by God in Jesus Christ.

Throughout its entire length, the great thanksgiving prayer makes all this possible in any number of different ways. Often, the prayer begins with a reminder that we are created primarily to offer God thanksgiving and praise. Then the mighty acts of God in Jesus are proclaimed, in thanksgiving for our redemption: Christ's offering on the cross, his passion, resurrection, and ascension are remembered and acclaimed. There will often also be specific thanksgiving for the saints and a looking forward to the fulfillment of the coming kingdom and reign of God. We pray too in that great prayer that God's Holy Spirit will sanctify both us and the gifts of bread and wine; here, too, is more cause for thanksgiving. But seminal to the prayer is the act of *remembering*. Remembering is indeed a key part of human experience. The philosopher Plato believed that all learning was remembering. He pictured our lives as being like a journey from a cave out into the world of reality. In the cave there are only images and shadows, copies or silhouettes of reality. As we journey through the cave toward reality, Plato believed that we learn by remembering the reality out of which we were born. Christian theology has always been far more rooted in history and in the mighty acts of God than this. We do remember, but we remember the saving acts of God in Jesus' life, death, and resurrection. As we remember them, so God in Christ is present to us every time we celebrate the eucharist. In this, we experience the redemption given by God, and we give thanks once again for that redemption and for our communion with and in Christ. This is why every time we celebrate the sacrament, at the heart of the eucharist, we repeat the words of Jesus, as recorded by Matthew, Mark, Luke, and Paul (John's account of the night before Jesus' death focuses on the footwashing, not the meal): we do this in remembrance of Jesus. Often the host and the chalice will be lifted up to remind us of Christ's sacrifice on the cross and to signify his nearer presence to us in the eucharist. The great prayer of thanksgiving is then a climax within the sacrament of the eucharist and it focuses the entire life of thanksgiving to which we are all called.

Life as Gift

We have, then, come full circle—back to living eucharistic lives. We have done so, however, by seeing how such lives must be rooted in the sacrament of the eucharist itself. It is the place, *par excellence*, where we are reminded of the patterning power of God's reign. It is the place where we see, through Christ's own sacrifice, how better to embrace life as gift and to offer ourselves in grace-filled lives. Christ's suffering and death are the culmination of a life of acceptance, of seeing life as gift. The effects of this transformation are seen not purely through the life of the individual. The eucharist is itself unavoidably a *corporate* rite. Indeed, another reason why the experience at Taizé is so moving and vivid is the sheer fact of numbers. Often five thousand or more people, from a great variety of traditions, come together to receive communion; the sacrament of thanksgiving sends them out to live eucharistic lives, powered by the mystery of Christ's redemptive sacrifice. This means the possibility of transformed communities alongside transformed individuals. This has its own theological impact. What might that impact be?

Even within Christianity itself there is a tendency to absolutize earthly principles. This is just one of the tendencies that helps keep Christ's Church divided. It also stands at the heart of divisions within individual churches; contemporary problems within both Roman Catholicism and the Anglican Communion stem partly from such absolutizing. This process of absolutizing makes belief in God as a gracious creator superfluous; the instincts implied earlier on, captured well in Durrell's writing, are sidelined. Life is no longer celebrated or seen as *gift*. Bringing thanksgiving back to the center of Christian faith is the essential antidote to these tendencies. Thanksgiving is not simply an added luxury alongside other modes and moods of prayer. Instead, thanksgiving for "life as gift" effectively relativizes the claims of earthly absolutes. It also relativizes the claims of dictators and the prophets of consumerism and other alternative heavens! Eucharistic living is authentic Christian living. A pattern of living rooted in thanksgiving cannot avoid seeing life as *gift*. If we return to Paul in Philippians, he puts this all in context:

> Rejoice in the Lord always; again I will say, Rejoice. Let your gentleness be known to everyone. The Lord is near. Do not worry about anything, but in everything by prayer and supplication with thanksgiving let your requests be made known to God. And the peace of God, which surpasses all understanding, will guard your hearts and minds in Christ Jesus. (Philippians 4:4–7)

This also places thanksgiving squarely alongside intercession, and reminds us that we *offer* ourselves in prayer rather than simply act as if we are customers in some sort of vast divine market.

Vocation

We have now seen, then, how thanksgiving is one of the fundamental instincts of the Christian life. We have seen, too, that the eucharist "incarnates" that principle for us and acts as a focal center for eucharistic lives. It does so both in our individual lives, but also in its effects upon the Church and potentially in the wider community. How do we see this being made effective in people's lives? One starting point is balance in both Christian theology and Christian life and prayer. So, it is essential for the Christian faith to take seriously the ambiguities of our world and of our experience. It is, for this reason, that *theodicy* is an essential part of the Christian tradition. Theodicy seeks to take seriously the problem of evil. How, if we believe in an almighty and loving God, do we explain the existence of evil and suffering? What logic can there be for the occurrence of earthquakes and flooding, of painful and crippling diseases? How do we account for the fallenness of humanity? In his "An Essay on Man," Alexander Pope summed this up very sharply: "Created half to rise, and half to fall; Great Lord of all things, yet a prey to all; Sole judge of truth, in endless error hurled; The glory, jest, and riddle of the world."[5]

Clearly, Christian theologians must answer these questions seriously and responsibly. Indeed, it is that final question about human fallibility that prompted the exclamation within the *Exsultet*, the ancient hymn used on Easter Eve: "O felix culpa!" O happy fault! For it was that fault, the hymn reminds us, that helped win us so great a redeemer in Jesus Christ.

But eucharistic living is by no means only a contemporary concern. Even a cursory glance through Christian literature makes this plain. Nor, indeed, does the ability to offer thanksgiving depend purely upon the sort of golden experiences recounted by Gerald Durrell in his Corfu childhood. Looking back to the twelfth century, for example, we encounter Peter Abelard, who, through his love for Éloise, suffered untold suffering, indignities, and tribulations. Out of the suffering, however, issued one of the great hymns of praise still regularly printed in our hymn books and sung in our churches. His hymn *O Quanta Qualia* ("O what their joy and their glory must be," *Hymnal 82*, no. 623) begins by singing of the "endless Sabbaths" the blessed enjoy in the fullness of God. Such Sabbaths are "crown for the valiant, [and] to weary ones rest." Later in his great hymn, Abelard is realistic about our trials and challenges, but still it is praise and thanksgiving that are the instinctive response: while "seeking Jerusalem," the heavenly home that is our "dear native land," we nevertheless yearn for this "with hearts raised on high." In the verses of his great hymn, Abelard combines our experience of suffering and joy, but offers it up in an individual and community song of thanksgiving.

A very different example of thanksgiving triumphing over grief and tragedy are found in many of the entries in the diary of Francis Kilvert.[6] Kilvert, an Anglican clergyman in the late nineteenth century, was struck down by ill health and died

---

5. Alexander Pope, "An Essay on Man," 1734, II.15–18.

6. For further information on Kilvert, please consult the website of the Kilvert Society: www.thekilvertsociety.org.uk.

when he was just thirty-eight years of age. Two extracts from his diary offer us the responses of a very different eucharistic life. First of all, echoes of resurrection:

> It was very sweet and lovely, the bright silent sunny morning, and the lark rising and singing alone in the blue sky, and then suddenly the morning air all alive with music of sweet bells ringing for the joy of the resurrection. "The Lord is risen" smiled the sun, "The Lord is risen" sang the lark. And the church bells in their joyous peeling, answered from tower to tower. "He is risen indeed."[7]

God's creation was often what awakened thanksgiving in Kilvert's heart. Here he captures well the different and contrasting moods suggested by landscape and weather:

> The afternoon had been stormy but it cleared towards sunset. Gradually the heavy rain clouds rolled across the valley to the foot of the opposite mountains and began climbing up their sides wreathing in rolling masses of vapour . . . The Black Mountains were invisible, being wrapped in clouds, and I saw one very white brilliant cloud where the mountains ought to have been . . . [*then later—emphasis added*] There was not a flake of snow anywhere but on the mountains and they stood up, the great white range rising high into the blue sky, while all the rest of the world at their feet lay ruddy rosy brown. The sudden contrast was tremendous, electrifying. I could have cried with the excitement of the overwhelming spectacle.[8]

Elsewhere in this same piece, Kilvert reflects: "One's first involuntary thought in the presence of those magnificent

---

7. April 16, 1876. William Plomer, ed., *Kilvert's Diary: Selections from the Diary of the Reverend Francis Kilvert, 1870–1879* (London: Jonathan Cape, 1944), 133–34. Kilvert's diary is easily accessible online, and this extract especially has been widely anthologized.

8. Plomer, ed., *Kilvert's Diary*, 133–34.

sights is to lift up the heart to God and humbly thank him for having made the earth so beautiful."

This response is not unusual in Kilvert's writing. It is there despite the harshnesses of life's experience for him. Such instinctive thanksgiving does not negate or ignore the reality of suffering. That would be to allow the theological balance to become over-weighted in the other direction. Suffering, however, which is oblivious of thanksgiving and eucharist, ignores an essential part of Christian prayer.

Another classical example of such eucharistic writing comes again from an Anglican pen and also, like Kilvert, from a country rectory in Herefordshire. This time the writer springs from the seventeenth century. Thomas Traherne wrote a series of reflections or "instructions" on the Christian life which were later called *Centuries of Meditations*, since they had been composed in discrete collections of one hundred per piece. He wrote the *Centuries* when he was thirty-five years old, just two years before his death in 1674. Traherne gave the book no title himself, but had he done so it may have been *The Way to Felicity.* Much of his writing picks up the theme of felicity or happiness and so captures again our theme of thanksgiving. He wrote: "An empty Book is like an infant's Soul, in which any Thing may be written. It is Capable of all Things, but containeth Nothing. I have a mind to fill this with Profitable Wonders."[9]

Throughout his *Centuries,* the theme "Are not praises the very end for which the world was created?" remains at the center. Just two extracts offer something of this mood of prayer and thanksgiving:

> You never Enjoy the World aright, till you see how a Sand exhibiteth the Wisdom and Power of God. And prize in evry thing the Service which they do you, by Manifesting his Glory and Goodness to you Soul . . . Your Enjoyment of the World is never right, till evry Morning you awake in Heaven: see your self in your father's Palace: and look upon the Skies and the

9. Thomas Traherne, *Centuries, Poems and Thanksgivings* (Oxford, UK: Clarendon Press, 1965), 3.

Earth and the Air, as Celestial Joys: having such a
Reverend Esteem of all, as if you were among the
Angels . . . You never Enjoy the World aright, till the
Sea it self floweth in your Veins, till you are Clothed
with the Heavens, and Crowned with the Stars.[10]

Later in a separate reflection he writes:

Your Enjoyment is never right, till you esteem evry
Soul so great a Treasure as our Saviour doth: and
that the Laws of God are sweeter than the Hony and
Hony Comb because they command you to love them
all in such Perfect Manner. For how are they God's
Treasures? Are they not the Riches of his Love?[11]

In all this, then, is embraced the whole of God's economy for
the world and, indeed, the universe, in the mind, heart, and
spirit of Traherne. His reflections offer instruction on how we
might begin to pattern our lives after the reign of God. The
creation as we experience it at present, our future-promised
bliss, and our fellow men and women are brought together
within these "profitable wonders." It is a world framed by an
attitude of thanksgiving. Prayer flows out into a structure
and pattern which fashions human life both for us individu-
ally and within community.

At this point, prayer as thanksgiving is not far from the
prayer of adoration or even contemplation. Prayer at this point
is integrally related to the pattern of our moral life. We have
seen how such prayer helps us to appreciate "life as gift." It
helps us apprehend that element of grace that is at the heart
of the gospel. It thus frees us from ourselves. Iris Murdoch,
in both her novels and philosophical writings, applauds contemplative prayer since it helps to unself us. This brief extract
from her novel *The Bell* shows what she is about. Dora, one of
the key characters, is in the National Gallery:

Dora was always moved by the pictures. Today
she was moved, but in a new way. She marvelled,

---

10. Traherne, *Centuries*, 14–15.
11. Traherne, *Centuries*, 19.

with a kind of gratitude, that they were all still here, and her heart was filled with love for the pictures, their authority, their marvellous generosity, their splendour. It occurred to her that love at last was something real and something perfect. Who had said that, about perfection and reality being in the same place? Here was something which her consciousness could not wretchedly devour, and by making it part of her fantasy make it worthless.[12]

The answer to her question about perfection and reality is Plato. Plato was foundational for Murdoch, but the point about the pictures and about reality can equally be said of our contemplation, adoration, and thanksgiving to God. God's perfection takes us out of ourselves, God "unselfs us," allows us to embrace life as gift, allows us to live "grace-filled" lives. It changes the basis of our behavior, our attitude to the world, and the way we relate to others. This is what Traherne saw in his "profitable wonders." More recently, the novelist Salley Vickers has given us a glimpse of this in the unlikely and transformed heroine of her novel *Miss Garnett's Angel*. We have increasingly been able to see, then, that thanksgiving as a mode or mood of prayer is positively life-transforming. It lifts us out of ourselves, places us firmly in the hands of God and within the context of the whole of creation and the wider human community. All of this is brought together uniquely in the celebration of the eucharist. But finally, then, how can this help us to understand thanksgiving more widely and outside the confines of the eucharist itself? Is thanksgiving a mood or mode of prayer that is transferable to *any* aspect or moment within human life?

"Yes"

The beginnings of an answer to this question may be discerned in a lyrical section of Paul's second letter to the Corinthians. Paul writes:

---

12. Iris Murdoch, *The Bell* (London: Chatto and Windus, 1958), 190.

For the Son of God, Jesus Christ, whom we proclaimed among you, Silvanus and Timothy and I,
was not "Yes and No"; but in him it is always "Yes."
For in him every one of God's promises is a "Yes."
For this reason it is through him that we say the
"Amen" to the glory of God. But it is God who establishes us with you in Christ and has anointed us,
by putting his seal on us and giving us his Spirit
in our hearts as a first installment. (2 Corinthians
1:19–22)

Two key points emerge from this brief extract. First of
all, it confirms our belief that Jesus Christ sets the pattern
for the divine reign, that pattern which fashions eucharistic
lives, lives of thanksgiving. Jesus offers himself entirely to
God: in Jesus, every one of God's promises is "Yes." But this
leads on to a further corollary: God establishes us and anoints
us, giving us his Spirit. God thus stands as the ground of our
being, as the reason why life is meaningful rather than meaningless. At the beginning of John's gospel a similar point is
made, but in a very different way. Here God is described as
the *word*. Word here, however, translates a Greek word that
is rich and multi-layered in its resonances. The Greek word
logos is translated in antiquity in a variety of ways: word,
reason, wisdom, purpose, ground—even *meaning*. Picking up
Jewish classical resonances then, God gives meaning to our
world and God is perfectly revealed in Jesus who is also the
word or *logos*.

It is then in response to the meaningful nature of our
lives and of our world, as seen in God, that we are provoked
into a mood of gratitude and thanksgiving. This is captured
perfectly in Paul's image of Jesus. Jesus lives out a eucharistic life to perfection, and from this the eucharist itself
emerges. So, in one sense, there is no separate mode or mood
of prayer that is thanksgiving. It is the context within which
all other prayer is formed; it is that context of meaningful-
ness and gratitude for all—even the trials and sorrows that
help fashion our lives. Now we can see life as gift. This sets

the context for all moods of prayer. *Intercession*, for example, fits into that pattern as we align our wills with the will of God. *Confession* calls us back to a life of thanksgiving when and where we have fallen away from our grace-filled vocation. *Praise* is the natural response to this instinct for gratitude and thanksgiving.

There are, of course, moments in individual lives where thanksgiving pours out abundantly within our prayer. There are countless examples of this—from the birth of a child, to healing from disease; from the exhilaration provoked by God's creation, to deliverance in times of trial. Similarly there are moments for thanksgiving in the lives of communities and nations. Here are specific moments in the life of our world which call forth from us focused prayers of thanksgiving. In our own life of prayer, too, it is important to remind ourselves of this instinct of thanksgiving. The needs of our world focused in intercession and the penitence expressed in confession for our falling away can both obscure that ground basis of gratitude for our creation, preservation, and redemption by God.

Books of Common Prayer across the Anglican Communion include the *General Thanksgiving*. Written by Bishop Reynolds of Norwich and first found in the 1662 Book of the Church of England, it is now a classical resource for prayer, usable by people of all traditions. At its heart, it captures something of the same spirit that we encounter in Traherne, an all-encompassing response to God for everything that we receive as gift:

> We bless thee for our creation, preservation, and
> all the blessings of this life; but above all for thine
> inestimable love in the redemption of the world by
> our Lord Jesus Christ, for the means of grace, and
> for the hope of glory.[13]

Later on, rather like Traherne's instructive *Centuries*, it re-calls us to live eucharistic lives:

---

13. Found, for example, in BCP 1979, 101.

And we beseech thee, give us that due sense of all
thy mercies, that our hearts may be unfeignedly
thankful, and that we show forth thy praise, not
only with our lips, but in our lives; by giving up
ourselves to thy service, and by walking before
thee in holiness and righteousness all our days.

Probably because of its position, among occasional prayers
and thanksgivings, it is easily forgotten. It is a magnificent
prayer in its original form and still a good prayer in its contemporary form. It might well be used more than it is by all
of us as individuals and in corporate worship, or even when
starting or finishing meetings. It helps to remind us to frame
all our doings and all prayer in the context of thanksgiving
and so to live eucharistic lives. We do so not naïvely ignoring
the evils of our world, but allowing our thanksgiving to
embrace evil as well as good, as a part of our life's experience.
There is a magnificent prayer that does just this; it was found
on a piece of wrapping paper in Ravensbruck, the largest of
the concentration camps for women. It asks:

O Lord, remember not only the men and women
of goodwill but also those of ill will. But do not
remember all the suffering they have inflicted
upon us; remember the fruits we bought, thanks
to this suffering, our comradeship, our loyalty, our
humility, the courage, the generosity, the greatness
of heart which has grown out of this; and when
they come to judgement, let all the fruits that we
have borne be their forgiveness.[14]

Thomas Traherne understood the ambiguity of Christian
thanksgiving too, so let him have the last word: "Thou wast
slain for me: and shall leave thy Body in the field O Lord?
Shall I go away and be Merry, which the Love of my Soul and
my only Lover is Dead upon the Cross."

---

14. This prayer is widely anthologized (for example, in George Appleton, ed., *The
Oxford Book of Prayer* [Oxford, UK: Oxford University Press, 1985], 112) and put to
liturgical uses, for example in the Chapel of the Holy Innocents in Norwich Cathedral,
England.

CHAPTER 2

Praise

Mark Earey

*"Thank you, God,
for the chance to be here
to praise you once again."*

S O BEGAN A TIME OF prayer in a service I attended recently. Phrases and sentiments similar to this are commonplace in informal worship and more formal liturgical services throughout the church, but they raise some interesting questions. Why would we be grateful for the chance to praise God? What does it mean to praise God, anyway?

It is easy to see the "purpose" behind other forms of prayer: if I recognize my failures, then confession is a good place to start; if my heart is breaking at the state of God's world, then intercession allows me to share God's heart of compassion and to express longing for change. But what about praise? What does praise do and what is it for? Does God need it and why do we need to offer it? Is God so insecure that constant praise is necessary? Or does God have such a massive ego that praise is needed to massage it night and day, year on year into eternity? These questions are not often asked in church, but they need to be faced if we are properly to understand praise as a mood and mode of prayer.

What Is Praise?

In ordinary life it is fairly straightforward to understand praise. Perhaps the most obvious context in which we encounter "praise" is when we praise a child who has tried hard, crossed a road safely, brushed their teeth thoroughly, or done well at sports day or in exams. The intention is to boost their confidence, to encourage them to do well, to reinforce patterns of behavior that we consider to be good. None of this seems relevant to praising God. We also praise our peers, of course.

We might praise a colleague for a brilliant presentation, or praise a friend for a lovely meal, but the danger of sounding patronizing in these situations is ever present, highlighting just how dominant the adult-child model of praise is. And praising someone who is our superior is doubly problematic; so what are we to make of "praising God"? To say to God that we "praise you for your glory" (as we do in the ancient hymn known as the *Gloria in excelsis*) is definitely not to say, "Well done God, for being so glorious!"

Perhaps we need to start somewhere else with praise, with an experience of praise which is different. At the end of a play or a concert, we might praise the cast and musicians with a standing ovation, a prolonged round of applause, or a call for an encore. The same sort of mood and action often marks the end of a football match (at least it does for the supporters of the winning team). This too is praise, but we don't often label it as such. It's partly about thanking; it's partly about appreciating and recognizing talent; but it is also primarily about celebrating—together—a truly great experience, and recognizing it as such. It is about relationship. To praise in this sense is to be bonded to those (or the one) praised, and with others praising, in an explosion of emotion which feels, albeit briefly, like touching or glimpsing a deeper reality.

We often recognize that intercession is not about changing God's mind, but about aligning our wills with God's (see the chapter on Intercession later in this volume). Perhaps we need some similar thinking to clarify what praise is about, too. Praise is not about changing God or getting God on our side. It is not sycophantic "sucking up," and neither is there a danger that God, through constant praise, will become big-headed or arrogant. Our praise of God can only, realistically, be the praise of creatures to the creator, but it doesn't *feel* like that. It feels much more like the joint celebration of something truly wonderful, in which we discover who we are. In praise, we recognize our creatureliness, not to have our noses rubbed in it, but in order to recognize that God took on this same creatureliness, redeemed it and transformed it, so that we might now be treated as friends of God, brothers and sisters of Christ, and sharers in the Holy Spirit.

Because praise is a celebration, it is normally expressed outwardly. It shows itself in words, noise, music, ceremonial movement, art, color, even smell, allowing us to tell the story in a way that we can all share. You can adore God in your heart; you can thank God in your own prayers; but praise is most naturally communal, even if circumstances sometimes restrict the company to the saints and angels.

Between Adoration and Thanks

Praise basically results from something wonderful. It falls somewhere between adoration and thanks. When we adore someone, we express love and affection and delight in that person simply for who they are; when we thank someone, it is usually for something done for us. Praise hovers somewhere between the two: you might say that praise is the pivot point between adoration and thanks, like the midpoint of a see-saw.

This applies in our worship of God, just as it does in other aspects of life. There is an element of adoration in praise—simply to gaze on God in awe, wonder, and love. There is also an element of thanks—to be grateful for all that God has done in every time and place, and in our own lives, or church, or nation. When adoration moves toward thanks, it passes through praise, and vice versa—which means that the boundaries between the three are sometimes blurred. At the root of all of them is an acknowledgement of the "Other." It recognizes what God has done, but is not limited merely to what God has done for *me* (which is what thanks tends toward).

> As soon as thanks focuses on whom it is addressing,
> it becomes praise and the overflow of appreciation
> searches for appropriate words and actions.[1]

Praise is firmly focused on the one being praised—whether that person is a child, a peer, or the creator of the universe. It is related to what that person has done, but never in isolation from who that person is. It is inherently generous and giving, overflowing and abundant—it can never be self-interested, self-conscious, restrained, or miserly.

Consider, for instance, the ancient Christian song usually known by its Latin first line, *Gloria in excelsis*: "We worship you, we give you thanks, we praise you for your glory. . . ."[2] The context is assumed to be corporate. It's "we," not "I." The focus is on God. It passes through thanks but moves straight to the heart of the matter: praise. Praise for what? In this case, nothing but God's glory.

This makes praise more generic and perhaps more central to worship than thanks, confession, or intercession—for praise depends on God and not on what God has or hasn't done for us, or what we have or haven't done for God. Praise is universal. It does not, ultimately, depend on circumstances (though it can often feel easier in some circumstances than others). It can take place with the same enthusiasm in Soweto as it does in Surrey (indeed, probably with more enthusiasm in Soweto, if the truth be known), because it does not depend on life being comfortable or conditions being conducive.

Why is that? Because praise springs from two facts which no human experience can diminish: the generous and loving acts of God in creation and salvation:

---

1. David F. Ford and Daniel W. Hardy, *Living in Praise: Worshipping and Knowing God* (London: DLT, 2005). First published as Daniel W. Hardy and David F. Ford, *Jubilate: Theology in Praise* (London: DLT, 1984).
2. BCP 1979, 356.

> You are worthy, our Lord and God,
> to receive glory and honor and power,
> for you created all things,
> and by your will they existed and were created.
>   (Revelation 4:11)
> Worthy is the Lamb that was slaughtered
> to receive power and wealth and wisdom and might
> and honor and glory and blessing! (Revelation 5:12)

So what do we do when life is kicking us, and the last thing we feel like is praising? There's a line of thought that says that to praise in those circumstances is hypocrisy. Better to cut it out—fold your arms, keep away from church services, wait until things improve. But this is to misunderstand praise. Praise is not about how we feel, it is about the reality of God and God's action in the universe. Praise in difficult circumstances is not hypocrisy, it is *formation*. Praise does not just express what we feel and experience, it also shapes us—who we are, how we understand ourselves, how we fit into the big scheme of things, how we live.

How Do We Praise?

In the church today, "praise" is often used to mean "singing joyfully." A service advertised as "Evening Praise" evokes different expectations from one calling itself "Evening Prayer." The mood at the former, you might expect, will be more upbeat, the repertoire more "contemporary," and the style more informal than at the latter. But though praise certainly encompasses questions of mood and style, it does more than that.

We have seen that praise springs from who God is and what God has done. This means that a core means of praise is to recount those great deeds, to tell that story. This is a primary means of celebration and praise in any context. When something wonderful happens, we celebrate by telling the story (again and again!). We notice, we give our attention, and we just have to keep talking about it, recounting it, wondering at it. This is partly why praise is so naturally corporate—it is harder (though not impossible) to praise on one's own, because there is no one to share the story with.

We recount God's actions in history and in our lives, and we rejoice in God's character, not for God's sake but for the sake of celebrating the truth. This is the dynamic of praise. Other questions—shall we sing, or dance, or shout, or paint or chant or proclaim?—are secondary to this primary means of praise which is, one way or another, to celebrate by telling the truth together about God.

Praise in the Eucharist

Given all of this, it is only natural that praise is at the heart of all worship. So where do we expect to find praise in the eucharist? There are obvious places (hymns and songs, for instance), but praise is actually woven into the fabric of the eucharist from start to finish.

Hymns and Songs

This is probably the obvious place where most congregation members would expect to find and experience praise in any act of worship, though not all hymns and songs are purely praise—thanks, adoration, confession, and intercession all get a look-in too. But there is something about the combination of music with words that makes singing a natural vehicle for praise—from the psalms to modern worship songs. Music adds to the intensity of what is being expressed, without taking away from the content of the words, and this echoes the dynamic of praise itself—overflowing and magnifying what is already full and perfect.

Gloria in Excelsis

Glory to God in the highest . . .
Lord God, heavenly King,
almighty God and Father,
we worship you, we give you thanks,
we praise you for your glory . . .

For you alone are the holy one,
you alone are the Lord,
you alone are the Most High, Jesus Christ,
with the Holy Spirit,
in the glory of God the Father. Amen.

The *Gloria* is really just a very ancient hymn, and in many churches it will be sung, sometimes to a metrical setting (i.e., a hymn tune). In many other churches, though, it will be spoken, especially in quieter services on Sunday or during the week.

It exhibits the typical attributes of praise—caught up between thanks, petition ("you take away the sin of the world: have mercy on us . . ."), and simply recounting things that God already knows, but which deepen in the telling.

Glory to God

If a psalm is being used as part of the liturgy of the word, then it may well conclude with one of the doxologies:

Glory to the Father and to the Son
and to the Holy Spirit;
as it was in the beginning is now
and shall be for ever. Amen.

or

Glory to God, Source of all being,
Eternal Word and Holy Spirit;
as it was in the beginning is now
and shall be for ever. Amen.[3]

Doxologies are common in Christian worship: hymns often conclude with them (a verse praising the persons of the Trinity), and the prayer that Jesus taught ("Our Father in heaven . . .") often finishes in worship with a doxology ("For thine is the kingdom, the power and the glory . . ."), which was not part of the prayer recorded in the gospels, but has

3. *Common Worship: Daily Prayer* (London: Church House Publishing, 2006), 648.

been added by regular use in the church's worship. The eucharistic prayer itself also concludes with a doxology.

Why has the church wanted to add these "glory words"? In the case of the Psalms, to give a trinitarian (and, therefore, Christian) conclusion to a text that originated in the Old Testament context—that is, to give the last word to the understanding of God revealed in Jesus. In other cases, perhaps because of an instinctive sense that all prayer and worship should find its ultimate meaning in sheer praise of God, so that, once again, praise has the last word.

Responding to the Gospel

Similarly, the introduction and response to the reading of the gospel are not requests for help, affirmations of belief, or expressions of thanks, but simply ascriptions of praise:

> The Holy Gospel of our Lord Jesus Christ
> according to _____.
> Glory to you, Lord Christ.
> This is the Gospel of the Lord.
> Praise to you, Lord Christ.[4]

Eucharistic Prayer

The great thanksgiving ("eucharistic") prayer at the heart of the eucharist is a complex mix, including thanks, remembrance, petition ("send your Holy Spirit . . ."), and sometimes intercession ("Bless the earth, heal the sick, let the oppressed go free . . ." from Prayer F in *Common Worship*).

Central to its concerns, nonetheless, is praise. Consider, for instance, this selection:

> We praise and we bless you, holy and gracious God,
> source of life abundant. (Opening sentence, Prayer 2,
> Enriching Our Worship 1)
> All thanks and praise
> are yours at all times and in all places,

---

4. BCP 1979, 357–58.

our true and living God . . . (Opening sentence,
  Prayer 3, Enriching Our Worship 1)
To you be glory and praise for ever. (Optional
  response in Prayer A, *Common Worship*)
This is his/our story.
This is our song:
Hosanna in the highest. (Response from Prayer D,
  Common Worship)
You give us breath and speech, that with angels
  and archangels
and with all the company of heaven
we may find a voice to sing your praise:
Holy, holy, holy Lord,
God of power and might,
heaven and earth are full of your glory.
Hosanna in the highest. (Sanctus, and
  introduction from Prayer G, *Common Worship*)
Praise to you, Lord Jesus:
Dying you destroyed our death,
rising your restored our life:
Lord Jesus, come in glory. (Acclamation)
. . . we worship you, Father almighty,
in songs of everlasting praise:
Blessing and honour and glory and power
be yours for ever and ever. Amen. (Doxology,
  concluding Prayer A, *Common Worship*)

Sent to Praise

The prayer often said after communion gives us a clue to one of the other aspects of praise: it shapes and forms us for Christian living. Praise is not just an act for public worship, praise is a shape of living, a direction in which to face. The praise of corporate worship has to shape us for living in praise, so that our whole lives inspire others to praise God too.

Almighty God,
we thank you for feeding us . . .
Send us out in the power of your Spirit

to live and work to your praise and glory. Amen.
(Prayer after Communion, *Common Worship*)

Why Does It Matter?

If we were to extract praise from the eucharist, would it matter? At first sight, maybe not. We could leave adoration and thanks, and confession and intercession. But that would not be Christian worship. Without the pivot point of praise, adoration and thanks fall flat, with nothing to propel them beyond themselves. Praise also lays the foundations for other forms of prayer. Praise establishes the sort of God we believe in. We praise God for love, compassion, mercy, power, wisdom. Without that foundation, we lose our confidence to come with our confession, we lose our boldness to come with our needs and the needs of the world—what if God is not interested, doesn't care, or is preoccupied? Praise shapes us for other forms of prayer.

Praise is a big-picture response to God that goes beyond the particularities of my life or our situation. Praise says God is still in charge, there is someone bigger than all this: praise is an act of hope, and it is a truthful act because it doesn't avoid a (sometimes painful) realism about the particular way things are now. Thanksgiving prayer looks to the past; praise draws on the past and turns to the future—God's nature and action in creation and salvation is the sure hope for the present and the future. That's why it may not always be easy to thank God, but it is always right to praise God, because the nature of God doesn't change.

Praise Is Dangerous

There's a sense in which no one worries too much whom you adore—this is largely a private matter. Put up posters of who you like in your own bedroom, or on your own fridge. You can, likewise, confess your faults to anyone you choose, and few will be concerned. And you can ask for things if you dare to, from anyone. But whom you praise matters. Praise is a political act, which has the potential to de-throne idols. As a corporate act, praise is therefore threatening to the powers—both earthly and heavenly. In the early centuries of the Christian church this was obvious—to fail to praise the emperor (and to make this public and plain by refusing to offer incense before his image), or to replace praise of him with praise of another, was tantamount to treason. At various times and in various places the empire chose to force this choice, and many Christians gave their lives for the sake of praise—by refusing to offer praise to anyone but the true and living God.

Such pressure is not unique to the early centuries of Christianity, and neither is it unique to those regimes whose leaders will not tolerate praise of anyone except themselves. In Western culture too, praise is subversive and political (in the broadest sense, though sometimes in more specific ways) and praise can put you at odds with those around you. Whom we choose to praise (and maybe how we choose to praise—see below) sets the foundations for how we live. Praising God (and no one but God) may put us at odds with political leaders, but it may also put us at odds with big business, multi-national corporations, advertisers, and the media . . . not to mention our own friends, neighbors, and families. It means that we will not sit quietly and conform to the praise of the false gods of celebrity, consumption, youth, and beauty. Perhaps if we were more aware of this, we would be less hasty in rushing into praise?

There are also implications here for the content of our praise and how we imagine and picture the one whom we praise. Many have questioned traditional assumptions about how we address God—is it appropriate, truthful, or helpful always to name God "Father" and "almighty"? How do we make room for other ways of naming God and other images for the God who is beyond all names and whose image is given to the whole human race? Is it appropriate to use male pronouns for the God who is neither male nor female, but in whose image male and female are created? If we praise God mainly for power, triumph, strength, but not often for vulnerability, warmth, risk, compassion, are we shaping our living and our hopes in only one dimension? Have we balanced our songs about a God who always wins with ones about the God who also urges, invites, laments, agonizes, and implores—the God who sometimes puts aside triumph in favor of freedom? If we emulate, and are shaped by, that which we praise, then these questions matter, not just for how we picture God as individuals, but for the image of God we share with the world and the way we are shaped as a community of those who love that God and seek to follow Christ.

Can Anglicans Praise?

The question is facetious, but it makes an important point. When I started going to church as a teenager, I encountered the service of Evensong from the Book of Common Prayer for the first time. I was amazed by the versicles and responses.

> O Lord, open thou our lips
> **And our mouth shall shew forth thy praise . . .**
> Praise ye the Lord.
> **The Lord's name be praised.**

There was no denying the praise-focused content of the responses (once I'd worked out what "shew forth" meant), but the mood and tone in which they were sung seemed unlike the mood of any other sort of praise that I had encountered, either in church or in other contexts. I was assured by long-standing church members that this sort of praise reflected a "deep joy" rather than a frothy, superficial sort of happiness, but I wasn't entirely convinced.

The Psalms of praise suggest a very different mood for praise:

> Rejoice in the Lord, O you righteous. Praise befits
> the upright . . .
> Sing to him a new song: play skilfully on the
> strings with loud shouts. (Psalm 33)

Clap your hands, all you peoples; shout to God
with loud songs of joy. (Psalm 47)
Make a joyful noise to God, all the earth; sing the
glory of his name;
give to him glorious praise. (Psalm 66)
O come, let us sing to the Lord;
let us make a joyful noise to the rock of our
salvation! (Psalm 95)
Praise him with trumpet sound; praise him with
lute and harp!
Praise him with tambourine and dance;
praise him with strings and pipe!
Praise him with clanging cymbals;
praise him with loud clashing cymbals! (Psalm 150)

It is important to remember that there is more to the Psalms than just praise, but when praise is central, then it is undoubtedly varied, physical, and exuberant.

Praise can certainly take many forms, but I am not persuaded that it is possible to praise in a truly understated way. This is why I ask (with my tongue in my cheek) whether *Anglicans* can praise, because for many Anglican congregations (in England, at any rate—it would not be true of Anglicans in other parts of the world), understatement seems to be a common mode and mood in worship. I certainly don't want to suggest that sadness, frustration, or pain should never be expressed in worship (and one only needs to turn to the Psalms again to find plenty of that), simply that praise is also valid and necessary. And there does seem to be something inherently and non-negotiably upbeat, positive, exuberant, and joyful about praise, and we shouldn't be embarrassed by it.

Perhaps one of the gifts that the Pentecostal churches and the charismatic movement have given to the wider Church is the gift of enthusiasm without embarrassment. Caricature and stereotype are always a danger, but there is no denying that Pentecostalism has helped other parts of the church to see again that praise is not just a cerebral matter or an inner disposition—it can (and should) show on the outside and we mustn't be frightened of it. If we clap and stand and cheer to praise a football team or the cast of a great show, why not do the same to celebrate the love and glory of God? Perhaps the starting point for a renewal of praise in the eucharist is to release the mood to match the mode. Perhaps it is time to stop understating, and time to let rip—just sometimes. That might mean a broader repertoire of styles of music; it might mean popular culture mingling with the "high" culture frequently encountered in parish churches; it might mean taking our eyes off ourselves and focusing on the one being praised. As the children's song puts it, jumping and dancing might make us "look funny," but "that's all right" if one has "got to (woo! woo!) praise the Lord!"[5] It's not my favorite worship song, and the theology is not the most profound, but I can't help feeling that the sentiment is right. English Anglicans (and others influenced by that culture) are not good at doing "looking funny" (apart from the clergy, obviously)—and maybe a little less self-regard, and a little more passion and enthusiasm would do us all good—and prepare us for the worship of heaven.

Praise for Life

To finish, let's remind ourselves of the purpose of this praise in the eucharist. As with all aspects of liturgy, praise is formational—it shapes us for living. It may be risky to give the last word again to the children's song, but it takes us to the heart of the renewal of praise, that praise may renew us, singing that the whole of life may be a song of praise, of intent "to worship God in every way," and correlating the actions that accompany the song and its singers' every action: "I want my actions every day" to praise God's name.[6]

If there's something I would want to change in the song, it would be to make it plural—for praise is *us* celebrating God together, and living praise means us, *corporately*, in the shape of our common life, as well as in our individual lives, living in ways that show God is real and God is to be celebrated.

---

5. Judy Bailey, "I Reach Up High," Daybreak Music Ltd, Silverdale Road, Eastbourne, East Sussex, UK, 1993.

6. Bailey, "I Reach Up High," verse 2.

CHAPTER 3

Confession

Harriet Harris

W HEN THE PRODIGAL SON IN Jesus' parable turns back toward home and is met by his father, he begins his confession: "Father, I have sinned against heaven and against you; I am no longer worthy to be called your son" (Luke 15:18–19a). His father intervenes and sends his slaves to fetch a robe, ring, and sandals for his son, and to prepare a feast.

The father, it seems, barely hears the confession. He is already filled with compassion for his son, and had embraced and kissed him even before the son began to speak. It is not much of a confession anyway, but more a plan of action in which the son is building up to saying "treat me as one of your hired hands." The father interrupts him before he can make this proposal, which, it turns out, is based on a misunderstanding of the father. Despite the misconceived and incomplete confession, the father holds a feast. The feast consummates the father's reconciliation and makes it public. The household and community will join in, even though their natural reaction might have been to reject the boy for bringing shame upon them. They will see the father's forgiveness and will celebrate with him.

This parable affords some insights into confession. Confession does not cause God's mind to change toward us. God may not need to hear our confession (though we may need to make it). Nor, if we are properly sorry for our sins (which is debatable in the prodigal son's case), does confession make us worthy to receive communion. God's mind does not change toward us, and the eucharist is not for the worthy.

Nor does confession cleanse us or reconcile us to God. God does these things because God is abundantly loving and forgiving. The eucharist itself is given for our reconciliation.[1] This is why repentance and confession are bound up with it.

But how are they bound up with it? We tend to think of repentance and confession as preliminary preparation for receiving. However, in truth, we are better at feeling sorry after we have received forgiveness. The father's embrace and reconciliatory feast challenge the prodigal son's expectations and will change the way he approaches his father. He had returned home intending to earn his way within his father's household, but he will begin to learn how his father sees things. So it is with us. We become better at confessing the more often we receive forgiveness, and as we get into a cycle of receiving and confessing. To be welcomed by the father once does not mean that we have fully realized the extent of the father's love or the nature of his judgment. We are shaped by doing so repeatedly. We are disciples, that is to say, pupils who are disciplined or shaped by what we learn.

The eucharist schools us in confession because it schools us in repentance. It does that by helping us to share the father's sorrow at the state of his lost children, and his joy at being able to reconcile them. We "truly repent" when we genuinely share the father's sorrow, rather than merely feeling sorry for ourselves or attempting to pay our dues. We truly repent

---

1. On the eucharist as given for our reconciliation, see Jean-Marie Tillard, "The Bread and Cup of Reconciliation," in Edward Schillebeeckx, ed., *The Sacramental Administration of Reconciliation* (London: Burns & Oates, 1971), 38–54; Alexander Schmemann, "Confession and Communion," Report to the Holy Synod of Bishops of the Orthodox Church in America, accepted and approved by the Holy Synod of Bishops of the Orthodox Church in America, February 17, 1972.

when this sorrow turns us toward Christ in a longing for our reconciliation and the reconciliation of the world.

Since the eucharist schools us in confession, what sense do we make of confessing before we come to receive?

A way into this question is to ask why the prodigal son attends the feast while his older brother does not. The father loves them both. The father wants both sons to come to the feast, but his older son, who had been loyal during the younger son's profligate years, stays outside.

He stays outside because he thinks the feast should not be held. After all he has done, working for his father and suffering with him the shame of his brother's actions, he cannot bring himself to come. Understandably, he feels that it is he who deserves a feast. But in thinking like this, he is looking upon the father's gift as something that should be earned.

One role that confession plays, then, in relation to the eucharist is to teach us that we cannot earn this gift and are never worthy of it. In short, confession teaches us that we are sinners. We have a lot to learn in this regard. It is not obvious to the older brother—and may not be obvious to us either—that he is in sin, that is to say, that he is enslaved to something. Yet refusing to come to the feast is both evidence of his enslavement and a deepening of it. He is held captive by his grievances, tied up with self-pity, resentment, and self-righteousness, all of which are understandable, but all of which bind him. Feeling wronged does not exempt him from the need for forgiveness. Those who are hurt need release from the grievances that hold their hearts captive.[2] For this to happen, they first need to recognize their slavery; to see their sin. Below we will explore the moment of realization when those who do not imagine that they are in sin come to realize that they are.

Furthermore, the older brother wants the repercussions of his brother's actions to be played out, not dissolved. He keenly

---

2. See Miroslav Volf, *Exclusion and Embrace: A Theological Exploration of Identity, Otherness, and Reconciliation* (Nashville, TN: Abingdon Press, 1996), 114. Actually being wronged does not exempt us from the need for forgiveness either. Those who are oppressed also need release from the grievances that enslave them.

feels the injustice of the feast. Forgiveness breaks the chains of causality that justice pursues, because these who forgive take upon themselves the consequences of what others have done. "Forgiveness, therefore, always entails sacrifice."[3] The older brother rejects the father's sacrifice, which is the forgiveness of his child, and would rather his father sought recompense.

So a second role that confession plays in relation to the eucharist is to reveal the nature of the father's forgiveness as moving us into a new kingdom of values where recompense is no longer relevant. Further on, we will explore our movement out of the slavery of sin and into the kingdom of God's forgiveness.

A third role of confession is to reconcile us to our brothers and sisters. We are instructed in Scripture and the teachings of the early church to be reconciled to one another before we make our offering, and not to celebrate the eucharist with divisions among us lest we make a mockery of it (Matthew 5:23–24; 1 Corinthians 11:17–34; *Didache*, chapter 14).[4] This is why, in most eucharistic liturgies, we share the peace just before the offertory and always after we have made our confession. The discipline of confessing brings to mind our divisions and hopefully prompts us to seek peace with one another.

The parable of the Prodigal Son might seem particularly relevant on this point, given its picture of division between the two brothers in the family. Yet, here the analogy between the eucharist and the feast in the parable breaks down significantly. The older brother is not reconciled to his younger brother and so cannot bring himself to attend the feast. Had he attended, he would have opened himself up to the possibility of reconciliation. Had he come to the feast but refused to make peace with his brother, he might have ruined the evening. However, he would not have made a mockery of the feast, for this was not the feast of the body of Christ. Its guests were

---

3. Dag Hammarskjöld, *Markings,* quoted in Judy Hirst, *Struggling to be Holy* (London: Darton, Longman and Todd, 2006), 60.

4. *Didache,* chapter 14 says: "But every Lord's day gather yourselves together, and break bread, and give thanksgiving after having confessed your transgressions, that your sacrifice may be pure. But let no one who is at odds with his fellow come together with you, until they be reconciled, that your sacrifice may not be profaned."

recipients of the father's sacrificial love, and they would hopefully go out from the feast accepting one another, but they
were not being substantially re-made into a new community
of sacrificial love. They were not being constituted and uni-
fied as the body of Christ on earth. It is our constitution as
Christ's body, rooted in Christ's own bodily sacrifice, that we
profane if we celebrate the eucharist with divisions among us.

Paul cautions the Christians in Corinth that if they do
not make peace with one another, they should not make the
eucharist (1 Corinthians 11:29–30). His stark warnings have
sometimes put others off, with the result that some individuals and church communities have refrained from the eucharist too readily or too often. In order to address this problem,
we end with an excursus on Paul's exhortation to self-examination (1 Corinthians 11:28). Paradoxically, we can become
proud judges of our own state of unworthiness, and so with-
hold ourselves from the eucharist rather than giving ourselves
to God's loving judgment and reconciling action.

A fourth aspect of confession, to which the parable of
the Prodigal Son obliquely applies, is that it articulates a
response that is natural for human beings in the presence of
God (cf. Isaiah 6:5). When approaching the heavenly throne
(Hebrews 12), we are aware of our unworthiness. We might
try to hide our unworthiness, or we might decide the time
for pretense is over and so endeavor to take off our masks.
Confessing is how we remove our masks. This is where
the parable becomes relevant, for in it both sons seek the
approval of their father, in the effort to obtain what they
deserve. The father, however, relates to them as a parent
who delights in his children. Timothy Radcliffe captures the
significance of the difference between approval and delight:
"The mechanisms of approval train us in deceit. Delight
invites us to come into the open and be seen as we are."[5]
The father's embrace pre-empted the prodigal son's preten-
sions and his endeavor, masked as a confession, to go on providing for himself as a slave in his father's household. There

5. Timothy Radcliffe, *What Is the Point of Being a Christian?* (London: Burns and Oates, 2006), 61.

is scope for the father's embrace to go on transforming both sons. The "Prodigal Son" is an open-ended parable, leaving room for both sons to learn that the father's love is itself fundamental. It does not depend on their gaining approval, nor is it apportioned to what they deserve.

Learning that We Are Sinners

The peacemakers Jean Goss and Hildegard Goss-Mayr visited Poland ten years after the end of World War II. They asked some Polish Christians if they'd be willing to meet with other Christians from West Germany. They said no. One of their number exclaimed: "What you are asking is impossible. Each stone of Warsaw is soaked in Polish blood! We cannot forgive!" Before the peacemakers parted, the whole group said the Prayer That Jesus Taught together. When they reached the words "forgive us our sins as we forgive," everyone stopped praying. Tensions built up, until the Pole who had spoken most vehemently said, "I must say yes to you. I could no more pray the Our Father, I could no longer call myself a Christian, if I refuse to forgive. Humanly speaking, I cannot do it, but God will give us strength."[6]

At first the sin of the Polish Christians was not obvious, and even presented itself as a good. They were honoring the Polish blood that had been spilt. Their withholding of forgiveness seemed justified and even righteous. But provoked by the familiar words of the prayer Jesus taught us, they realized that they had to put to death their sense of righteous indignation. Only thus can a new life built on the risk of mercy and peace be born. The confession was at one and the same time a realization of the sin: "I could no longer call myself a Christian, if I refuse to forgive."

---

6. Walter Wink recounts this episode in *Engaging the Powers: Discernment and Resistance in a World of Domination* (Minneapolis, MN: Fortress, 1992), 275–76. He takes it from Jim Forest, *Making Enemies Friends* (New York: Crossroad, 1988), 76–78. For Jean Goss and Hildegard Goss-Mayr's reflections on their peacemaking endeavors, see Gerard Houver, ed., *A Non-Violent Lifestyle* (London: Marshall, Morgan & Scott, 1989).

Sin can be understood as giving a minor good priority over the most important good.[7] To say that we are all sinners is to say that we all make this mistake: we prioritize some goods over the thing that is really important. The prodigal son's older brother prioritized dutiful behavior and a sense of fairness over the most important thing, which was the father's love for his sons; for *both* of his sons. The Poles prioritized, in honor of their people, the remembrance of harm done. Both were offended by the wideness of God's mercy, and both were perhaps totting up their own merits. They had to die to their offense and to their own sense of virtue so that God's love could come first.

All of Christian life, and the fulcrum of Christian spirituality, is the dying and rising with Christ. We often do not know that we are sinners, or refuse to believe that we are, and so we justify ourselves. Indeed, we can even turn confession into a polishing of our own haloes. When we are in such a state, God is hidden from us, and instead we see a punitive, vengeful god whom we either fear for our own sakes, or whom we expect to chastise others. We do not see the God who forgives and goes straight on to celebrate.[8] When we confess with true repentance, we are broken open: "The sacrifices of God are a broken spirit: a broken and a contrite heart, O God, thou will not despise."[9] We allow ourselves to be destroyed by God's love and remade; crucified and raised from the dead. We die to ourselves, no longer seeing ourselves or our perspective and priorities as things to possess and be proud of.

Writing about private confession, such as one might make to a confessor on the evening before a eucharist, Dietrich Bonhoeffer says:

> In confession occurs the break-through to the Cross.
> The root of all sin is pride, *superbia*. I want to be

---

7. See Herbert McCabe, OP, *God, Christ and Us* (London: Continuum, 2003), 30.

8. McCabe, *God, Christ and Us*, 75–7·6; Herbert McCabe, *Faith within Reason* (London: Continuum, 2007), 156.

9. Psalm 51:17, used as a preliminary sentence from scripture before the exhortation to confession in the order for morning prayer, and for evening prayer in the Book of Common Prayer.

my own law, I have a right to my self, my hatred and my desires, my life and my death . . . Confession . . . is the profoundest kind of humiliation. It hurts, it cuts a man down, it is a dreadful blow to pride . . . In the deep mental and physical pain of humiliation before a brother—which means, before God—we experience the Cross of Jesus as our rescue and salvation.[10]

Bonhoeffer's words are true also of corporate confession within a service of the eucharist, so long as that confession is spoken not with unthinking familiarity but with true repentance.[11] For although we do not articulate particular sins to a Christian brother or sister during the eucharist, we most directly conform ourselves there to Christ's reconciling action: "The old man dies, but it is God who has conquered him. Now we share in the resurrection of Christ and eternal life."[12]

Learning How to Live under God's Forgiveness

Confessing sin and confessing faith are two sides of the same coin: conforming ourselves to the God in whose loving sacrifice we die and are born into new life.

God is like the king in Jesus' parable of the unmerciful slave (Matthew 18:21–35). When the king cancels the slave's debt, he dies to the world of calculation and control, and takes his slave with him. They are both dead to that world. They are free of it, and life for the slave begins anew. Yet, when he leaves the king's court, he reverts to the usual pattern of calculation, control, and violence, and in particular the violence that he knows as an oppressed slave. He shows no mercy to his fellow slave, probably not because he is unusually mean,

---

10. Dietrich Bonhoeffer, *Life Together* (London: SCM Press, 1954), 89–90.

11. True repentance, as explained above, involves sharing God's sorrow at our lost condition and the brokenness of the world, and longing for reconciliation, and turning ourselves toward Christ.

12. Bonhoeffer, *Life Together*, 90.

but because he is carrying on as he is used to. He still does not have any money, so he does the usual things a slave in a violent slave economy would do, to get the money someone else owes him.

It is terribly easy to hold on to a spirit of slavery, and so to fail to be transformed by God's love. The slave's own situation had been changed by the king's cancellation of his debt, but he did not let that change work through him. Likewise the Polish Christians stood forgiven, but at first resisted letting forgiveness work through them.

This, in essence, reflects the problem of post-baptismal sin, with which the Church has struggled since New Testament times (Hebrews 6:4–8; 10:26–31; 1 John 1:7–9, 3:9). In baptism we are given a new nature in Christ, and sin is deeply incongruous with this nature. Christ's blood cleanses us from sin, and those who are born of God cannot sin (1 John 1:7, 3:9). However, we do sin. Confession is given to us to deal with this problem, and thereby mediates the way between baptism and participation in the eucharist.

In baptism we die with Christ and are raised in him to new life, but we do not automatically remove ourselves from the slave culture. We still live with a spirit of slavery, not realizing that we have been made children of God (Romans 8:15), or that in being made God's children we live in a new kingdom with a new set of values. We claim to have communion with God while walking in darkness (1 John 1:6). The question of post-baptismal sin is whether we thereby lose what our baptism has bestowed.

The answer is no. God has a way of maintaining the relationship. By confessing our sins we open ourselves up to God's forgiveness: "If we say that we have no sin, we deceive ourselves, and the truth is not in us. If we confess our sins, he who is faithful and just will forgive us our sins and cleanse us from all unrighteousness" (1 John 1:8–9). The eucharist itself consummates God's forgiveness, for it is through Christ's atoning sacrifice that we are forgiven, and the eucharist extends and mediates that sacrifice through time: "My little children, I am writing these things to you so that you may not sin. But if anyone does sin, we have an advocate with the Father, Jesus Christ the righteous; who is the atoning sacrifice for our sins, and not for ours only but also for the sins of the whole world" (1 John 2:1–2). The eucharist puts us in touch with the once-for-all paschal event. It makes sacramentally present and communicates the act that remits sins. For this reason, "the forgiveness which makes the Christian fit to receive the Lord's supper *truly* is directly produced by the memorial itself."[13]

The eucharistic community, if it has understood all this, is made up of those who know themselves to be in slavery to sin, who dare to be honest about that, and who know that although we are sinners we can still walk with God (whereas, not to know oneself as forgiven by God is not to know this[14]). Our time in the waters of baptism need not happen again, but our dying and rising with Christ must recur continually as we make our passage out of the world of sin and debt, and are transformed into Christ's likeness.

> Grant, Lord, that we who are baptized into the death of your Son our Saviour Jesus Christ may continually put to death our evil desires and be buried with him; and that through the grave and gate of death we may pass to our joyful resurrection; through his merits who died and was buried and rose again for us, your Son Jesus Christ our Lord."[15]

Each time we confess, we die a bit more, and we ask that we might be granted to serve God "in newness of life." The prayer of absolution is a prayer to further our transformation and sustain us under God's reign: "confirm and strengthen us in all goodness, and keep us in life eternal." Therefore the *kyrie*, the thrice-repeated plea for mercy, is not the cry of the condemned, but a prayer for all that God has to give. God's mercy is God's perfection, and we are called to be perfect as

---

13. Tillard, "The Bread and Cup of Reconciliation," 47, 50.

14. D. Z. Phillips, *The Concept of Prayer* (New York: Schocken Books, 1966), 67–68.

15. Collect for Evening Prayer on Friday, *Common Worship: Daily Prayer* (London: Church House Publishing, 2005), 190.

our father in heaven is perfect, that is, to realize our life in the kingdom of heaven and be transformed into God's merciful likeness (Matthew 5:46–48; Luke 6:32–36).

Being Reconciled to One Another

We confess not only for our own sakes, that we might become inhabitants of God's kingdom, but for the sake of the church and the world. We confess so as to lessen the obstacles of sin that we keep tripping over as we try to walk with Christ, and to heal our divisions with our sisters and brothers. When the Poles repented and confessed, they died to their sense of righteousness and let forgiveness transform them. They thereby let go of the impossible debt to which they had been holding the Germans. They and their German neighbors could both die to that debt, and life could begin afresh. Indeed, lifelong relationships were established between the Polish and German Christians involved.[16]

Followers of Christ are called to make the sacrifice of forgiving others: to take upon themselves the cost of wrongs done, for the sake of restoring our relationships. "The eucharist is human participation in the reconciliation of the world that Christ accomplishes," writes William Cavanaugh. And he cites some words of St. John Chrysostom to show how we are both united to and become agents of that reconciling work:

> The Son of God came down for this purpose, to reconcile our human nature to the Lord. But he did not come down for that purpose alone, but also for the purpose of making us, if we do likewise, sharers of His title. . . . You, according to human capacity, must do what the Onlybegotten Son of God has done, be an agent of peace, for yourself and for others. For this reason, at the very time of sacrifice He recalls us to no other commandment than that

---

16. Wink, *Engaging the Powers*, 276.

of reconciliation with one's brother, showing that it is the greatest of all.[17]

If we are not reconciled to one another, we bring upon ourselves the danger of celebrating the eucharist whilst failing to embody the righteousness of God.[18]

The earliest picture we have of a eucharistic community is of the fledgling and divided community in Corinth. Paul reprimands the Corinthian Christians because they are not sharing the meal in a companionable way (and to keep "company" means literally to "break bread with"). Indeed, Paul says, it is not really the Lord's supper that you are eating, for each of you eats your own supper and some are left hungry. "What!" says Paul. "Do you show contempt for the Church of God and humiliate those who have nothing?" (1 Corinthians 11:22). Paul warns them not to eat the bread and drink the cup in an unworthy manner. "Examine yourselves," he says, "[f]or all who eat and drink without discerning the body, eat and drink judgment against themselves" (1 Corinthians 11:28–29).

The meaning of "discerning the body" is the subject of much debate. Some ancient manuscripts say "discerning the Lord's body," and there is a tradition, which includes Augustine and Aquinas, which takes this to mean appreciating a sacramental change in substance from bread to the body of Christ. Paul may, however, mean "body" in a collective sense, such that the Corinthians failed to discern the distinctive reconciled nature of the Church as the body of Christ. These two interpretations are not unrelated. Paul's moral point seems to be that while we proclaim the death of Jesus, we only pretend to share in that death for us if our behavior is not recognizable as a proclamation of the Lord's death.[19] In the very flesh

17. William T. Cavanaugh, "Discerning: Politics and Reconciliation," in Stanley Hauerwas and Samuel Wells, eds., *The Blackwell Companion to Christian Ethics* (Oxford, UK: Blackwell, 2004), 203.

18. Robert Song, "Sharing Communion: Hunger, Food and Genetically Modified Foods," Hauerwas and Wells, *The Blackwell Companion to Christian Ethics*, 399.

19. Cf. Anthony C. Thiselton, *1 Corinthians, A Shorter Exegetical and Pastoral Commentary* (Grand Rapids, MI: Eerdmans, 2006), 187–88.

of Christ, God offers the possibility of new life, so overcoming the confinement of sin. The new life must by the Holy Spirit become manifest in the way we live. This is how the Church is born and becomes the body of Christ.[20] If we maintain or increase division among us, then we turn the eucharist into its opposite—we turn companionship into division, and make a mockery of the eucharist. We show nothing of Christ's sacrifice and its power to reconcile us to God and to one another.

The eucharist brings with it judgment, and therefore renders the insight to judge ourselves (consider 1 Corinthians 11:31–32). Vincent Donovan, a missionary to the Masai people in the 1970s, saw how this can operate in practice. The Masai people would not make a sacrilege and call themselves the Body of Christ when there was hatefulness, lack of forgiveness, or selfishness among them.[21] In one tribe, the way that peace was offered and maintained was by taking a tuft of grass (grass is regarded as sacred to these largely desert-dwelling people) and passing it around the village. If anyone refused to accept the grass as a sign of the peace of Christ, the elders of the tribe would, on those occasions, decide that the eucharist could not be made.[22]

Paul exhorted the Christians in Corinth to judge themselves with this kind of discernment. The eucharist was challenging the basic ordering of their society, whereby the poorer laborers and the wealthier merchants each ate according to their custom, and did not eat together. It challenged their social standards. If they could not be reconciled over this matter, it would be better if they refrained from celebrating the eucharist. However, the ultimate goal was that the judgment of the eucharist would bring about a change in them, reconciling them to one another so that they could truly celebrate. Donovan witnessed how the eucharist challenged

20. Tillard, "The Bread and Cup of Reconciliation," 39.

21. Vincent J. Donovan, *Christianity Rediscovered: An Epistle from the Masai* (London: SCM Press, 1982), 127. For exploration of the complex ways in which churches are morally shaped by their worship, see Christian Scharen, *Public Worship and Public Work: Character and Commitment in Local Congregational Life* (Collegeville, MN: Liturgical Press, 2004).

22. Donovan, *Christianity Rediscovered*, 127.

the basic ordering of Masai society. When he celebrated the eucharist with the Masai people, the men and women had to come to terms with eating together. This was against their custom.[23] If males and females are not used even to seeing one another eat, how challenging is the intimacy of the eucharist, in which the chalice is passed round and one person's lips touch where another person's lips have been? The eucharist is a great leveler and unifier. It is especially good news for those who have been brought low or excluded by social norms, as the Masai women and girls testified![24] Had the Masai refused the leveling and unifying effects of the eucharist, they would have made a mockery of it. However, the eucharist was their judgment, and they conformed themselves to it.

An Excursus on Self-Examination

Paul's exhortation to self-examination (1 Corinthians 11:28) is to the Christians in Corinth collectively. The point is that, as eucharistic communities, we judge ourselves and repent so that we can live together in a way that is fitting to the eucharist, and therefore to Christ himself.

Nevertheless, Paul's words are sometimes heard as a call for intense introspection, rather than as a warning to the Corinthians not to provoke divisions among themselves.[25] Necessarily, corporate and individual reflection go hand-in-hand. However, where the emphasis falls heavily upon introspection, people can tend to judge themselves too unworthy to come to the eucharist. Hence some individuals refrain from receiving communion, and some church communities celebrate the eucharist only once a year or once a quarter.

The rationale for infrequent communion is simple: the fear of bringing judgment upon ourselves (1 Corinthians 11:29).

---

23. Donovan, *Christianity Rediscovered*, 121.

24. Donovan, *Christianity Rediscovered*, 121.

25. Richard B. Hays, *First Corinthians: Interpretation, A Bible Commentary for Teaching and Preaching* (Louisville, KY: Westminster John Knox Press, 1997), 200.

"Dearly beloved in the Lord," begins Cranmer's third exhortation in the Book of Common Prayer:

> Ye that mind to come to the holy Communion of the Body and Blood of our Saviour Christ, must consider how Saint Paul exhorteth all persons diligently to try and examine themselves, before they presume to eat of that Bread, and drink of that Cup. For as the benefit is great, if with a true penitent heart and lively faith we receive that holy Sacrament; (for then we spiritually eat the flesh of Christ and drink his blood; then we dwell in Christ, and Christ in us; we are one with Christ, and Christ with us) so is the danger great, if we receive the same unworthily. For then we are guilty of the Body and Blood of Christ our Saviour; we eat and drink our own damnation, not considering the Lord's Body; we kindle God's wrath against us; we provoke him to plague us with divers diseases, and sundry kinds of death.[26]

Cranmer had intended people to receive communion weekly, but the practice of a weekly eucharist fell away in the Church of England, and was not restored until the catholicizing trends of the nineteenth and twentieth centuries made regular Sunday parish communion the norm.

The holiness and awe-fulness of the eucharist is emphasized not to discourage us from attending it too often, but rather to encourage us to attend with a humility or brokenness of spirit, without which the eucharist can do little of its healing work, either for us or through us.

We cannot, in any case, avoid accountability to God by staying away from Christ's table. Thinking back to the story of the Poles; they did not decide to refrain from saying the Lord's Prayer, lest they be convicted by it. Rather they said it and allowed themselves to be changed by it. They were changed by the very saying of it. We are changed by our very

---

26. The Third Exhortation, to be said at the time of the celebration of the Communion, Book of Common Prayer.

participation in the eucharist. The eucharist brings both judgment and reconciliation. It thereby shows us that God's judgment is not the opposite of God's love. It is that love turned toward us when we have got ourselves lost. We might prefer God to look away, but God will not do so. God is faithful and persistent and will not look away. God's judgment is simply God's faithfulness, and God's faithfulness is simply God's love.

Approaching the Heavenly Throne

We learn to confess within that relationship of divine judgment to divine love. We approach the heavenly throne (cf. Hebrews 12:22–24), and this rightly makes us tremble. The light shines brightly and shows us for what we are.

> O Lord, you have searched me out and known me . . .
> you discern my thoughts from afar . . .
> and are acquainted with all my ways.
> For there is not a word on my tongue,
> but you, O Lord, know it altogether.
> You encompass me behind and before
> and lay your hand upon me. (Psalm 139:1–4[27])

If it were not for God's love, we could not bear to be laid bare. But because God has come to save sinners, we want to be known by him: "Search me, O God, and know my heart; test me and know my thoughts. See if there is any wicked way in me, and lead me in the way everlasting" (Psalm 139:23–24).

Beau Stevenson, diocesan advisor in pastoral care in the Diocese of Oxford and a former mental health chaplain, tells about a time when he was taking the eucharist in the hospital chapel where he worked, and a realization was creeping up on him that something was not quite right.[28] Then he realized what it was: someone was standing there without any clothes on. Beau asked the man to put his clothes back on, but he

---

27. Common Worship: Services and Prayers for the Church of England (London: CHP, 2000).

28. In conversation with the author.

said he would not until he had received communion. The rest
of the congregation did not mind. Only the organist found it
funny, because the offertory hymn was "Just as I Am." The
man was enacting the realization that all we can do is place
ourselves, just as we are, in God's hands. And so he removed
his outer protection.

"Be glad!," Bonhoeffer writes:

> You can hide nothing from God. The mask you
> wear before men will do you no good before him.
> He wants to see you as you are, he wants to be gra-
> cious to you. You do not have to go on lying to your-
> self and your brothers, as if you were without sin;
> you can dare to be a sinner. Thank God for that.[29]

Because in Christ the love of God comes to the sinner,
through Christ we can be sinners, and only so can we be
helped. All sham is ended in the presence of Christ.[30] To know
this "is liberation through truth"[31]; "[t]o be seen by Jesus is an
experience of truth"; "Jesus's delight in us is not vacuous affirmation: it is our painful joy in being stripped of pretension."[32]

So it is that at the start of a service of the eucharist we
acknowledge "Almighty God, to whom all hearts are open,
all desires known, and from whom no secrets are hidden."
It is from this acknowledgement that we go on to make our
confession. The fact of coming before God is what makes a
penitential rite appropriate early on in the liturgy, because
confessing is the response we make to the God who knows
even the secrets of our hearts.

Closing Reflection

The liturgy also affords many subsequent opportunities to
confess, outside of the penitential rite: in collecting our thoughts

29. Bonhoeffer, *Life Together*, 86.
30. Bonhoeffer, *Life Together*, 87.
31. Bonhoeffer, *Life Together*, 86.
32. Radcliffe, *What Is the Point*, 62.

in relation to the Collect, on hearing from Scripture, in sharing the peace, and when praying the *Agnus Dei* or prayer of humble access, or, indeed, at any point throughout a service including after receiving communion. The following post-communion prayer is especially evocative of a confessional attitude. It incorporates gratitude, a sense of our own unworthiness, alignment with Christ's dying and rising, and a turning toward Christ for the sake of our own freedom and that of others:

> Father of all, we give you thanks and praise, that when we were still far off you met us in your Son and brought us home. Dying and living, he declared your love, gave us grace, and opened the gate of glory. May we who share Christ's body live his risen life; we who drink his cup bring life to others; we whom the Spirit lights give light to the world. Keep us firm in the hope you have set before us, so we and all your children shall be free, and the whole earth live to praise your name; through Christ our Lord.[33]

The multiple opportunities to confess throughout a service of the eucharist are as fitting as the penitential rite early on, given that the eucharist is schooling us in repentance.

What we learn through repenting and confessing is none other than the gospel itself. We learn that we can come to God in no way other than unworthily. Our only "worthiness" in receiving communion is the recognition of our unworthiness. We confess our unworthiness and come for our reconciliation. If we keep ourselves away from communion on the grounds that we are not worthy, we deny God's mercy, and may even proudly hold ourselves back from dying to God's forgiveness. By confessing our sins, we humble ourselves and accept communion as a gift, rather than something we could ever deserve.

---

33. *Common Worship: Services and Prayers for the Church of England* (London: Church House Publishing, 2000), 182.

CHAPTER 4

Intercession

John Pritchard

I FIRST KNEW SOMETHING WAS AMISS with the intercessions when I realized my concentration time was down to about five seconds. My mind would wander off to such faraway places as the football results, the damp patch on the wall above the pulpit, Sunday-lunches-I-have-known, the clothes sense of the person in the pew in front, and so on.

But wasn't this time of intercession in the eucharist meant to be rather crucial? Weren't we supposed to be holding open a world of need to the infinite resources of a loving God? Had not Karl Barth said that to clasp the hands in prayer was the beginning of an uprising against the disorder of the world? So wasn't it a bit of a come down to be worrying about a late penalty conceded by Newcastle United?

I began to analyze why intercessions in public worship so often seemed to lose their way. One problem, I decided, was our habit of speaking to God in such huge *generalizations*. I know it's good to pray for "the church throughout the world" and to mention the obscure (to us) dioceses in the Anglican cycle of prayer, but I wanted to know what precisely I could be praying for. Was it more priests, the healing of divisions, a new program of evangelism, or what? I know we have a responsibility to pray for "peace and justice in all places of violence and oppression," but what about the latest outrage splashed over this morning's newspapers? Couldn't we be more specific? Such generalized prayers don't give God a lot to go on.

Another problem I began to recognize was that of *blandness* in prayer. It was all so polite, so moderate, the epitome of an Anglican church in which the bland lead the bland. Is the world not full of passion and color, of argument and struggle, of beauty and horror? Could not our prayers be more colorful and gritty? Would God be offended if we expressed our outrage and desolation in more desperate phrases that truly reflected our feelings? Could we not risk a bit more ecstasy at the wonderful gifts of life?

I had a similar complaint about the *limited range* of our intercessions. We would regularly pray for clergy, teachers, and the medical profession. We might even pray for our political leaders—although we would be very careful to avoid any whiff of political bias. But when did the intercessions last include prayers for checkout staff at the supermarket or refuse disposal teams or people who run our power stations or tend our public parks, or play representative sport or draw cartoons? The agenda we present to God can be very limited. A visitor to church might wonder what narrow world we Christians inhabit.

Another presenting problem was that of *repetition*. I suppose all of us have a default setting that returns to safe ground and established routines whether we're getting up in the morning, telling our life-story, or choosing what television programs to watch. But surely a congregation's patience is severely tested (let alone God's) if we have the same list of trouble-spots, the same list of clerical hierarchy, the same list of the sick, week after week. Sometimes I would long for a rogue trouble-spot to appear or for just a morsel of information about why we had prayed for Sam Stringfellow every week for the last five years.

There is more to the intercessions than filling in the time between the Creed and the Peace. Mighty issues are at stake. Renewing the eucharist includes revitalizing our prayerful approach to God so that prayer is as it were, "taking the

chalice to the fountain to be filled." In intercession the chalice
to be filled is not just our own; it's the chalice of the world.

The Significance of the Moment of Intercession

The placing of the intercessions in the eucharist is significant. They come immediately after we have stormed the
liturgical heights in the reading of Scripture, the interpretation and application of the Word in the sermon, and the
solemn response of the Church in the weighty statements of
the Creed. We now respond in a more particular and personal
way by praying for the world and its people in the light of both
the great purposes of God and the details of the world's life
as we know it.

It is, therefore, a major opportunity to participate in
God's mission. Let no one trivialize the place of prayer in the
economy of God. It's not just religious small-talk. When one
pastor was asked to "get things going with a little prayer," he
fantasized his response: "I will not! There are no *little* prayers!
Prayer enters the lion's den, brings us before the holy, where
it's uncertain whether we'll come back alive or sane, for it's a
fearful thing to fall into the hands of a living God."[1] That's
more like it. Intercession gives us the awesome opportunity
of cooperating with God in the sustaining and healing of the
world. We hold before God this glorious, damaged world and
offer ourselves as part of the process of restoring all things to
their own truth and purpose.

Moreover, this time of intercession is a high point of our
love for God's people. We cannot do anything more valuable
for people than place them intentionally in the hands of the
God who loves them beyond measure. Intercession is therefore
one of the most profound ways we have of loving someone. One
writer imaginatively described intercession as: like throwing
sticks and stones into the river as it flows past.[2] The stones
we throw are those prayers that have the dead weight of

1. Quoted in Eugene Peterson, *Working the Angles* (Grand Rapids, MI: Eerdmans, 2000), 46.
2. Michael Adie, *Held Together* (London: DLT, 1997), 79.

selfishness, and sink quickly to the bottom. The sticks are the prayers that, though light and fragile, are taken by the flow of the prayer of Christ to the generous ocean of the Father's love "where all our needs are satisfied." The intercessions in our eucharistic worship give us the opportunity lovingly to throw these sticks of prayer into the river.

A Supporting Theology

If, however, we are to believe in what we are doing as we intercede, we need to have a practical theology of intercession which lets us pray with confidence. If people pray too easily for the healing of someone with apparently terminal cancer, we may be leading some people in the congregation into an intellectual and spiritual corner. Can they pray this? If God could heal this particular condition, what other conundrums does that pose? The question then becomes whether this kind of prayer increases faith for people or undermines its credibility. The way God uses our prayer is, of course, a mystery to all but God. Nevertheless, we have to have a working framework in which to place our praying for others.

Let's be clear from the outset: intercession isn't about changing God's mind. It's about laying hold of God's willingness rather than overcoming God's reluctance. It's more to do with aligning our will in a creative synergy with God's good purposes. When our desires, expressed in prayer, begin to resonate at the same frequency as the purposes of God, something new may happen, but that's very different from concluding that we've changed God's mind and persuaded God that we've got a better answer than God had. A simple illustration is to think of a ship coming into port. The sailors throw their ropes to the quay. They aren't trying to draw the quay to the ship, but rather the ship to the quay. When we pray, we aren't trying to pull God toward our way of thinking; we're trying to draw our way of thinking into alignment with God, and so contribute to the release of God's energy in that particular situation.

Intercession is about the stretching of possibilities. We work with a too-limited view of what might be possible in our created order, and this restricts our expectancy. Much more is possible in a world with the kind of open texture that quantum physics now describes to us. Chaos theory and the Uncertainty Principle show us a world of openness, unpredictability, and connectedness that make all kinds of conversations possible.

Christians say that prayer contributes to a stretching out of the possibilities inherent in a given situation. When these possibilities are stretched to their maximum, the unexpected may happen, which people sometimes refer to as "miracles." More properly, they might be seen as the further reaches of an inherent potentiality. Or as Malcolm Muggeridge said many years ago: "The supernatural is just the infinite projection of the natural."[3] God rules from within his created order, rather than *intervening* from outside. You could say that he *under-rules* rather than *overrules*.

It follows, of course, that there are intrinsic limits to the range of possibilities in any given situation. In the (continuing) creation of a universe, there is clearly a limit to the number of variations possible within its manner of operation. You have *this* universe rather than *that* one, just as when a couple have a child, they have *this* child rather than another one, and work with the limitations and wonders of this particular personality. The parents can seek to love, persuade, cajole, or bribe their child, but they no longer have the infinite possibilities about a child such as they had before this child's conception. So it is with the world as we have it. There are intrinsic limitations to its variability. You can't have dry rain or square circles.

In terms of prayer, there are important implications. When a cancer reaches a certain stage, it will normally be beyond reversal. However—and this is crucial—we don't know when that point has been reached, so our responsibility is to pray

3. Malcolm Muggeridge, *Something Beautiful for God: Mother Teresa of Calcutta* (London: HarperCollins, 1971), 171.

that all the possibilities of healing and comfort inherent in that situation may be given to that person. We don't know where the limits of inexhaustible love lie, but they often seem to be far beyond what we had a right to expect. Jesus was always experimenting with divine love and seeing what it could achieve, and in prayer we do the same. In a created universe there are bound to be limits to these possibilities, but as we don't know what they are, we can pray hopefully and then leave the outcome to God, working through the fabric of God's own creation. John V. Taylor wrote: "The truth about God is not so much that he is omnipotent as that he is inexhaustible, and for that reason he will always succeed."[4]

Our public intercession, therefore, has to find a delicate balance. It needs to be faithful and hopeful, but not unrealistic and naïve. The wording of prayer matters, if not to God, then at least to the people of God, seeking to find a way of praying appropriately and honestly in a hard situation. Intercession is about putting our love and care at God's disposal. God will use our prayer in the best possible way. Our prayer might not be very subtle; indeed it may be misconceived, knowing as little as we do. Nevertheless the loving intention of our prayer is what matters, and God will be able to take and use that love for God's good purposes.

Ultimately the meaning of all prayer is that we get hold of God, not of God's "answers," for God is the One we most deeply need in every situation, whether of pleasure, pain, or the large territory in between.

Lively Intercession

What, then, makes for lively intercessions that engage people and help them to pray?

1. Consider the context. We have to ask ourselves what makes this particular service distinctive. Every Sunday has its own character, given to it by its place in the Church's

---

4. John V. Taylor, *The Christlike God* (London: SCM Press, 1992), chapter 7.

year, or its place in the narrative of the local church with its celebrations and remembrances. Moreover, the service might be a formal civic service or an informal all-age communion, a quiet midweek eucharist or an all-action Parish Mass. What will be the mood and color of the occasion? The intercessions may need to be reflective and spacious in one service, and faster paced and highly participative in another.

It's also important to know our congregation and what's likely to be in their minds and hearts as they come to church on this particular occasion. Are these the regulars who are used to praying in a church setting, or will there be a large family present who have come for a baptism and for whom liturgical prayer will be strange territory? What are the cultures people come from and what values, ideas, and priorities may be most prevalent? What issues are on many people's minds at present, perhaps because of the international news, local events, or personal crises? Will there be people there who are particularly sensitive to grief because of a recent bereavement, and if so, what manner of praying will help them most? There are many issues to consider, but they often come together as a package as we simply try to respond to the "personality" of the congregation as it is likely to be on that occasion.

We also need to consider what emotional range the congregation will feel comfortable with in the words and ideas we use. Traditionally people who lead intercessions have erred on the side of formality, but it is equally possible to err on the side of excessive emotion and sentimentality. The context is important. A short poem used in a local parish church may be quite out of place in a cathedral. Newspaper headlines might be very effective in a parish eucharist in one place but seem to be a gimmick in another.

2. Pray about the real world and not a narrowly religious one. People who come to church are no different from everyone else, except in the vital particular that they are seeking a Christian way through life's joys and turmoils. They are subject to the same disciplines and fragilities of work and family life, and the same pressures on their finances, their relationships, and their time. They have the same temptations and dark struggles. And yet it sometimes seems as if they are asked to take off their everyday humanity and leave it at the door of the church, to be collected again on the way out.

The intercessions, like the sermon, provide an opportunity for people to be helped to see how faith and everyday life interact. Intercession is about making connections, supremely a connection between God and the daily complexities of living. The intercessions can therefore provide real encouragement to thoughtful discipleship as people are offered ways of praying about their lives and the life of the bewildering world around them.

An interesting exercise for a training session on leading intercessions is to look at the sports pages and the celebrity pages of that day's newspapers and work out how to pray about those worlds. Given the quasi-religious significance of football to very large numbers of young men and the vast sales of celebrity magazines, this exercise isn't without its value in trying to make faith connections with every aspect of the world for which Christ came to bring life and hope.

3. Be particular. The intercessions weren't a liturgical high point in the theological college where I taught, and I was used to being bored. But suddenly here was a young man, back from time abroad, painting word pictures of various people in different parts of the world, describing their everyday lives, their families and their work, their plans and their frustrations, and using those pictures as pegs for us to pray about issues of survival and human flourishing in developing countries. I was involved; I had real people before my eyes; my imagination was engaged; I was praying!

I was experiencing what every good communicator knows, that the personal and the particular are key methods of enabling people to engage with important issues. We can pray about trade justice every week without feeling passionate, but tell us about Amir and the falling price of his crops or Bahati, a pregnant woman living with HIV, and we are immediately praying with conviction.

The principle of particularity is an important one in leading intercessions. Examples from life, quoting from up-to-date news reports, naming specific people (not just "political leaders"), using images rather than concepts—all these are ways of making intercessions immediate and compelling. In general, people who come to church know the theory; what they want is the practice. They want examples. They want a spark of imagination to light up the intercessions and bring them home. They look for reality.

On the other hand, we have to beware the danger of becoming so particular that we risk excluding those who cannot identify with the specific situations offered in the intercessions. It's like preaching about a film most people haven't seen; they can't identify with it and therefore it doesn't make the point the preacher intended. Similarly, our prayers may not resonate with others if they come too much from our own world of ideas and experiences. A balance is needed, but, if in doubt, err on the side of the specific!

4. Be vivid. Colorless language encourages no one but the most dedicated to pray. There is a danger that official liturgies opt for a limited "frequency range" in the use of language, avoiding the extremes of ecstasy and lament in order to embrace the majority on reasonably safe ground. The writers of many contemporary Anglican resources are to be commended for going further than almost all official liturgists since Cranmer in widening the emotional range, but there remains a certain safe "house" style. The intercessions give an opportunity to widen that range and to employ rich, colorful, image-laden language that excites the imagination.

The use of beautiful language and daring phrases can bring real pleasure and engagement to congregations as they pray. The naming of specific feelings that patrol the borders of normal emotions can be liberating for people frustrated with the conventional middle ground of religious language. It may be helpful to think of preparing intercessions as an exercise in painting rather than an exercise in writing. Such an approach corresponds to the fact that our minds are much more like art galleries than libraries; we experience life more through images than through ideas and concepts.

As ever, my Anglican temperament also makes me say, "But don't go over the top!" Language that is too flowery can easily seem contrived and designed to impress the congregation rather than to bring real needs before God.

5. Be aware of structure. It's not just an Anglican temperament that makes me encourage a clear structure in our intercessions. There is something in the deep processes of the human psyche that needs structure to give security and facilitate freedom. Order, structure, and a degree of familiarity enable people to relax into their praying. They sense a shape and a trajectory in the prayers, and so they are set free to participate.

This is one of the fundamental principles behind the breaking up of prayers with regular congregational responses. We can take it that most regular churchgoers know to respond to "Lord in your mercy" with "hear our prayer," or to "Lord, hear us" with "Lord, graciously hear us." But our imagination can roam widely on suitable responses, as long as the response is made clear at the start and isn't so long and difficult to remember that the congregation spends most of the time worrying about getting it right. The following are examples of simple seasonal variations:

- Advent: Your kingdom come your will be done.
- Pentecost: Lord, energize your Church with wind and fire from heaven.
- Harvest: For what we have received make us truly thankful.
- Ascension: At the name of Jesus every knee shall bow.

You could add:

- Every tongue confess him King of Glory now.

Another way of ensuring a sense of shape and direction to intercessions is to build in a movement from the local to the global or vice versa. Issues in the church can move on to the locality, then to the wider community, then to national issues, and finally to God's whole creation (or you can stop anywhere on route!). I've always met a positive response to prayers that go out in circles like the ripples caused by a stone dropped in a pond; you can pray for those closest to you in the innermost circle, then for those you usually only contact at birthdays and Christmas, then for those you meet in shops, at the gym, or walking the dog but whose names you don't know, and so on to the outer edges of the pond. Again, there's a sense of logical development.

Shape matters in prayer. We can pray in the countdown to Christmas for those who in various ways are anxious about that season—homemakers, hoping to cope, young people fearing an inner emptiness, older people feeling useless and alone, clergy fearing smaller numbers at church—each time punctuating the prayers with the words of the angel: "Do not be afraid. I bring you good news that will be for *all* people." In Holy Week we can use intercessions that involve the putting out of candles as each disciple or group of people desert Jesus on his way to the final darkness of the cry of dereliction. Again, the structure holds the prayer together and enables people to feel secure enough to enter the prayer themselves.

6. Be aware that prayers are addressed to God and biddings to the congregation. The two are often confused. "We pray for God to help Mrs. Peabody after her fall . . ." is not addressed to God, although it sounds like it. "Lord, we ask you to help Mrs. Peabody after her fall . . ." is addressed to God and is therefore prayer. A failure to distinguish the two modes of speech is one of the reasons why much intercession can feel somewhat remote and detached. It sounds as if it should be prayer, but actually it isn't directed to God and therefore keeps God at one remove.

The person leading the intercessions needs to be clear that a bidding is a very helpful lead into prayer, guiding the congregation toward the prayer itself, but that prayer is what we actually say to God. "We remember this morning the dreadful scenes from X that we saw on our television screens yesterday, and we want to pray for the victims." That's a bidding. "Father, protect and comfort those we saw on television last night. . . ." That's a prayer.

A further point to emphasize here is the need for the intercession leader to actually pray rather than to read notes.

Having labored long and with great care in the preparation, the leader may well be keeping very close to the script, but the crucial issue is the intention of the heart, and that will show in the way the intercessions are delivered. People know when someone is truly praying.

7. *Take risks, particularly with silence.* Mention has already been made of the value of stretching the normal range of content, language, image, and responses in the intercessions. This can be summed up as an invitation to take risks. It's usually when someone steps outside the norm that something memorable occurs. Convention gives us security; innovation challenges us and may help us to grow. People don't usually talk about things they are used to; they talk about things that have taken them out of their normal experience and given them something new to think about.

At the start of Lent or Holy Week, members of the congregation could be given a four-inch nail as a reminder of the road Jesus was travelling toward the cross, and that nail can be the focal point of the intercessions as we pray for those whose journeys are hard and painful. On another occasion each person can be given a sticky note on which to write a particular concern and then be invited to attach the note to a cross or the altar rail or place it in the empty tomb of an Easter Garden. In less formal settings, people can be invited to light candles and come forward to place them safely in a sand tray or on a stand. They may say a prayer, name the subject of the prayer, or simply do it all in silence. With advances in digital technology, many possibilities open up, such as the use of evocative images on a data projector, or even short scenes from the news or from a contemporary film. There are many books now offering creative ideas for riskier intercessions.[5]

A growing number of churches are now experimenting with an open period of "liquid prayer" when the congregation is able

---

5. For example, Julia McGuinness, *Creative Praying in Groups* (London: SPCK, 2005); John Pritchard, *The Intercessions Handbook*, new ed. (London: SPCK, 2005); John Pritchard, *The Second Intercession Handbook* (London: SPCK, 2004); Sue Wallace, *Multi-Sensory Prayer* (Milton Keynes, UK: Scripture Union, 2000).

to move around the building at their own pace and pray at a number of different "stations." At these stations there might be a prayer tree to pray for the sick, a map and night lights to pray for world needs, scripture readings on prayer at the lectern, a mirror for confession, candles at the font to pray for the newborn or newly baptized, a place for anointing, and so on. This will usually be too long an option for a parish eucharist, but elements of it might be used or it could be adapted for special occasions such as a parish weekend away.[6]

One of the major areas of risk, but one that can open up whole new vistas of reality in our intercessions, is the use of silence and space. Offering people the time actually to pray, rather than just to listen to someone else saying prayers, can revolutionize people's appreciation of this time of prayer. Our services are often awash with words, and many people long for some genuine space, some time for reflection, some rest from the constant assault of a culture talking itself to death. If you offer some people even a little silence in the intercessions, they will come and weep on your shoulder and write you into their will.

Of course it isn't quite as simple as that. Some people are made anxious by silence; they don't know what to do with it and soon get twitchy. There is also the anxiety of the person leading the intercessions to take into account; we easily lose our nerve and cut the silence short just when it's settling down. We need to hold our nerve and go through the pain barrier. It lets people know that we really are serious about offering them time to pray in their own way. The secret is in the way we lead people into silence. It needs to be clearly signaled that there will now be a silent period for specific prayer, and clear guidance needs to be given on how that time might be used. To say, "We'll now be quiet to pray by ourselves" is likely to leave many people floundering. On the other hand, we might say: "In silence, now, please pray for those one or two people

---

6. Consider, for example, the style of the kinds of "missional worship for the emerging church" described and commended in Mary Gray-Reeves and Michael Perham, *The Hospitality of God: Missional Worship for the Emerging Church* (New York: Church Publishing, 2010).

who are particularly in your mind and heart today. Pray for all that's best for them from the God who loves them immeasurably." This gives the congregation sufficient guidance to go on and leads them clearly into their own prayer.

8. *Training and feedback.* In recent years the Church has put a lot of resources into training people for the new services of *Common Worship*. Courses also abound in preaching, making music, taking all-age services, using IT, Godly Play, puppetry, even welcoming people to church. What has been slower to take off has been training in leading intercessions. However, the demand is growing. A Saturday morning or two evening sessions is not much to ask of a church that takes its praying seriously. Just as important, however, can be intercessors having their own feedback system with two or three trusted people ready to offer comment on what helped them to pray on that occasion and what hindered them. We may cross our fingers and hope the way we lead intercessions helps others, but it's far better actually to find out! Honesty is vital, as is the sensitivity of those friends in saying the positive things first—and generously—before pointing out the negatives.

Why It Matters

Prayer is one of the most basic instincts of humankind. Some people try to shake it off, but prayer simply emerges naturally in times of gratitude, distress, anxiety, or hope. According to research conducted by automobile associations, three out of four of us pray at times in the car, and 22 percent of us pray regularly in those little steel boxes. We are irrevocably praying animals.

What matters, therefore, is the quality and the growth of that prayerful instinct. We may start from the commercial standpoint, "Does it produce the goods?" But in due course, we would hope for a fuller appreciation and enjoyment of the possibilities of prayer. Prayer is a relationship, not a cashpoint. It's not magic, trying to bend the world to our will. Rather, it works the other way round. Nevertheless, we can believe that the instinct of people, always and everywhere, to pray for people and situations, is not without good reason. Things change when we pray. We can't be sure what things. It may be the person we're praying for, the situation itself, or even (especially) ourselves. And we can't attribute simple causality to the process by saying that our prayers caused such-and-such to happen. We are in the presence of much more mystery than that. But God seems to use our prayers as part of God's dynamic economy of love. God seems to have made things such that God needs our partnership in the sustaining and re-creating of the world.

And that's why intercession matters so much. This isn't simply an arcane religious ritual. It's a crucial part of the healing of a damaged world. Rabbi Jonathan Sacks said: "The world we build tomorrow is born in the prayers we say today."[7]

That's why it matters. Pray on.

---

7. Jonathan Sacks, *The Koren Siddur: New Translation and Commentary by Chief Rabbi Sir Jonathan Sacks* (New Milford, CT: Koren Publishers, 2006), xliv.

Part Two

Sacramental Actions

"LITURGY" IS OFTENTIMES TAKEN TO mean something like "work of the people," a notion that folds out neatly as an emphasis on participation. Vatican II's insistence that "full, conscious, and active participation" is the first principle of liturgical renewal has been commonly echoed by an ecumenical array.[1] At the same time, part of what ecumenical movement in liturgical renewal has secured for the churches was a shared dual emphasis on word and sacrament, with gospel proclamation and eucharistic prayer[2] at the center of each respectively.

In recent years, Anglican churches have published creative material on how scripture reading might be enhanced so as to invite greater participation.[3] But less material has emerged, at least at the same official level, on enhancement of participation in eucharistic prayer—though it seems that considerable effort of such kind may be needed, given recognition that "prayer at table" is apparently oftentimes considered to be the most "boring" part of the service.[4] There does not always appear to be much of the sense expressed in some early Christian great prayers of thanksgiving: raised with

---

1. *Sacrosanctum concilium*, 14.

2. *Common Worship* speaks of eucharistic prayer, other traditions of a "prayer of great thanksgiving" or "great prayer of thanksgiving," or the like.

3. For example, *New Patterns for Worship* (London: Church House Publishing, 2002), esp. 99–102.

4. For a spirited defense of eucharistic prayer in the face of suggestions to "'drop the long, boring bits' (also known as the eucharistic prayer)," see Robert Cotton and Kenneth Stevenson, *On the Receiving End: How People Experience What We Do in Church* (London: Mowbray, 1996), 16.

"open mouths" and "upturned faces,"[5] as if astonished and amazed.

Some of the *Common Worship* materials do, however, suggest that eucharistic prayer can be spruced up with song—and not simply mass settings but choruses, for which *Patterns for Worship* provides a model.[6] Following *Patterns for Worship*'s lead, not only the communion pieces included in major hymnals, but the kind of assembly song that characterizes charismatic church style might be explored—so, at least on occasion, "Open the eyes of my heart, Lord," "In the stillness of this hour," "Let our praise to you be as incense," "You are holy, you are whole," or any number of possibilities current in at least some contemporary praise resources.[7]

Song involves the body in ways that simply speaking may not, and some other—perhaps more daring—proposals about vivifying participation in eucharistic prayer involve quite intentional gesturing of the body in praise and sacrifice, that is, in the ancient *orans* posture of prayer. This posture (found, for example, in depictions in the catacomb spaces used by early Christians) has long been associated with the presider, but—perhaps in part because charismatic church style has distributed the gesture, as it were—it is now not altogether unknown, if not yet common, to find the gesture being adopted by the whole assembly.

The lack of attention to an apparent felt-need for more experiential involvement in eucharistic prayer among the assembly is perhaps odd, given that the same prayer has been a—if not *the*—major focus of academic study of liturgy. Indeed, courses in liturgy have sometimes been organized as histories of what

---

5. Cf. R. C. D. Jasper and Geoffrey Cumings, eds., *Prayers of the Eucharist: Early and Reformed*, 2nd ed. (Collegeville, MN: Liturgical Press, 1987), 43.

6. *Patterns for Worship* (London: Church House Publishing, 1989, 252) suggested that "Part or all of a song which is a version of 'Holy, holy' . . . may replace the 'Holy, holy'" and gave an example of such a song.

7. "Open the eyes of my heart": Paul Baloche, 1997, Integrity's Hosanna Music; "In the stillness of this hour": Scott Brenner, 1989, Mercy/Vineyard Music; "Let our praise to you be as incense": Brent Chambers, 1979, Scripture in Song Music; "You are holy, you are whole": Per Harling, 1990, Ton Vis Produktion. These songs—and many that share an accent on divine holiness—can be found in contemporary praise music collections.

it is possible to know about the development of eucharistic prayer,[8] and the immediately surrounding words and gestures of the communion rite. No doubt, this tendency relates to ways in which study of the prayer over time, and particular traditions' embrace of particular forms of it, reveal major eucharistic controversies which have done and continue to fracture the unity of the churches, divide Christian opinion, and threaten one another's theological sensitivities.

Some distinctive pathways through eucharistic controversies and questions have marked the traditions that contemporary Anglicans, despite their differences, share. Yet, past means of engaging and resolving the questions by previous generations of Anglicans are not the only trajectories shaping contemporary Anglican understanding. Ecumenical and liturgical movements in the twentieth century are also a very significant feature of the present Anglican liturgical landscape. This is to say that Cranmer and those who succeeded him in shaping the evolution of prayer books in the emerging Church of England, and many forebears along the way, might recognize only some and not all of what is commonplace in Anglican practice in different places in the world today. The fact that Anglicans in different places take up some different stances—shaped by some different, but of course related, historical moments, accidents, and intentional decisions—surfaces in the present collection in the fact that while all the authors write as members of the Anglican Communion, three in Part Two do so from within the Church of England, while one joins in from the Episcopal Church. This, apart from matters of church style (in older, more familiar, but gendered terms, "churchmanship"), means that the following pages contain somewhat different expressions—no doubt some imbibed, some intentional—on particular issues, practices, foci, and terms. This in itself might be regarded as a signal of the vitality and largesse that many Anglicans have loved in their tradition.

---

8. See Jasper and Cumings, *Prayers of the Eucharist*, as an influential example of this.

Parts of the ecumenical consensus to emerge in the twentieth century—to which Anglicans in different settings
responded in different and related ways—were, in fact, shaped
by Anglican thinkers. In relation to the four actions of gospel
memory—taking, blessing, breaking, and giving—with which
this part of this volume is concerned, Dom Gregory Dix, an
Anglican monk of Nashdom Abbey, is especially notable.
Although aspects of his understanding have been superseded
over time, now gaining less assent than several decades ago,
Dix's *The Shape of the Liturgy* has left an abiding mark on
liturgical studies and movements in ecumenical liturgical
renewal.[9] The shape he discerned is fourfold and drawn from
gospel stories that in fact suggest seven actions—bread and
wine are taken (=2), blessed (=2), and given (=2), and bread
alone is broken. Yet he asserts:

> The liturgical tradition reproduces these seven
> actions as four: (1) The offertory; bread and wine
> are "taken" and placed on the table together. (2)
> The prayer; the president gives thanks to God over
> bread and wine together. (3) The fraction; the bread
> is broken. (4) The communion; the bread and wine
> are distributed together.[10]

Although later scholars have not always shared Dix's confidence that "the liturgical tradition" mediates this shape
"with absolute unanimity" or that they constitute "the absolute invariable nucleus of every eucharistic rite known to us
throughout antiquity from the Euphrates to Gaul," it nevertheless remains, as Simon Jones remarks, that "it is difficult to over-estimate the influence which this simple and
apparently self-evident thesis has exerted over liturgical
scholarship and revision."[11] Dix's construct of the presider's

---

9. See Dom Gregory Dix, *The Shape of the Liturgy*, new ed. (London: Continuum,
2005). The book prefixes Dix's original 1945 text with a splendid essay by Simon
Jones setting out the enduring significance as well as contemporary questions of Dix's
book.

10. Dix, *Shape of the Liturgy*, 48.

11. Simon Jones, "Introduction," in Dix, *Shape of the Liturgy*, xv.

actions—the "manual acts"—at table is more or less broadly inscribed in countless ritual books and liturgical studies of the latter twentieth and early twenty-first centuries. Anglican appropriation of Dix's legacy—welcoming and resistant or expansive in different measures—can be traced in Inter-Anglican Liturgical Consultation ventures like *Our Thanks and Praise*[12]; and others' reception of Dix's basic construct, with various degree of questioning, can be traced in shared collections like the World Council of Churches' *Eucharistic Worship in Ecumenical Contexts*.[13]

The authors in Part Two continue the search to articulate spiritual practices that express the fourfold sequence. They take each of the actions in turn, inviting readers to ponder meanings of the taking, blessing, breaking, and giving of gospel memory. According to their particular expertise, they explore the actions liturgically and theologically, not so as to sketch a narrowly priestly spirituality—that is, open only or mainly to the one actually handling things through the manual acts—but inviting the participation of Christian assemblies at large.

Lizette Larson-Miller's ecumenical sympathies are reflected in her major study of the Roman Catholic rites for anointing the sick,[14] and she brings to her piece in the present volume her specialty as a liturgical historian, drawing on key voices from the past most relevant to her focus. Of particular interest in her essay on taking are the comparisons

---

12. David R. Holeton, ed., *Our Thanks and Praise: The Eucharist in Anglicanism Today* (Toronto: Anglican Book Centre, 1998). The Episcopal Church has become somewhat strangely out of step with majority Anglican practice in this area of ritual, and the previous volume in the Weil Series in Liturgics, Louis Weil, *Liturgical Sense: The Logic of Rite* (New York: Church Publishing, 2012), offers compelling advocacy for an alternative to current Episcopal Church ritual (see his chapter 7, pages 81–100).

13. Thomas Best and Dagmar Heller, eds., *Eucharistic Worship in Ecumenical Contexts: The Lima Liturgy and Beyond* (Geneva: World Council of Churches, 1994). For recent discussion of eucharistic practice in some other traditions, see Robert Gribben, *Uniting in Thanksgiving: The Great Prayers of Thanksgiving of the Uniting Church in Australia* (Melbourne: Uniting Academic Press, 2008), and Martha Moore-Keish, *Do This in Remembrance of Me: A Ritual Approach to Reformed Eucharistic Theology* (Grand Rapids, MN: Eerdmans, 2008).

14. Lizette Larson-Miller, *The Sacrament of Anointing the Sick* (Collegeville, MN: Liturgical Press, 2005).

she repeatedly raises between *Common Worship* and the Episcopal Church's Book of Common Prayer. Larson-Miller explores different takings in the communion rite, at the preparation of the table, perhaps as an action accompanying the institution narrative within the eucharistic prayer, and in the exchange of giving and receiving as the sacramental gifts are shared. In doing so, she draws our attention to the use of our hands "as an expression of the heart," to the meanings of tradition, and to the dialogical "dance" of the liturgy between God and God's people in their mutual "commitment to co-creation." In her evocative essay, Larson-Miller encourages us to relish the ambiguous depth of meaning in the rich juxtapositions of the liturgy: offering is preceded by giving, and God gives what we offer and offers what we take.

David Stancliffe contributes to this series with an essay on blessing—the action that gives eucharist its name. He does so as the chairperson of the Liturgical Commission for the Church of England at the time through which *Common Worship* was introduced to parishes. He oversaw, therefore, the group and process that produced the texts through which worshipers give thanks at table, as well as the rubrics that choreograph aspects of the ritual. In his essay for this collection, he complements his work in that representative role with a vivid piece of personal writing in which he locates his own experiences of celebrating the eucharist; his affection for particular rites, places, moods, and styles of prayer; and a strong sense of being graced by these things. He comments on some of the emphases of contemporary Church of England texts, and constantly recalls us to the wider context of the rituals, gestures, spaces, sounds, smells, and things that shape the ambience of liturgy. So while leaning into history of texts for the great prayer, he more stresses the non-textual dimensions of celebration in ways that open up thinking about eucharistic prayer in fresh ways.

Alan Bartlett writes a chapter on breaking, conscious of experiences of oppression, abuse, and damage. These experiences may be difficult to talk about, rendering the topic of breaking dangerous, with the possibly of opening persons to (further) pain. Nevertheless, he searches for what he calls "a healthy spirituality of brokenness," buoyed by confidence that the breaking of bread in the communion rite—also known as the fraction—links strongly to the cross of Christ where accompanying presence in pain may be found. Alan takes a relatively more conservative stance—among others, to Dix, as he acknowledges—in mapping the breaking of bread and the suffering of Jesus, and this lends a particular christological and passion-weighted focus to his reflections. For him, though, this finds its place alongside his stated sense that the father-figure of the parable of the prodigal son (Luke 15:11–31) is a—perhaps *the*—key image by which contemporary Anglicans picture the divine. So discussion of suffering finds its context in a wider orbit.

John Thomson brings a strong emphasis on mission and evangelism to his chapter on giving, drawing on the post-liberal insights of Stanley Hauerwas and others. While speaking throughout of worship in general and eucharist in particular, he chooses not to explore particular details and possibilities for the liturgical action of giving in the communion sequence. Rather, he pours his attention into a powerful and positive account of worship, of participation in the eucharist shaping worshipers as themselves the thing given in communion: worshipers are "gifts for the world." Practical examples and insightful anecdotes ground his understandings in a conviction that his vision can be realized. So we are challenged to believe that through "imbib[ing the] transforming grace of God eucharistically in word and sacrament," we might witness as "cascades of grace" to a "new society" emerging under God's reign, the church as a public service to the enveloping community.

CHAPTER 5

Taking

Lizette Larson-Miller

Take and Eat

I'VE ALWAYS FOUND IT A bit disconcerting when a young child comes forward for communion in parental arms, reaches out to take the consecrated bread in his or her hand, only to have the parent tell them "no" or pull their hand away. There is something so honest and connective in the reaching out to engage in communion that, setting aside differing Anglican canonical regulations and parents as first catechists for the sake of argument, there is a moment of sadness in the event of non-communion. More than simply appeasing a child's desire to have what others are taking, the desire to respond to the gesture of reaching out in that ritual moment, and reaching out toward God and fellow Christians, compels one to respond— and therein lies the mystery of this ritual exchange of taking and receiving on the one hand, and giving on the other.

The multiple communions that are layered beneath and above the human exchange of taking the gifts, the elements of the eucharist, at any given point in the liturgy are symbolic of communion encounters in life, as is the case for the liturgy as a whole.

> [Liturgy] is the way that the Christian community symbolically re-enacts its relationship with God.

> This liturgical spirituality implies the actual participation in the mission of the church as a means of opening ourselves to the saving power of Christ and the transforming actions of the Spirit. This spirituality is a concrete way of living the gospel under the inspiration of the same Spirit. There is, then, a direct relationship between social justice and the way liturgical spirituality leads the Christian to experiences of transcendence.[1]

This ritualization of relational give-and-take is symbolic of our ongoing relationship with God, a dialogue in word and action, in spirit and flesh.

This chapter focuses on both the liturgical action of taking at several places in the eucharistic liturgy, as well as the sacramental spirituality that shapes our understanding of, and flows from, the ritual action. As with any symbol, whether it be word, gesture, person, or place, the symbol gives "rise to thought."[2] What of our graced lives is reflected in the action of taking in the eucharist, and what is informed by this taking? What has been our inherited understanding through the richness of long Christian tradition, and what new insights are emerging as twenty-first century Christians now engage in these ritual actions? Looking first at the liturgical actions of taking and their trajectory from the gospels through liturgical practice to theological reflection, this essay then moves to the interaction between what we do in liturgy and its relationship to how we live as Christians—what difference does this ritual action make?

To Take—A Fundamental Liturgical Action

The fourfold action of take-bless-break-give, laid out in the synoptic gospels and in the Apostle Paul's First Letter to the

---

1. James L. Empereur and Christopher G. Kiesling, *The Liturgy that Does Justice* (Collegeville, MN: Liturgical Press, 1990), 15.

2. Paul Ricoeur, *The Symbolism of Evil* (Boston: Beacon Press, 1967), 347–48.

Corinthians, is presented as the pattern of Jesus and his disciples, and has been the primary template for celebrating the eucharist throughout Christian history: "While they were eating, Jesus took a loaf of bread, and after blessing it he broke it, gave it to the disciples, and said, 'Take, eat; this is my body'" (as recorded in the version of the last supper at Matthew 26:26). This sequence of actions has not only shaped the way the eucharistic liturgy took form throughout different centuries and in different cultures, but it has been highlighted from time to time as a way to understand the fundamental shape of the eucharist through actions, not just words, faithful to scripture and tradition.

The action of taking occurs several times in the eucharistic liturgy, but does it communicate a similar meaning each time? The first "taking" is, at heart, a practicality: the one who will bless and break and give the bread (with three parallel actions for the cup of wine) needs to get the bread (and wine) to begin the process, and so must take it from those who offer it. In *Common Worship* Order One, this part of the liturgy comes under the eucharistic rite proper "The Liturgy of the Sacrament" and is called "Preparation of the Table— Taking of the Bread and Wine." The sequence of rubrics notes the gathering and presenting of the gifts of the people, the preparation of the table, and ends with "the president takes the bread and wine."[3] In the 1979 Book of Common Prayer of the Episcopal Church, this liturgical action also comes under the eucharistic rite proper, here "The Holy Communion," and is called the Offertory. The rubrics say that the celebrant[4]

---

3. *Common Worship: Services and Prayers for the Church of England* (London: Church House Publishing, 2000), 175. This study will focus primarily on Order One of *Common Worship* (hereafter, *CW*), although the reformation-era construction of Order Two makes an interesting contrast with the ecumenical pattern of *CW* and the Episcopal Church of the USA's BCP 1979.

4. Note that in both *CW* and BCP 1979, the minister is a priest (unless noted as a deacon at the setting of the table), but that the BCP 1979 still uses the title "Celebrant," from the Latin *celebrare*, which carries the medieval ecclesial associations of the one who actually performs the religious rite, while *CW* has returned to an early church term of "President" or "Presider" from the Latin *praesidere*, the one who occupies the seat of authority in the assembly. Often celebrant and presider are used interchangeably, but the former carries a cultic performative association that the latter does not emphasize and represents one of the differences between the Episcopal Church and the Church of England.

may begin the offertory with a sentence of scripture, that
there may be music, and that representatives of the congregation bring "the people's offerings of bread and wine . . . to
the deacon or celebrant. The people stand while the offerings
are presented and placed on the Altar."[5] Both of these reflect
a normative Sunday morning pattern of the gathered church.

The second "taking" is a bit more intangible. This may
occur in the midst of the eucharistic prayer,[6] so-called literally
in Order One of *CW* and labeled "the Great Thanksgiving" in
the BCP. *CW* Order One has eight eucharistic prayers, the
BCP has six between Rites I and II, and in all of them, the so-
called "Words of Institution," which form a liturgical harmo-
nization of Jesus' words as recorded in the gospels, generally
come at the end of the anamnetic section of the eucharistic
prayer. This is the portion of the eucharistic prayer that
praises God by reminding God of all the wonderful things
that God has done for us, and concludes with the recitation of
what Jesus did at the Last Supper. Following this, the prayer
invokes the Holy Spirit over the gifts and the prayer shifts to
intercession, asking God to do these things now. In *CW* Order
One, the words of institution may be accompanied by manual
acts, although unlike Order Two, they are not narrowly specified.[7] In the Episcopal Church's BCP, the rubrics at the words
of institution are some of the most precise in the prayerbook:

> At the following words concerning the bread, the
> Celebrant is to hold it, or lay a hand upon it; and
> at the words concerning the cup, to hold or place a

---

5. BCP 1979, 361.

6. See *CW* 333, footnote 17, which reads in part, "The bread and wine must be
taken into the president's hands and replaced upon the table either after the table has
been prepared or during the Eucharistic prayer." (Compare note 16 on the eucharist in
the *Alternative Service Book 1980*, the authorized alternative to the 1662 prayer book
in the Church of England, prior to *Common Worship* which was introduced in 2000).

7. My sense that there are generally manual acts done comes from personal
experience, both in attending and participating in numerous eucharistic liturgies in
the UK and also in presiding at them; however, one person's experience is not always
the best indicator! See the recent discussion in Benjamin Gordon-Taylor and Simon
Jones, *Celebrating the Eucharist* (London: SPCK, 2005), 62–63.

hand upon the cup and any other vessel containing wine to be consecrated.[8]

So while the words of Jesus—"take, eat"—are heard, there is a literal taking of the bread and the cup by the hands of the celebrant which accompanies the words (or the words accompany the gesture!).

The third "taking" is at communion itself. In *CW* the simple rubrics state: "The president and people receive communion. Authorized words of distribution are used and the communicant replies "Amen."[9] In the BCP, the rubrics state: "The ministers receive the Sacrament in both kinds, and then immediately deliver it to the people." Communion is given with one of the authorized formulae listed.[10] The emphasis here is not on *taking* communion, but on *receiving*, but certainly there is a semantic and ritual dance that occurs in the giving to and the taking in at communion. One of the very interesting developments in the Episcopal Church has been an increasing adoption of the Eastern Christian practice of the celebrant/presider not taking communion him or herself (or giving it to oneself), but receiving it from one of the other ministers,[11] which has the effect of turning the emphasis away from taking and toward receiving with regard to the person of the priest, and toward a greater similarity in the reception of communion for all, celebrant and people.

These three ritual moments are the primary occasions for the action of taking, around which this essay centers. There are other points in the eucharist when the action of taking will occur, even involving the bread and the cup, but they are either secondary or occasional, so these three will be a sufficient base on which to build the following discussion of

---

8. BCP 1979, 362.

9. *CW*, 181.

10. BCP 1979, 365.

11. This is not an approved practice according to the rubrics of BCP 1979. For a discussion on the spirituality and theology of such a practice, see Robert Taft, *Beyond East and West: Problems in Liturgical History* (Washington, DC: Pastoral Press, 1984), 101–09.

spirituality and theology, preceded by a brief excursus on the symbolic importance of hands in liturgy and the ritual action of taking.

Into Your Hands
I Commend My Spirit

Judaism and Christianity are both religions that have much to say about hands. In the Hebrew Scriptures, hands, particularly the hand of God, are a repeating symbol of external action, a biblical sign of the outward action of God or of God's chosen ones. The gospel stories of Jesus touching and healing continue this trajectory of the hand as the symbol of the whole person and of power transmitted to another. In Christian liturgy, hands become the outward expression of the heart. "Lift up your hearts" is often outwardly enacted by lifting up one's hands, as "the body brings to prayer the image of the qualities of the soul."[12] Hands are used for blessing, to show honor to holy objects, are symbolically washed, and are the means of our communion, the giving and taking of the consecrated bread and wine.

The oldest Christian tradition of taking communion that we know of is in the hand. There are several brief mentions of how to receive communion in the early church, the most well known being Cyril of Jerusalem's description in the late fourth century in his instructions to the newly baptized.

> When you approach, do not go stretching out your open hands or having your fingers spread out, but make the left hand into a throne for the right which will receive the King, and then cup your open hand and take the body of Christ, reciting the Amen. Then sanctify with all care your eyes by touching the Sacred Body and receive it.[13]

---

12. Origin, *On Prayer,* 31.

13. Cyril of Jerusalem, *Mystagogical Catecheses,* 5.21.

Cyril's emphasis on the "how" of reception is dictated by the "what"—the recognition that neophytes (newly initiated) are receiving the very God to whom they have oriented their lives. But it is the hands that become both a dwelling for Christ's body and a vehicle for reception into the communicant's own flesh. This meeting between God, individual, and human community is a sacramental encounter of particular intensity. Not every liturgical tradition has stressed the communion procession, but such processions do provide a wonderful theological image—a mutual drawing in, God into us and us into God. The ancient call to communion, "holy things for holy people," is a call to recognize that, in spite of our sinfulness, this moment makes us "worthy" to stand in God's presence and to approach these mysteries. To receive by hand shows outwardly what we encounter inwardly: God from God, Light from Light. The Syrian theologian Philoxenus, writing in the early sixth century, gracefully put it this way:

> When you have extended your hands and taken the Body, bow, and put your hands before your face, and worship the living Body whom you hold. Then speak with him in a low voice, and with your gaze resting upon him say to him: "I carry you, living God who is incarnate in the bread, and I embrace you in my palms, Lord of the worlds whom no world has contained . . . as you have made me worthy to approach you and receive you—and see, my hands embrace you confidently—make me worthy, Lord, to eat you in a holy manner and to taste the food which is your body as a taste of your life."[14]

But this taking of communion is not just about our having been found worthy to receive, and our taking in of Christ (just as we put on Christ at baptism) is also a challenge to us to be open to how this communion might change us. We have often prayed in Anglican liturgies throughout history that we not

---

14. Philoxenus, translated by Aelred Cody, *Rule of Prayer, Rule of Faith* (Collegeville, MN: Liturgical Press, 1996), 62–63.

approach communion solely for our own comfort, but acknowledge the invitation that is presented to us. So the BCP:

> Save us from the presumption of coming to this Table
> for solace only, and not for strength;
> for pardon only, and not for renewal.[15]

This invitation is one of surrender and obedience, to put ourselves in God's hands. And this is to admit our dependence, our lack of total control. While with Philoxenus we say, "I carry you, living God . . . my hands embrace you confidently," we also stand in need of remembering that this is not a polite tea in which we participate, but a holy communion in which we may very well be taken. Our "Amen" to the declaration "the body of Christ" is also a commitment to a self-emptying that allows more room for God, and to both trust in God's wisdom in whose hands we now are and to accept that God may have plans for us not yet fully known to us.

We Possess a Treasure

To take something generally means to control it, to get possession of an object, a person, or a place by force. Conversely, to be taken *by* something often means that we are overwhelmed by another person or idea to the extent that it consumes us so that all other facets of our life become less important or even irrelevant. The similarities between the two circle around the connection between possession and relationship, and while the idea of possessing or controlling something seems quite out of place in a discussion on the eucharist, there is something passionate and intentional about the concept when used theologically. Communion is about relationship, our relationship first and foremost with God, and by necessary extension, in our relationship with every human being. Relationships require a dialogue; they are a two-way street. When we are offered something, we need to respond, by either refusing to take or

---

15. Here the American prayer book has adapted the older prayer and inserted it into Eucharistic Prayer C (BCP 1979, 372).

by taking. But having taken something, we need to further make a decision if that something will remain external to us or if we will be open to it becoming part of the very essence of ourselves, taking the chance that what we have taken in will overtake us.

If we reflect on the third ritual moment of taking discussed above, the taking of communion, we can begin to see the layers of meaning contained in the response of taking what is offered. We take the consecrated bread and wine, and enter into a communion, physical and spiritual, with that which we have taken. It is a communion with the living God, this bread of heaven and cup of salvation, that which keeps us in eternal life, but it joins us with all the other individuals taking communion too, a so-called vertical and horizontal communion, forming a cross at the center of our lives.

In the world in which Jesus himself lived, as well as in many cultures today, it matters with whom you eat. When individuals eat together, they are saying something about their relationship one to another. Even in the United States, there are still meals in the general culture that carry emotional meanings—bringing a boyfriend or girlfriend home to eat with the family for the first time, funeral meals, wedding banquets, etc. There is also a tremendous amount of writing on both sides of the Atlantic about the importance of the daily family meal—parents and children eating together. The meal is not just about physical nourishment, although that is important; it is also about social nourishment, the occasion to stop individual activities and do something together. Taking the initiative to be the domestic church, a community in communion for a while, helps makes sense of taking communion on Sunday morning, the one meal informs the other. We are part of something outside ourselves which then becomes part of the essence of who each of us is. In liturgical language, we "evermore dwell in him, and he in us" through this invitation to take and eat.

Take, Eat, This Is My Body

The second of the rituals of taking in the eucharist discussed above is that in the midst of the eucharistic prayer, when the presider is instructed to lay a hand on or hold the bread and then the cup at the words of institution. In Anglicanism, we try delicately (but often, in reality, very clumsily) to balance three different inheritances of ritual consecration at this moment in the eucharistic prayer. From a late medieval Latin tradition, we have inherited a focus on the words of Jesus and the accompanying manual acts of the priest to mark the moment of consecration. This was also the favored Protestant reduction of the Roman Canon, often using these words alone, or the Apostle Paul's version in 1 Corinthians. From Eastern Christianity, we have adapted and Westernized a focus on the work of the Holy Spirit in the eucharistic prayer by a trajectory that says it is the epiclesis that consecrates, with its accompanying gesture ("Sanctify them by your Holy Spirit" in Prayer A of BCP 1979, "grant that by the power of your Holy Spirit . . ." in Prayer A of *CW*). And from the contemporary ecumenical eucharistic perspective, we have inherited a theology that the entire eucharistic prayer is consecratory, mirrored in the downplaying of manual acts at both the words of institution and epiclesis in favor of a sustained posture throughout the prayer, as well as a pronounced elevation with the gifts at the end of the prayer. The focus of the conversation on the *moment* of consecration, or change, or blessing, for so many years has obscured many other potential starting points for theological reflection, such as the binary structure of thanksgiving and supplication that other scholars have seen as a better hermeneutic for understanding multiple eucharistic theologies.[16]

All of this is tied in with understanding the action of "taking" at this particular point in the liturgy because it has

---

16. "Talley's thesis is that the classic structure of the eucharistic prayer common to all its variants is the pattern of thanksgiving followed by supplication, that theological reflection on the eucharist ought to begin here, and that the obscuring of this structure has been the source of the major problems in Western theology, for example, the emergence of the idea of a 'moment of consecration'" (William R. Crockett, "Eucharistic Theology and Anglican Eucharistic Revision," in David R. Holeton, ed., *Our Thanks and Praise: The Eucharist in Anglicanism Today* [Toronto: Anglican Book Centre, 1998], 37).

often been difficult to see the words of Jesus (at least in the harmonized gospel version that we use liturgically) as part of the thanksgiving. This thankful remembrance of God's actions generally concludes with the anamnesis of what Jesus did and said at the Last Supper. Are these words part of the larger sacrifice of praise and thanksgiving, or are they a separate efficacious speech-act?

Arguing for one position or another is beyond the scope of this essay, but in the midst of this theological discussion is the command: "Take, eat." Is it an invitation said by a priest who by looking meaningfully at people is reenacting what Jesus did? Or is it a narrative and ritual action of *why* Jesus did what Jesus did? If one tends toward the latter interpretation and puts these highly charged words in their context, the actions of Jesus (and by extension, our symbolic actions and words) are always participating in the reality they symbolize and pointing beyond themselves. "Take, eat: This is my Body, *which is given for you* . . . This is my Blood of the new Covenant, *which is shed for you and for many for the forgiveness of sins.*"[17] To take this body and this blood is to not only take on the joys and obligations discussed above in the section on communion, but it is to make sense of taking in a Christian understanding. To take something is not to keep it for oneself, but to hand it on. *Traditio*, tradition. We remind ourselves who we are when we see this bread and cup taken and hear these words, and we remember that we are to hand on this treasure, not possess it solely for ourselves. This is the sacred meal, it is sacramental (which is not the opposite of real!). It calls to mind story upon story into which our own stories may be inserted and drawn up.

> Such a meal is generally accompanied with . . . an oral commemoration of the event, to which is then added, with the meal, a commemoration in sacrifice and communion. The evocation of the past event is made first at the level of memory, then at the level of the ritual meal. The liturgy of the word elicits

17. As cited in BCP 1979, 362–63. Emphasis added.

the liturgy of the meal, which actualizes here and now the past event, or at least renders present the divine benevolence manifested in the event.[18]

So a Christian taking, particularly at this point where the presider is taking and telling the story outwardly for all who are gathered around to celebrate the eucharist, is to take not just for oneself, but for the good of the Church and the world.

Earth Has Given and Human Hands Have Made

Finally, we come back to the first ritual of taking, the taking of the bread and wine brought to the altar at the preparation of the table (or the "offertory" in the American prayer book). The Book of Common Prayer has no prescribed text to accompany the presentation and placement of the gifts on the altar; *CW* has a set of twelve prayer options, which begin with a variation of a prayer (already a variation of a verse from the Revelation of John) included in a number of prayerbooks throughout the Anglican Communion:

Yours, Lord, is the greatness, the power, the glory, the splendour, and the majesty; for everything in heaven and on earth is yours. All things come from you, and of your own do we give you.[19]

"All things come from you, and of your own do we give you." This wonderfully brief sentence summarizes the first of the two theological conundrums that arise at this point in the liturgy: How can we take, bless, break and give something that is not ours to begin with? And what exactly are we doing with these gifts that are not ours—are we offering them to God, God who has already offered God's Son, the offerer and

---

18. Philippe Rouillard, "From Human Meal to Christian Eucharist," in R. Kevin Seasoltz, ed., *Living Bread, Saving Cup: Readings on the Eucharist* (Collegeville, MN: Liturgical Press, 1987), 136.

19. *CW*, 291.

offering?[20] What does the ritual action of taking have to do with these two theological issues? Again, to stay with the focus on the action of "take" is to enter into these issues to the extent of reminding ourselves that they exist and are understood to mean different things. The gifts of bread and wine (and often, money)[21] are brought up and taken, handed over, *traditio*, in an action that is part of a chain of handing over: from God—to us—to God—to us—to the world.

As presider, to take the bread and wine from the hands of others is to express outwardly a covenant of commitment to use the gifts as intended for the good of all. The rite in the Book of Common Prayer for the ordination of a priest describes this in two ways: "may she . . . rightly administer the sacraments of the New Covenant" and "As a priest . . . you are to share . . . in the celebration of the mysteries of Christ's Body and Blood."[22] The two phrases are expressing two different aspects of the presiding priest's role—both the administrator, the presider acting "rightly," with integrity for the good of the community, and as one of a whole community that is celebrating. All are "doing" the eucharist, all are participating, but there are different roles, just as there are different ministries and gifts in the church. The Apostle Paul's wonderful analogy of the church as a body in 1 Corinthians 14 is a perfect reminder that if we all try to perform the same role, the same function, we do not have a body—all we have is a group of spleens, or ankles. It is only in the diversity of roles and functions, working together toward the common good, that we have a whole body. And so here, at this point in

20. The Episcopal Church has been a bit more comfortable with the language of offering and sacrifice than the Church of England, although newer liturgical books have made less of this difference. For an extended study on offering and sacrifice in Anglican eucharist, see Kenneth Stevenson, *Eucharist and Offering* (Collegeville, MN: Liturgical Press, 1986); and Kenneth Stevenson, *Accept This Offering: The Eucharist as Sacrifice Today* (London: SPCK, 1989); as well as John Macquarrie, *A Guide to the Sacraments* (London: SCM Press, 1997), chapter 13.

21. The prayers at the preparation of the table in *CW* remind us that the order is money first, and then the gifts of wine and bread by the very order of the prayers: the first prayer is inclusive of everything, the second and third specifically mention money, the fourth through eighth focus on the bread and wine, the remainder are metaphorically related to the gifts at table.

22. BCP 1979, 534, 531.

the liturgy, the necessary and life-giving diversity of life and of the church is symbolized by the reality that some give and one takes, just as throughout the liturgy some lead, others follow, some initiate, others respond. At this point in the liturgy, this person, the presider, has been appointed to take the bread and wine, to place them on the table, and to begin the great prayer of thanksgiving in which the whole church, in heaven and on earth, joins.

Another theology can be drawn from the prayers at the preparation of the table in *Common Worship*, specifically from the set of blessings borrowed from the Roman missal (which were in turn adapted from Jewish table prayers) and presented as the fourth option.

> Blessed are you, Lord God of all creation: through your goodness we have this bread to set before you, which earth has given and human hands have made. It will become for us the bread of life. Blessed be God forever.
>
> Blessed are you, Lord God of all creation: through your goodness we have this wine to set before you, fruit of the vine and work of human hands. It will become for us the cup of salvation. Blessed by God for ever.[23]

This borrowing of a Jewish blessing, blessing God who has already blessed us, points to a wonderful image in relation to both the bread and the wine: the necessary partnership in creating bread and wine. Bread is co-created, started by and through the God of all creation, fruit of the earth, but then finished by human hands. Wine is also not a natural substance, it does not grow on the vines alone, but is finished through the work of human hands. This co-creative partnership is an exemplar of both what happens in liturgy and what flows from and to liturgy in our lives. The divine-human relationship expressed here as co-creative, however, is one that endures in a necessary tension.

---

23. *CW*, 291.

The ecumenical and liturgical movements of the twentieth century opened windows that allowed Christians to look at patterns in liturgy and ecclesiology that were no longer life-giving or iconic of God's work in the world and in people. But like any movement of correction, the swing of the pendulum to one extreme resulted in both a necessary balance to the previous theology and, eventually, an overemphasis on the new perspective. With regard to liturgy, one of the primary issues was a previous overemphasis on the transcendent nature of God, stressing the difference between God and humanity. Often the liturgy was about distance, the inaccessibility and mystery of God, and by extension, the same attributes were extended to those perceived to be closer to God than the majority of the congregation. The correction was to restore the biblical and early church emphasis on the priesthood of all believers, the people of God, as the documents of Vatican II stressed.[24] As this was increasingly applied to the renewal of liturgy in many ecumenical circles, however, the overemphasis became a liturgical short-sightedness that focused solely on what *we* do in liturgy. The primary goal in liturgy planning in some circles was to prepare a liturgy that reflected where people were, and what they stood for. Recent liturgical theology has named and recognized the issue and helped restore a balance between what we do in the liturgy and what God is doing in the liturgy, while returning a focus on the people of God worshipping God, not themselves or particular political issues.[25] The co-creativity named in the optional prayers at the table, as the bread and wine are taken, reflect not only the differentiation of roles so poetically expressed by the Apostle Paul, but also the necessary tension and balance between the divine and human initiatives in liturgy. The traditional expression of the dual purposes of eucharistic liturgy, the glorification of God and

---

24. This theme is woven through many of the conciliar documents, but most especially *Lumen Gentium* (Dogmatic Constitution on the Church), chapter 2.

25. See Michael Aune's two-part article, *Worship* 81 (2007): 46–68 and 141–169; and John Baldovin, "The Uses of Liturgical History," *Worship* 82 (2008): 2–18.

our sanctification,[26] resonates with the widespread cultural phenomenon of the late twentieth century in which a hunger for the transcendent often takes the form of people professing that they are spiritual, but not religious. The duet danced throughout the liturgy is a dialogue, a partnership, a commitment to co-creation, to faithfulness and to transformation, always with God and always through our interactions with our neighbors, confirming that Christian spirituality and the ritual enactment of faith (*religio*) are inseparable.

We Offer Ourselves,
Our Souls and Bodies

Take, bless, break, give—the fourfold action begins with take, yet in both the liturgy and in our Christian lives, the taking itself is preceded by an offering, a giving. Is it God who takes and we offer? Yes. Is it God who offers and we take? Yes. We who are God's can only offer what already belongs to God, but we also take what is both not ours and already ours.

We offer ourselves as a "living sacrifice of praise and thanksgiving." The offering is ours because it is first given to us. Our lives do not take on meaning and deep joy until they are given for others. So we offer ourselves, "our souls and bodies, to be a reasonable, holy and living sacrifice."[27] This is because we first acknowledge our very existence as a gift from God. Indeed, in the Christian life we say that we can only love God and give ourselves to God because "Christ first loved us." As Don Saliers has written, "Giving ourselves over to the mercy and to the compassion of the One who cre-

---

26. Stated and re-stated in many ways throughout liturgical history, it has become a topic of recent interest in evangelical Christian circles, where the idea of sanctification has intrigued many online conversationalists (for the multiple entries, simply type in to a search engine: "God's glorification and our sanctification"). For sacramental understandings, see *Sacrosanctum Concilium,* 10: "From the liturgy therefore, and especially from the eucharist, grace is poured forth upon us from a fountain, and the sanctification of men in Christ and the glorification of God to which all other activities of the church are directed, as toward their end, are achieved with maximum effectiveness," which became the basis for many contemporary theological discussions.

27. *BCP 1979,* 336.

ated all things and called them good is to discover our own best being."[28]

This ritual action of taking (and implied offering) is headed toward conversion and transformation.[29] The bread and wine are taken/offered to be blessed, broken, and given so that we may be taken and blessed and broken and given so that the world might be transformed. Another word or meaning of "take" might be "accept"—our relationship with God is a two-way relationship, initiated by God but calling for a response from us. We accept, take, what God offers us in order to transform our lives in accordance with the plan laid out for us in the life and death and resurrection of Christ. "Liturgy is the way that the Christian community symbolically re-enacts its relationship with God"[30]: may this liturgical pattern of ritual action guide our daily living into union with God.

28. Don E. Saliers, *Worship and Spirituality* (Philadelphia, PA: Westminster Press, 1984), 82–83.

29. Saliers, *Worship and Spirituality* (1984), 83.

30. Empereur and Kiesling, *The Liturgy that Does Justice*, 15.

CHAPTER 6

Blessing

David Stancliffe

T HE SPIRITUALITY OF THE EUCHARISTIC prayer is concerned with that pattern of transformation that is at the heart of all sacramental acts, and of the eucharist in particular. What happens? How are we being changed "from one degree of glory into another" (2 Corinthians 3:18)? What are the processes and patterns that God in Christ lays before us and that we try and inhabit each time we "make the offering," as our early forebears in the faith described their participation in the eucharistic action? How do we enter into that "upward call of God in Christ Jesus" (Philippians 3:14), that sense of being drawn out of ourselves and into the sacrificial self-offering of Christ to God? Before we begin to focus on this central prayer of the community's worship, we need to reflect on its place in the eucharistic action.

Drawn together from busy lives with their complex, private agendas, the individuals who are coming to be made one again in Christ have gathered to form the eucharistic assembly. As they begin, they sing God's praises and are confronted by divine majesty. This may bring them to their knees as they acknowledge how far from Christ they are.[1] The promise of God's forgiveness and the renewed confidence it brings have welcomed them into the gate of heaven and raised them to their feet to sing *Gloria in excelsis Deo*, and then to say "Amen" to the presidential prayer that collects and offers their aspirations as they stand before the throne of grace.

Drawn together in prayer and praise, they are ready to set the story of their lives against the timeless story of what God has done for his people in the Liturgy of the Word; they have risen to their feet as the Book of the Gospels has been carried into their midst, and have heard Christ—the living Word—speaking to them face to face, "as one speaks to a friend" (cf. Exodus 33:11) The interplay between their story and God's story has been explored and the implications teased out in the sermon and turned into intercession in the prayers of the people.

From Cerebral to Sensate

At the hinge point between the Liturgy of the Word and the eucharist, between worship in the Temple and the breaking of the bread in their homes as Acts 2:43 describes it, the Church reassembles to exchange the peace and prepare the gifts.

What has happened hitherto has been a process of engagement: God's people have come to set their story today against *the* story of what God has done for them in Christ, and to ponder its implications for them and their lives in the days ahead. But what will change? Is anything going to happen as a result? At this point, the eucharistic action shifts gear from the verbal to the practical, from the cerebral to the sensate, from the personal to the communal, from the past to the present, from the incarnational—God's coming among us to share our life—to the redemptive—the way in which God in Christ changes things.[2] Here we enter not merely a

---

1. For Coventry and an account of why the cathedral was built as it is, see David Stancliffe, *The Lion Companion to Church Architecture* (London: Lion, 2008), 252–56; for Cefalu, see page 24.

2. See David Stancliffe, *God's Pattern: Shaping Our Worship, Ministry and Life* (London: SPCK, 2003), esp. 14–20.

reflective process of instruction and pondering, but into the
eucharistic action where the redemptive action of Christ in
his dying and rising actually transforms the poverty of our
life into the riches of divine glory. As the presider may pray
as she adds water to the wine in the chalice on the altar, we
seek that we may come to share in the divinity of Christ, the
one who humbles himself to share in our humanity.[3] How is
that prayer fulfilled and made real in what follows? How does
the eucharistic action change and form us into what in baptism we are called to be—the body of Christ?

First, the preparations: how are the altar and its vessels
and the people who surround it with their gifts prepared?
Those tokens which have been brought to the altar and prepared upon it represent all the hopes and longings generated
by the people present and represent their prayers; indeed,
nothing less than their whole lives is there as bread and wine
are brought and laid before God, offered to him to be transformed and given back to make those scattered people one. As
St. Augustine says:

> It is the mystery of yourselves that is laid on the
> table of the Lord; that mystery you receive. To
> that which you are, you answer "Amen," and in
> answering you assent. For you hear the words
> "the Body of Christ" and you answer "Amen." Be a
> member of the Body of Christ that the Amen may
> be true.[4]

Because the connection between the prayers of the people
and the tokens laid on the altar seems so tenuous, as movement in the geographical focus of the action, the exchange
of peace and a chant or song has come to break the ancient
connection, this gap—this "soft point," as Robert Taft[5] calls

---

3. A prayer to this effect is part of the Roman rite as the wine is prepared on the
altar before the eucharistic prayer itself.

4. St. Augustine of Hippo, Sermon 272.

5. Kenneth Stevenson, "Soft Points in the Eucharist," in Michael Perham, ed.,
*Liturgy for a New Century: Further Essays in Preparation for the Revision of the
Alternative Service Book* (London: SPCK, 1991), 29.

it—has been filled over the centuries with a plethora of explanatory prayers and signs. There have been "offertory prayers" or "the little canon," anticipating the offering of the gifts to God in the eucharistic prayer itself. Almost universal in Western rites since the 1960s have been processions with the gifts, mirroring in some ways the Great Entrance of the Eastern rites, and in some cultures a major point of participation by the whole of the assembly as they bring the work of their hands over the past week to be offered for God's blessing and—apart from the bread and wine set upon the altar—distributed according to need by the deacons at the end of the liturgy.

First the Taking

In early days, this procession of gifts was accompanied by the reading of the diptychs, the list of donors living and departed to be remembered in prayer. To make the connection between the people and the gifts, as the visible link became more tenuous, both were censed in quick succession, and by the Middle Ages, when the assembly no longer took part in any offertory rite, such a link was virtually forgotten. No longer was even the bread and wine the stuff of daily life; both elements were—and remain in many places—the arcane secret of nuns and suppliers of religious perquisites.

How do such "offertory processions" relate to the first of Jesus' four dominical acts—taking, blessing, breaking, and sharing? In the Church of England in the preparation of the *Alternative Service Book 1980*, the taking became a distinct action after all had been prepared on the altar—perhaps by the deacon. The president was then instructed to take the vessels holding bread and wine into his hands, and without saying anything, replace them on the altar before beginning the eucharistic prayer.[6] The temptation to say something at this point proved so irresistible to many that without the

6. *Alternative Service Book 1980* (London: Mowbray, 1980), 129–30 (hereafter, *ASB 1980*). The *ASB* was authorized for use in the Church of England from 1980 until 2000, when *Common Worship* was introduced.

popular Roman *berakoth* prayers from the Missal of Paul VI ever being printed, the response "Blessed be God for ever" was grudgingly admitted.[7] A more satisfactory pattern has always seemed to me to be that which I have experienced in the newly reordered Duomo in Milan.[8] In the Ambrosian rite, after the exchange of the Peace,[9] the gifts are brought to the presider at his chair. The presider then takes them formally, blessing the people who bring them, and hands them over to the deacons who prepare the altar, only moving there himself to cense the gifts, pray the prayer *super oblata*, and begin the Creed.[10]

Among those that use the Roman rite, the most satisfactory preparation of the gifts that I experience is at the fine Romanesque abbey church of St. Benoit-sur-Loire. Here the altar, a substantial and significant white marble block (though not much more than a meter long), stands freely in the chancel presbytery on a carpet pavement of distinctive Cosmati mosaic. On it, the deacon spreads a large cloth and then two large vessels; that is all, there is no clutter of little chalices and no vast missal-stand dominating them all. One is a dish-like paten with a large flat loaf of unleavened bread, and the other a substantial calyx (or goblet), holding perhaps three liters. The presider breaks the bread at the fraction and places particles in the ciboria that those who are going to distribute communion bring to the altar; at the same time, as *Agnus Dei* is sung, the deacon fills the chalices which are brought to altar by those who are going to administer them.

All this alerts us to the fact that it is what is done, and how it is done, that is central to the spirituality of the eucharist, what is being conveyed in terms of our formation in the eucharistic prayer in particular. Of course, the text of the

7. For the battles that surrounded the passage of this part of the rite through the General Synod of the Church of England, see chapter 6, "The End of the Offertory," in Colin Buchanan, *An Evangelical among the Anglican Liturgists* (London: SPCK, 2009).

8. See Stancliffe, *Church Architecture*, 262–63.

9. In the Ambrosian rite, the peace is introduced by Matthew 5:23–24.

10. *Messale Ambrosiano Festivo* (Milano: Marietti, 1976), 640–42.

prayer remains central, but to the worshipper, what counts is the way in which the whole action of the liturgy transforms our human nature into the divine life.

Then the Great Prayer

It is over these gifts and all that they represent that the Church gives thanks in a prayer that has always been central to the church's understanding of what it does in making eucharist. That prayer has taken many forms, and so has the manner of its praying, but what essentially is expressed is what the Church believes about what God in Christ has done to transform our lives and make us one with God, and how we are caught into this life-changing pattern.

There are two main threads in this. First, is our transformation a continuous process or is it a sharp transaction? This is the same question that we ask of baptism and coming to faith. Does our coming to faith seem to us a discernable moment in time, when once we were stumbling around in darkness but now, like St. Paul on the Damascus road, have seen the light? And does our baptism mark our recognition of this moment or is baptism rather to be understood as God's act, claiming our life for divine service and starting us off in company with others on a path of growth in self-understanding that leads in time to maturity in faith, where belonging leads to believing?

Historically, there is a sharp moment—or so it seems. At the center of our faith, at the heart of the eucharist, is Christ's death on the cross, where the body was broken, the life poured out for our redemption. Yet even that moment, described in St. John's gospel as a moment of triumph and the completion of the new creation, is a moment that telescopes what St. Luke, for example, spreads over a considerable timeframe. Luke, as part of the synoptic tradition, records the triumphal entry, the last supper, the betrayal, arrest and trial, the crucifixion and burial, the resurrection, the appearances on the way to Emmaus and at the lakeside, the ascension, and the day of Pentecost. All these events, like a series of vignettes in a strip cartoon, reveal Luke's linear sense of history, Luke's tendency to historicize into an ordered sequence that central saving event, originally celebrated in the church in that one long night between the Saturday and Sunday we now call Holy Saturday and Easter Day. Holy Week as we know it depends on that kind of pattern, and raising the question is like asking how would we celebrate at the festival of the incarnation if we did not have Luke's gospel, but only Mark's or John's.

What is most significant is that, whether historicized as separate events or held as one whole, the connection between the event of Christ's death and resurrection and us has always required an interlocking unpacking of event and interpretation. Would the events of the Last Supper and their significance for the pattern of Christian worship have been understood without the journey to Emmaus and the way that the penny dropped for the disciples just as the stranger broke the bread at the supper table? Event and interpretation are indissolubly linked.

We come to these questions with a strong sense of the supremacy of the Lukan, linear, historicized pattern in our minds. That is how we have come to read the gospels. And yet the unbroken liturgical tradition, which predates the formation of the gospels as they stand, gives a more integrated pattern where *anamnesis* (that difficult word to translate, which means more our re-living now of what once took place than the usual translation "remembrance" conjures up), gratitude, and longing for what is to be are united in our celebration of Christ's presence in our midst, focused in the daily bread— the ordinary things—transformed before us.

Smell the Difference: Stories of Sensate Worship

How does the prayer, the way it is celebrated, how we dress and stand, what gestures we make, how we pray and sing together, give expression to all this? Like many others, I was brought up with a "Western," transactional theology of what happened in the eucharistic action. Later on I would come to recognize the various models of the theology of atonement at work, but the individualistic piety of my devout Irish grandmother and the hymns of my childhood, like Mrs. Alexander's "There is a green hill far away" did much to reinforce a sense of personal redemption re-enacted in the memorial meal. I sang to God, mindful of the love "that bought us" unequivocally on the tree of Calvary.[11]

Brought up on such hymnody, and the Communion Service in the 1662 Book of Common Prayer, it was little wonder that my early recollections of the eucharistic action began to melt away. I had enjoyed the music, the ceremonial, the vestments, and the processions—especially when one of the candle-bearers, Mr. Pullinger, winked at me. Words spun out of the liturgical wallpaper with a random, but sometimes surprising force: I listened hard in the creed, but "I acknowledge three baptisms" is what I knew I should have heard when there were three new prams in church. I thought the banners fine, but was mystified by the one that depicted rays pouring out of what appeared to be a large boiled egg in its egg-cup: no one had thought to explain devotion to the Blessed Sacrament to me at that stage! Instead, the sacrament was clearly a private affair for special people: "You can't go until you are confirmed, dear," said my grandmother, when we had moved to a traditional Church of England parish, where matins was the norm.

That turned out not to be the case, and staying with her in London occasionally meant a visit to St. Jude's on the Hill in Hampstead Garden Suburb for the eucharist rather than to my grandfather's city church for matins. This was an exciting world, where the smoke of the incense rose in clouds into the mysterious brick domes, and everything—including the readings—was sung. Much later, that experience was to be more formative of how I thought of going to church, when as a teenager, we lived in Westminster and my parish church became the Abbey. Going out on a Sunday morning into the East End for an exotic high mass to play the organ at the instigation of

---

11. The allusion here is to William Bright's hymn, "And now, O Father, mindful of the love." See *Common Praise* (Norwich, UK: Canterbury Press, 2000), no. 279.

an organ-builder friend or down the road to smell the difference of the chant-filled, smoky interior of the amazing Westminster Cathedral[12] was an eye-opener that prepared me to fall in love with Sir Ninian Comper's St. Cyprian's, Clarence Gardens,[13] or Thaxted—the first church I went to with no pews—or Blisland, a small church on the edge of Bodmin Moor, apparently untouched by the reformation. Here, and in the Comper chapel of Pusey House in Oxford, I became familiar with a rite that was integrated and mysterious, sung and splendid, yet focused on the personal and pietistic. The clergy were angelic beings, and their acolytes otherworldly; and as we knelt and sang at the end of the Prayer of Consecration the eucharistic hymn of William Jervois, which gives praise for God's "well-beloved, all-perfect offering," "sacrifice immortal," "spotless oblation" who "pleads" for all God's people "living and departed," I knew that we were in heaven.[14] Fuelled by reading Dom Gregory Dix's *Shape of the Liturgy* and John Moorman's *History of the Church in England*, I developed a romantic love of the Tractarian ideal, which led me to train for ordination at Ripon College, Cuddesdon, and then on to a curacy in the great smoke-blackened church of St. Bartholomew's, Armley, Leeds.[15]

Broadening Experience

But we were now in a new world, and visits to the continent of Europe were broadening my experience, as well as worship in a number of downtown, back-to-back parishes in Leeds. The new Roman Catholic cathedral, with the altar in the center of its circular space, had been built in Liverpool. St. Paul's, Bow Common, gave us a different image of eucharistic worship in the Church of England, and there was great excitement at the first offerings—*Alternative Services: First Series*—of a newly instituted body, the Liturgical Commission. We sang psalms

---

12. See Stancliffe, *Church Architecture*, 241.
13. See Stancliffe, *Church Architecture*, 234.
14. See *Common Praise*, no. 332.
15. See Stancliffe, *Church Architecture*, 232–33.

and a mass setting by Joseph Gelineau, and a jazzy Mass of St. Andrew by Malcolm Williamson, but the main diet was still Merbecke and Martin Shaw's Anglican Folk Mass.[16] What remained unchallenged as yet was the shape and theology of the eucharistic prayer, still firmly in a tradition that had a short and variable preface leading to the *Sanctus*, followed by an epicletic formula over the gifts and the Institution Narrative, an *amanesis* leading to the offering of the sacrifice of praise and worship[17] and a prayer for faithful reception before the doxology.

Over the past forty years, much has happened to broaden my experience as well as to change the way the church worships. One of the patterns of giving thanks over the bread and the cup that was formative for me was that prayed at Ewell Monastery, an adapted barn in Kent, where a small Anglican Cistercian community worshipped. The barn was bare, with a group of stools in a semicircle at the "west" end, and a circular table with a circular ring with six candle-sconces suspended above it at the "east" end. Those gathered with the community to celebrate moved from the stools at the west end to form a circle round the table at the east end for the thanksgiving. The presider stood in the circle with all those present, not alone at the table. Holding his hands in the *orans* position throughout the prayer without variation, the presider only approached the table with the gifts to break the bread at the fraction. The prayer, written and used in the Abbey of West Malling with the permission of their then visitor, Archbishop Michael Ramsey, is a continuous doxology, rehearsing the whole of salvation history, rather in the manner of the great Passiontide hymn of Venantius Fortunatus, *Pange Lingua gloriosi proelium certaminis*,[18] which is sung in the liturgy on Good Friday:

---

16. Originally written for Percy Dearmer's successor at St. Mary's, Primrose Hill, Arthur Duncan-Jones, who was later to be Dean of Chichester.

17. An idea reaching back as far as Irenaeus in the second century, and developed from Romans 12:1 and 1 Peter 2:5.

18. For the following translation, see David Stancliffe, *The Pilgrim Prayerbook*, 2nd ed. (London: Continuum, 2007), 153–54.

Sing, my tongue, the glorious battle,
Sing the ending of the fray;
Now above the Cross, the trophy,
Sound the loud triumphal lay:
Tell how Christ, the world's redeemer,
As a victim won the day . . .

The narrative of the Last Supper is woven into the prayer, which ends with the *Sanctus* in the form given in Revelation 4.8. But perhaps the most significant part of the experience is that the prayer is sung from beginning to end to a simplified preface tone.

Sounding the Fabric of Our Being

Singing the eucharistic prayer, like singing the creed, takes our praying beyond the realm of intellectual comprehension and assent into the fabric of our being. "One who sings, prays twice," says St. Augustine,[19] trying to explain how what you sing becomes part of you in a way that what is read or simply spoken does not. And we have for too long, even in a so-called Sung Eucharist, become accustomed to hearing only the *Sursum Corda* and the preface sung, a relic from the days when the rest of the canon in the Tridentine rite was spoken *sotto voce*, while the choir sang an elaborate setting not only of the *Sanctus*, but more especially of the *Benedictus*.[20] What more appropriate to sing than "Blessed is he who comes in the name of the Lord," as the transformative moment in the Roman Canon approached. That at least was how it was thought of in the *Haggerston Catechism*, an Anglo-Catholic manual produced in the 1930s which told children to look up for the elevation when they heard the bells ring, because they warned us that Jesus was coming, and we shouldn't miss the

19. Cf. St. Augustine, *Enarratio in Psalmum*, 72.1.

20. As in the so-called Little Organ Mass, the *Missa brevis Sancti Joannis de Deo*, by Joseph Haydn, where the *Sanctus* lasts about a minute, but the elaborate Benedictus for more like five and a half.

moment, like those foolish virgins in Matthew 25:1–13 who missed the coming of the bridegroom, being unprepared.

That was how the Roman Canon had come to be viewed: as a linear and logical sequence, where, in characteristic Latin fashion, the historicizing, cause-and-effect model of the logical engineer's language helped the theologians of the Middle Ages to identify a moment of consecration, a calling-down of the Holy Spirit by the priest whose ordination had bestowed the power to confect the sacrament and so effect that transubstantiation which was demanded by the logic of Thomist theology. While the species, the outward form of the eucharistic gifts, remained unchanged, their substance—the underlying reality—was now the body and blood of Christ.

At that moment, bells were rung, the host elevated—sometimes for a considerable time—and censed, while the faithful adored the sacrament. This was the moment that came to be repeated on its own, isolated from the canon of the mass, in what was called Benediction, where the host, enshrined in a monstrance, was adored and then used to bless the worshipers.

These practices, developed over many years, shifted the focus in eucharistic celebrations from communities' celebration of the transforming presence of Christ in their midst to the eucharistic species in itself, the bread and the wine, their transformation, adoration and—somewhat occasional for the majority of worshipers—reception in communion.[21]

A relic of these attitudes emerged—somewhat surprisingly—in the General Synod of the Church of England, as the eucharistic prayers that were to form part of *Common Worship*, the new texts authorized from 2000 onwards to replace the experimental *Alternative Service Book 1980*, were being considered before that authorization. There emerged a slightly inarticulate anxiety focused on the work of the Holy Spirit, the epiclesis. Did our calling on the Holy Spirit in prayer suggest an unwelcome instrumentality? Was it right to celebrate the power and the presence of the Spirit in a way that might

---

21. For a compact account of this change, see Stancliffe, *Church Architecture*, 109–11, 136, 142–44.

suggest we were summoning God to change the inanimate gifts on the table into something else, and not just to change us by our receiving them?[22] A solution was found textually in the majority of the eucharistic prayers by linking the invocation of the Spirit on the gifts and on those who received them in the same breath, refusing to make a prayed-for change in ourselves instrumentally dependent on a prior change in the elements. But the rite is more than words. The traditional gesture in the West of the presider raising, joining, and then lowering his hands over the gifts, signing them with the cross and then signing themselves at this dual epiclesis, does much to establish the indivisibility of the prayer as a whole.

But if the whole prayer is doxological, and the whole eucharistic action—taking, blessing, breaking, and sharing—is what brings about our transformation, even if the focus of this is the bread and wine now consecrated to be the body and blood of Christ, then we are no longer looking for a moment of consecration in the prayer, but for a prayer to rehearse in its entirety the saving acts of God in Christ in which we find the key to our transformation and a style of worship that complements it.

Words for Prayer

One of the features of the eight eucharistic prayers in *Common Worship* is the variation of structure. While Prayer A is a lightly revised redaction of prayers 1 and 2 in the *ASB 1980*, Prayer B a version of Prayer 3 in the *ASB 1980* (based on the Apostolic Tradition, until recently ascribed to Hippolytus—whose name was often used as a shorthand reference to the prayer), and Prayer C a slightly conservative revision of Prayer 4, the remaining five prayers are new for the Church of England. While Prayer E has its origin in a prayer from those provided for children's masses in the Roman Catholic Church, prayers F and G have a different

---

22. For a whole monograph on the subject, and especially for an account of the synodical process leading up to *Common Worship*, see David J. Kennedy, *Eucharistic Sacramentality in an Ecumenical Context* (Aldershot, UK: Ashgate, 2008), esp. 159–66.

theological pattern. Dubbed Eastern or Antiochene in shape,[23] this means that they use a richer and more vivid range of imagery employed by the early churches, have an extended and unchanging narrative of praise before the *Sanctus*, and have a clearer Trinitarian structure underscoring each prayer.

In the first section of Prayer F, Old Testament images of the covenant relationship with God predominate, and the narrative line relates them to the initiative of the Father. This is in the section that concludes with the *Sanctus*, the angelic hymn described in Isaiah's vision in the temple (Isaiah 6:1–8). As the prayer moves into the christological heart of our redemption, the story of our salvation is treated anamnetically, recalling the supper, death, and resurrection in temporal sequence, but without making the command to "do this in remembrance of me" isolated, or the formula "this is my body" appear consecratory. The third section of the prayer, before the doxology and the great Amen conclude it, is consciously epicletic, calling down the Spirit on the gifts and the celebrating assembly, and then praying for that wholeness for which we long to include the most vulnerable and needy. The inclusion of intercessory material in the eucharistic prayer is a welcome corrective to an over-personalized understanding: praying for the poor and marginalized, as well as for the departed and recently baptized, like joining your prayer with those of the saints, alerts the assembly to its union with fellow-Christians in time and space. Such a prayer is more in the (Anglican) tradition of the West Malling prayer, and owes more in its theology (though not in its length!) to the anaphora of Basil.

Prayer G has its origin in a freshly written prayer composed by the Roman Catholic Commission for English in the Liturgy in 1984 but never authorized for use. An adapted version was floated in *Patterns for Worship* in 1989, but its pattern of threefold seasonal insertions was judged too complicated. It

---

23. For a full and competent analysis of the elements of the eucharistic prayer or anaphora, see Enrico Mazza, *The Celebration of the Eucharist: The Origin of the Rite and the Development of its Interpretation* (Collegeville, MN: Liturgical Press, 1999), esp. 49–62, 281–94.

was reintroduced for its use of vivid paradox (such as "silent music of your praise") and feminine imagery ("as a mother tenderly gathers her children"), and like Prayer F, has a dual epiclesis and optional intercessions for the church before the doxology. These two prayers are more clearly a doxological whole than any previous Anglican prayers.

Doing the Words

One of the consequences of such a structure is that the traditional manual acts—taking the bread and cup into the presider's hands and elevating them after the institution narrative, for example—feels otiose. Should the presider merely indicate the bread and the cup when they are referred to in the narrative of the prayer, and leave the more demonstrative gestures to the epiclesis, and the elevation of the elements to the doxology? The Church of England has been reticent about mandating gestures in recent rites,[24] but experience of praying these prayers with a community indicates that this might well be a better course. Some prayers use optional refrains, which may change through the prayer. This cries out for the deacon or cantor to lead it, and for a sung response, which in turn raises the question of whether such a prayer should not be sung or inflected against an instrumental background—perhaps a soft chord sequence changing in each section, with the significant words articulated by strokes on a set of resonant but untuned gongs to slow the pace and give it a heightened, unhurried, timeless feel. Musical settings for the prayers enable an assembly to join in singing the prayer and can create a sense of continuous worship with the church throughout the ages.

---

24. Note the discussion of difference between the Church of England and the Episcopal Church's practice in Lizette Larson-Miller's contribution. Note also Marion J. Hatchett's acknowledgement and discussion of change around the Anglican Communion since the Episcopal Church's BCP 1979 in his essay, "Unfinished Business in Prayer Book Revision," in Paul Marshall and Lesley Northrup, eds., *Leaps and Boundaries: The Prayer Book in the 21st Century* (Harrisburg, PA: Morehouse, 1997), 28.

As far as movement and gesture are concerned, should not the whole assembly be ringing the altar, and if the presider is part of that extended circle, should not the assembly too be raising their hands to join in praying the prayer? After all, it is now common practice—except perhaps in those churches when there is still an almost Pavlovian reaction to the invitation to pray to fall to one's knees!—for those praying the prayer that Jesus taught together to extend their hands. Such common gestures do much to draw people into common prayer and out of either daydreaming or the personal introspection that passes for devotion. We have a good deal to learn from our Muslim brothers and sisters about the importance of uniform gesture embedding prayer into how we are formed as a praying people.

But these styles of praying, patterns of movement, and gestures have long been commonplace in other parts of the Christian world.

In the majority of the Churches of the East, the eucharistic prayer will be recited by the bishop or priest who presides at the altar from behind a screen, or iconostasis. Much of it will be inaudible, as well as the gestures invisible, and many of the chants and litanies that accompany it will obscure its shape. I remember going high into the Caucasus Mountains in Georgia one damp Sunday in November, and as I approached the monastery church of Anuri hearing the unmistakable voice of the soprano, Emma Kirkby. Of course it wasn't Emma, but in the nave of the resonant church stood a young woman, singing most beautifully. As I stood transfixed at not only the beauty of her voice, but her rapt attention, I heard from behind the iconostasis the very bass voice of the priest, probably her husband. They were entirely alone, save for the angels, but every note of the liturgy—probably lasting some two and a half hours, was being sung. In the West, there were few variations during much of the previous millennium, and until the 1960s the presider would have most likely turned his back to the congregation, and presided at something that looked more like a sideboard than a table, surmounted by a suitable devotional carving or picture. In the Roman Catholic West, the majority of the prayer would not only have been in Latin, but also recited silently, so room for conscious participation would have been limited.

It was part of Cranmer's desire, given expression in the 1552 Prayer Book, to make the prayer audible to the congregation, and for the whole communicant body to be incorporated into the action. They were to "draw near with faith" when invited, which meant entering the Chancel where the altar would be standing table-wise in the middle, and gathering all round it. Cranmer tried to dramatize the prayer itself, letting the actions of taking, blessing, breaking, and sharing the bread and cup form a dramatic accompaniment to the prayer itself, so that the "Prayer of Consecration" would be followed by the dramatized action of giving the sacrament, and concluded by what became known as the "Prayer of Oblation," a pattern which was followed nowhere else in Christendom and which the new rites of the Church of England have eschewed, except for a version of the Prayer Book rite in vaguely updated language.

A Beauty about It

What do these reflections tell us about the way in which emerging patterns of praying the eucharistic prayer in the liturgy are shaping the Church's spirituality? First, there is a recovery of the sense of doxology, of the praise of God's glory in creation, incarnation, redemption, and the continuing work of the Spirit, at the heart of the great thanksgiving. Second, the prayer is a single prayer, culminating in a timeless vision of the heavenly banquet, of which this action here in time and space is a foretaste. Third, our engagement in the prayer, and our almost creedal rehearsal of the events of our salvation, has a transformative rather than a transactional significance: we are becoming what we are—the body of Christ. So our worship should have a beauty about it, a life-changing sense of transformation that comes with a passionate longing for God.

We should expect of our "making the offering" no less than Prince Vladimir's envoys felt when they reported home after their experience of worship in Hagia Sophia:

> We knew not whether we were in heaven or on earth. For on earth here is no such splendour or such beauty, and we are at a loss how to describe it. We only know that God dwells there among men, and their service is fairer than the ceremonies of other nations. For we cannot forget that beauty.[25]

---

25. The Russian Primary Chronicle, translation and commentary by Samuel Hazzard Cross and Olgerd P. Sherbowitz-Wetzor, *The Russian Primary Chronicle*, Medieval Academy of America, Publication No. 60 (Cambridge, UK: Mediaeval Academy, 1953), x.

CHAPTER 7

Breaking

Alan Bartlett

The Spirituality of the Fraction

"WE BREAK THIS BREAD, TO share in the body of Christ."[1] The eucharistic presider is required to say these words, or similar, on every Sunday or Holy Day as she breaks the bread.[2] In many congregations, the presider will then break the wafers or tear the bread into pieces as the *Agnus Dei* is said or sung. "Jesus, Lamb of God, have mercy upon us." But what does this mean? And what is its significance for the presider and for the people gathered with her or him?

I write this as someone who has had the privilege of presiding at the eucharist for many years, constantly conscious of being unworthy of this privilege, and in remembrance of the words of George Herbert:

---

1. *Common Worship: Services and Prayers for the Church of England* (London: Church House Publishing, 2000), 179.

2. *Common Worship,* 334, note 20. This comment must be qualified straight away. There is an alternative. It is also permissible for the president, on non-Principal weekdays, to break the bread in silence. Therefore, this essay is an exploration primarily of one liturgical interpretation of the fraction, although the fraction itself is essential. Note also that in this essay I will normally prefer to use the term "breaking" as shorthand for "breaking of the bread" and as an alternative to the more technical term, "fraction."

> The Country Parson being to administer the Sac-
> raments, is at a stand with himself how or what
> behaviour to assume for so holy things. Especially
> at Communion times he is in a great confusion,
> as being not only to receive God, but to break and
> administer Him.[3]

Whatever our theology of the eucharist, the awesome privilege of standing *in persona Christi*, and taking the profoundest symbol of Christ's presence with humankind, and breaking it so as to share it, still brings me to a place of gratitude and trepidation. I can speak only for myself, but it is the place where I am most conscious of being in the presence of Christ. This is where I most feel that I am "with God with the people on [my] heart."[4]

But I also write, wary of the way in which the language of "brokenness" has been used by the Church to justify excessive demands on people to obey, to sacrifice themselves, as well as intersecting with theologies which depict God as a father into a bloodthirsty punisher of an innocent son.[5] Is there a way of appreciating spiritually the "breaking of the bread" without slipping into sadism or masochism?

In this essay I am going to explore, briefly, the biblical and liturgical roots of the fraction, and then suggest some

---

3. George Herbert, *The Country Parson* (London: Everyman, 1974), 226; first published in 1652.

4. Michael Ramsey, *The Christian Priest Today*, revised ed. (London: SPCK, 1987), 14.

5. "They contemplate Christ's passion aright who view it with a terror-stricken heart and a despairing conscience. This terror must be felt as you witness the stern wrath and the unchanging earnestness with which God looks upon sin and sinners, so much so that he was unwilling to release sinners even for his only and dearest Son without his payment of the severest penalty for them . . . And if you seriously consider that it is God's very own Son, the eternal wisdom of God, who suffers you will be terrified indeed. The more you think about it, the more intensely you will be frightened." Martin Luther, *A Meditation on Christ's Passion* (1519), as cited in Timothy F. Lull, ed., *Martin Luther's Basic Theological Writings* (Minneapolis, MN: Fortress Press, 1989), 167. Or in a more modern vein, read the song composed by Stuart Townend, "How deep the Father's love for us," in which we are invited to sing of a "searing loss" as the Father turns away his face from his Son, and the wounds of the Son bring many other "sons to glory." And more starkly, also by Townend, his song, "In Christ Alone," in which we may sing that the wrath of God "is satisfied" on the cross of Jesus.

theological and spiritual responses, which could enable a more healthy spirituality of brokenness. I will make three key points: that the breaking is a reminder of a sacrificial death and that the linkage to the *Agnus Dei* remains appropriate— sin still needs to be confronted, dealt with, and forgiven; that the breaking is a reminder of the depth of the meaning of the incarnation—that brokenness is part of the human condition and that Christ is present with humankind in the most extreme of situations; and that the breaking is a warning about the likely cost of Christian discipleship—but that discipleship does not find its meaning in the brokenness but rather in commitment to new life, with the risk which that entails.

I want to begin with two personal anecdotes. The first exposes some of the ugliness of breaking. As a young man I attended a lively youth group at a local charismatic Baptist Church. There was much about that church and that period of life for which I am very grateful, but I remember one particularly fierce talk challenging us about the depth of our love for God and assaulting our pride. We were invited to break a symbol of our pride. I went home and systematically but passionately smashed my favorite model tank! As I write now as an adult, I feel embarrassed and queasy because of this excess, but it is, of course, a small example of the spirituality of the breaking of human pride and will that was such a profound feature of much Christian faith and practice.[6] There was something cruel, let alone disproportionate and unnecessary, about forcing this sort of choice on a young man, but the rhetoric is familiar. "Jesus' body was broken for you. What will you break for him? (And if you won't break for him, you break him again . . .)."

The opposite example, much more serious, comes from my time as a curate in West Newcastle. We had invited a team to run a training session for our youth and children's workers on child sexual abuse. One of the team was a "survivor" whose story broke our hearts (especially mine as a newly ordained priest, because the first person she had

---

6. Alan Bartlett, *Humane Christianity* (London: DLT, 2004), chapters 1 and 3.

disclosed to was her vicar who told her that "Daddys sometimes do these things . . ."). I was presiding the following
morning, and as I broke the bread and stared at the deep red
wine in the chalice, I was reminded of the way that her body
and soul had been violated and broken. It was a profoundly
distressing moment, but it helped me to know that even in
this most extreme of places, Christ was to be seen.

Broken to Be Shared

The breaking of the bread is, in one sense, the most natural of actions.[7] A loaf is to be shared at a meal. It is broken
and torn so that all can have some. A society with bread
knives can forget this, but it was an everyday occurrence in
the ancient world! Jesus of Nazareth would have broken bread
thousands of times in his life and probably hundreds of times
with his disciples. The word *klao* (to break in pieces, especially bread) is commonplace, found in most strands of the
New Testament (Matthew, Mark, Luke, and Paul, although
not John). However, this simple action already had a complex
significance and soon came to acquire other deep theological,
spiritual, and liturgical meanings.

The precise actions of Jesus at the Last Supper and their
exact interpretation are, properly, a matter for serious scholarly debate.[8] (It is in itself both shocking and liberating for
modern Christians to realize that their most deeply loved
liturgical texts—here the words of the institution narrative—
vary between the gospels and are, in fact, composite texts.)
Here I simply state my own working assumptions: that Jesus
identified himself with the bread, saying, at least, "This is
my body"; that this was a sacrificial image in the context
of a Passover meal; that Jesus blessed, broke, interpreted,
and shared bread at a crucial point in the meal; and that

7. On the breaking, see Paul Bradshaw, Gordon Giles, and Simon Kershaw, "Holy
Communion," in Paul Bradshaw, ed., *Companion to Common Worship, Volume 1*
(London: SPCK, 2001), 95–147, 129–30.

8. See, for example, texts from different scholarly traditions: Jochaim Jeremias,
The Eucharistic Words of Jesus (London: SCM Press, 1966), or I. Howard Marshall,
Last Supper and Lord's Supper (Exeter, UK: Paternoster, 1980).

he intended his disciples to repeat these actions in memory of him. Whether there is a specific connection between the action of breaking the bread and Jesus' conviction that his body was to be broken is less clear. Gregory Dix is interesting on this:

> But though there is nothing in the record of the last supper to suggest that our Lord made any point of the broken bread representing His own Body "broken" on the cross . . . the symbolism was bound to suggest itself to somebody.[9]

I am less sure than Dix about this lack of connection—especially if the early variant reading of 1 Corinthians 11:24 is accepted, "This is my body, broken for you"—but in either case, I want to suggest that there is a symbolic connection between Jesus' breaking of the bread and the fact that his body was soon to be broken. This is the scriptural and traditional basis from which this essay builds.

Dix argued that the fraction became a universal feature of the ancient eucharistic liturgy, featuring with "absolute unanimity"; part of the "four-action shape of the liturgy."[10] As he reminded us, this marked an unarticulated change from the New Testament pattern of the bread being blessed and shared first, before the blessing and sharing of the wine. This was already a dynamic example of tradition.

Twists in the History of the Fraction

For Anglicans, there is a complex twist in the history of the fraction. Cranmer's growing liturgical Protestantism meant that, while in his reformed prayer books he kept the

9. Gregory Dix, *The Shape of the Liturgy* (London: Continuum, 2005), 81. Cf. Jeremias, *Eucharistic Words*, 220, and Marshall, *Last Supper*, 86. This understanding of the creative potential of developing tradition to bring new meanings to biblical texts is well explored by David Brown, *Tradition and Imagination: Revelation and Change* (Oxford, UK: Oxford University Press, 2002).

10. Dix, *Shape of the Liturgy*, 48–49.

institution narrative as a prayer (thereby establishing a distinctive liturgical trajectory for Anglicanism),[11] he did not specify a fraction.[12] It was only in 1662 that the manual action of a fraction was specified, in keeping with the slightly more visibly Catholic theology and style of that book, but it was during the Prayer of Consecration, not subsequent to it. It was much later, owing to Dix's direct influence, that a separate fraction, after the eucharistic prayer, was re-introduced.[13]

In the *Common Worship* liturgy, the fraction is first described, following Paul (1 Corinthians 10:16–17), as a way of expressing the unity of Christ's body, the Church, even as (also because) his sacramental body is broken and shared: "We break this bread to share in the body of Christ: Though we are many we are one body." It is secondly described as a means of proclaiming the Lord's death and return, also Paul (1 Corinthians 11:26): "Every time we eat this bread and drink this cup, We proclaim the Lord's death until he comes." Thirdly, the singing or saying of the *Agnus Dei*, which may take place as the bread is actually being broken, is a profound expression of Christ's body being broken so that it may be shared, so that blessing, forgiveness, and healing may come. When sung *to* Christ's presence *within* the element of bread, it becomes an action of deep responsive devotion to the love shown in the breaking of Christ's body on the cross.

11. Alan Bartlett, "How Protestant was Cranmer's 1552 Prayer Book?" in David Loades, ed., *Word and Worship: Essays Presented to Margot Johnson* (Oxford, UK: Davenant Press, 2005).

12. Dix, *Shape of the Liturgy*, 49, footnote 1, in fact argues that the earlier point for the fraction was, apart from the dominical example, a "temporary fashion all over Christendom in the fifteenth–sixteenth centuries, which died out again in most places, but happened to 'catch on' among Copts and Anglicans."

13. Bradshaw, Giles, and Kershaw, "Holy Communion," 130: "Here, at last, the third dominical action was clearly laid out in Anglican liturgy." While the historical and thus liturgical case for this has been very widely accepted, as a mere presider, I am conscious of some loss of coherence and visible significance, by re-placing the unbroken bread on the table, only to lift it again to break it after we have said our "Amen." While the Anglican liturgical tradition has not required a slavish obedience to reconstructions of the Last Supper as the exact model for later liturgical practice, to pronounce the words of breaking but to leave the bread unbroken, for me, adds some unreality to the saying of the Institution Narrative within the eucharistic prayer. This is compounded by the insertion of the Prayer That Jesus Taught between the eucharistic prayer and the fraction. I wonder whether if, in the spirit of trying to enable greater and deeper participation by the whole people of God with the eucharistic actions, this might be once again a topic for conversation.

Sober Joy

This is where we will begin the theological and spiritual appreciation of the breaking: I want to suggest, first, that the breaking *is* a symbol of the breaking of Christ's body on the cross, and that we can understand the meaning of this as being a reminder of Christ's death, which sets humankind free from slavery to sin.

What was once an undisputed, if not fully elaborated, understanding of the significance of Christ's death has become a contested piece of theology. Why did Christ die? What is meant when Christians say, "Christ died for us"? In a short essay it is impossible to explain or argue between the different theories of the atonement.[14] Instead we will base our reflection on the words and actions of the liturgy itself.

The broken bread reminds us that Jesus died. Whether we subscribe to a more sacrificial understanding of the eucharistic action or not, as the bread is torn we are reminded of a broken body and of death. This can remind us of the costliness of grace; that forgiveness of sins is not lightly achieved or given. This forgiveness cost God in Christ everything. One of the most poignant expressions of this was written by Ronald Bainton, paraphrasing Luther:

> In Christ, only in Christ. In the Lord of life, born in the squalor of a cow stall and dying as a malefactor under the desertion and the derision of men, crying unto God and receiving for answer only the trembling of the earth and the blinding of the sun, even by God forsaken, and in that hour taking to himself and annihilating our iniquity, trampling down the hosts of hell and disclosing within the

---

14. For a good summary, see Stephen W. Sykes, *The Story of the Atonement* (London: DLT, 1997). For a modern Anglican perspective from a diverse group of theologians comprising the Doctrine Commission of the Church of England, see *The Mystery of Salvation* (London: Church House Publishing, 1995). See also the influential text, Gustav Aulen, *Christus Victor* (London: SPCK, 1931). For a flavor of the most modern controversy, see Steve Chalke and Alan Mann, *The Lost Message of Jesus* (Grand Rapids, MI: Zondervan , 2004).

wrath of the All Terrible the love that will not let us go.[15]

I have already had cause to criticize Luther's theology of the atonement, but this piece of writing remains a vivid portrayal of the cost of forgiveness to, as we would say now, God the Trinity.

Open Hands

In an era of "cheap grace," when we attend church and see the bread broken yet so often it has no impact on us,[16] or when the very possibility of "atonement" is denied,[17] I want to argue that God has made atonement by taking back into Godself the hurtful consequences of a risky creation and of the evil done by free humankind. I would go further, and in a re-working of the classic Protestant doctrine of "justification by faith," suggest that on the cross, and so in the breaking of the bread, we are reminded that we are truly forgiven by and before God. Evil has a tangible quality. We cannot wish it away. And a world without justice is an unbearable world of frustration. But on the cross, and now re-expressed visibly in the breaking of the bread, Christ takes the blame and frees us from blame.[18] In his dying, the Church believes, as Cranmer wrote in the Book of Common Prayer, Christ takes away the sins of the "whole world" (not just limited atonement, which is an un-Anglican idea). Sin is dealt with. In the words of the *Agnus Dei,* he *is* the one who "takes away the sin of the world." We are set free. So the breaking is a moment of sober joy.

---

15. Roland Bainton, *Here I Stand: A Life of Martin Luther* (London: New English Library, 1950), 302. Frustratingly, Bainton gives no references. See also Jurgen Moltmann, *The Crucified God* (London: SCM Press, 1974), esp. 235–49, for a rich trinitarian account of the passion.

16. Dietrich Bonhoeffer, *The Cost of Discipleship* (London: SCM Press, 1982), 35–38 (first published in 1937).

17. This is the point of Ian McEwan, *Atonement* (London: Vintage, 2002). See discussion in Bartlett, *Humane Christianity,* 129–33.

18. See the fuller discussion in Bartlett, *Humane Christianity,* 133–36.

And yet we remain sinners, who need to plead for mercy. That we believe mercy is already offered and is freely given does not relieve us from the healthy and life-giving duty of honesty, of confronting our own sinfulness and asking for forgiveness. The problem with the Church's abuse of the doctrine of sin is not that sin is not a real problem for real human beings, but rather that the Church has been dishonest about its own sinfulness, has been distorted in its evaluation of sinful actions and sinful humanity, and above all, has focused on the disease (sin) rather than on the cure and the purpose of the cure: liberated life-filled human beings enjoying God for ever.

The conviction that Christ died for our sins has often been used by the Church as the most powerful of its tools for generating a response from its people. There is a fine but vital distinction between presentation of the sacrifice of Christ, which can draw out from us a freely given response of gratitude and an imposition of a sense of response that is a form of coercion. Some Christian spirituality sounds to our ears a little like gracious invitation: to pick a very popular example, C.F. Alexander's hymn "There is a green hill far away" reads as if because of the dear love of Christ, "we must love him too," trusting in his "redeeming blood" and trying to do "his works."[19] The very simplicity of this hymn, and its place in the Church's work with children over the generations, should make us more alert to its dynamic of requiring love because of a bloody death. But, conversely, because we are so often hard-hearted, we need to be sensitized. Indeed I wonder if lack of love is our greatest sin rather than, as "classically" thought, pride.[20] Therefore a broken wafer or torn bread as a symbol of divine and human brokenness may touch our cool and well-defended hearts. So how can we distinguish between these two approaches? This is crucial when we may be offered the

---

19. See *Common Praise*, no. 123.

20. Bartlett, *Humane Christianity*, 58: "If the core of my and human sinfulness is selfishness, self-centeredness, a sort of egotistical self-pre-occupation, which encompasses indifference to God and to others, then the core spiritual task may be to soften and open up my heart to the love of God and of others. Love to be received by me so it can be given by me."

broken body of Christ, Sunday by Sunday, and be exhorted to respond.

The distinction lies in the sense of gift, and so in the confidence in the depth of love in the giver of the gift, and so in the patience of the giver. It is for this reason that as a eucharistic presider I hold out the broken bread to the congregation after the fraction and again at the words of invitation. We are "blessed" to be invited to this supper. And as the new eucharistic prayers make clear, God will not "abandon [God's] own." Again and again God draws us into "a covenant of grace," and as a patient mother, even when we turn away and rebel, God tenderly gathers and embraces us again, because God's love is "steadfast."[21] This is a renewed understanding of God. As I have argued in *A Passionate Balance:*

> Eventually, the *enthusiastically and recklessly forgiving* God of the parable of the prodigal son has moved to be the controlling image of God in Christ for Anglicans.[22]

This is how we can know when the broken bread that we are being offered is not tainted by coercion, when it is given freely. God is not a bully or a deceiver. God respects humankind too much to do that. Jesus, by the way he treated people, showed us that truth. As C. S. Lewis wrote most perceptively of God's relationship to human beings:

> But you see now that the Irresistible and the Indisputable are the two weapons which the very nature of his scheme forbids him to use. Merely to override a human will (as his felt presence in any but

---

21. *Common Worship,* Eucharistic Prayers F and G, 198, 201.

22. Alan Bartlett, *A Passionate Balance: The Anglican Tradition* (London: DLT, 2007). Italics original. A bold claim perhaps, but notice that Rowan Williams' list of "successors to Westcott" (*Anglican Identities* [London: DLT, 2004], 83) includes Vanstone, the archetypal theologian of this perspective. See W. H. Vanstone, *Love's Endeavour, Love's Expense: The Response of Being to the Love of God* (London: DLT, 1977). From within evangelicalism, note John Stott, with his recognition of the breadth of Anglicanism and sensitive commendation of the theology of the cross, in John Stott, *The Cross of Christ* (Leicester: IVP, 1986), and John Stott and David Edwards, *Essentials* (London: Hodder and Stoughton, 1988).

the faintest and most mitigated degree would certainly do) would be for him useless. He cannot ravish. He can only woo.[23]

This must have an impact on how we live as Church: if God is like this, then how can the Church have been so different? Walter Moberly spells this out sharply: "The Church cannot be permitted to try to sustain itself by those very means which Jesus renounced."[24] The torn bread is offered with open hands.

Tearing

The second aspect of the breaking that I want to explore is how this relates to our doctrine of the incarnation. It is too easy to be glib and painless in our incarnational theology. There is something almost shocking as a priest about the action of breaking a wafer or tearing a loaf. Its very physicality reminds me that Jesus' body was literally broken by torture and execution. In the North East of England, some churches use our local bread bun, the Stottie, as our communion bread. These fresh but tough rolls take some tearing! The body that was broken during the passion was a real body. It took much effort to break it, effort by the cruel representatives of an oppressive state. In other words, as we break the wafers or tear the bread, we are reminded that we are remembering a real flesh-and-blood human being. As I tear the Stottie, I cannot forget the real death of a beautiful human being.

One of my theological teachers, Professor Ann Loades, once asked me what we should learn from the death of Christ. I ran through a variety of options in my head but she said simply, "Never again." We (humankind) should in some sense have learned that it is wrong to treat a human being in this debased way. It had never occurred to me before to think that way. But of course the more real our sense of the real human

---

23. C. S. Lewis, *The Screwtape Letters* (New York: HarperCollins, 2001), 39.

24. R. W. L. Moberly, *The Bible, Theology and Faith* (Cambridge, UK: Cambridge University Press, 2000), 235.

being whose death lies behind our ritualized breaking, the more we may be inspired to work for peace and the protection of human beings.

We need to remember the reality of the death of Jesus because it is only if his death is real that the liberating hope of the doctrine of the incarnation has reality for us. Again, it would be possible to engage in complex (and proper) theological discussion of the incarnation, but as before we will the fraction itself to drive our theological reflection.

Jesus and Things

Following Jesus, we take real bread and break it.[25] Rowan Williams has suggested a deep theological significance for this. He first notes that the association of Jesus with bread transcends later theological divisions.

> Whatever the particular theology of eucharistic presence in a tradition, there is inevitably a setting-aside of the elements and a narrative recalling Jesus' self-identification with the bread and wine as "representative" bits of the created order . . .[26]

He goes further:

> Jesus "passes over" into the symbolic forms by his own word and gesture, a transition into the vulnerable and inactive forms of the inanimate world. By resigning himself into the signs of food and drink,

---

25. I should note here that while the logistics of many communicants means that wafers are more practical, and respecting the sense of devotion that has wanted to honor Christ's presence in the consecrated elements and so prefers wafers which scatter few crumbs, Cranmer's healthy wisdom to use the best local bread seems to me to offer a more vivid sense of the reality of the body which lies behind our symbols. Cf. David Stancliffe, "The Fraction and the Shape of the Rite," in Stephen Conway, ed., *Living the Eucharist: Affirming Catholicism and the Liturgy* (London: DLT, 2001), 101.

26. Rowan Williams, "Sacraments of the New Society," in David Brown and Ann Loades, eds., *Christ: The Sacramental Word: Incarnation, Sacrament and Poetry* (London: SPCK, 1996), 95. It is partly because the spirituality of encountering Christ in the eucharist seems to me to transcend the classic theological divisions that I have allowed myself to ignore the issue of the "presence" of Christ.

putting himself into the hands of other agents, he signifies his forthcoming helplessness and death. He announces his death by "signing" himself as a thing, to be handled and consumed.[27]

Again, this is shocking. Jesus, the beloved one of God, associates himself with a "thing." It goes beyond our classic understandings of incarnation. But in so doing it reminds us of the profound physicality of the Christian doctrine of the incarnation, a physicality so often lost in the tradition or transferred into a reverence for manufactured objects, not for real people or living creation. The point is simple: in his death, in the breaking of his body, Jesus left a divine legacy of utter involvement with the human condition and the fate of the natural world and an assurance of the ultimate value of human beings in all their embodiedness. Williams sums this up starkly when he writes of the sacraments: "Let them still speak of nakedness, death, danger, materiality, and stubborn promise."[28]

This has a simple liturgical expression. The bread that is broken is "consecrated" bread which has been set apart to be Christ for us. It is Christ incarnate in the form of bread which is broken. As David Stancliffe writes, "There, before our eyes . . . is the sign of the death, of the body broken on the cross."[29]

What is the "human condition"? A former colleague, a trained counselor, used to wonder out loud whether everyone was "broken" or was it just the people who came to talk to her? In our conversations over time, we came to feel that everyone is, in some real way, broken, but that some people are better at hiding it! What did we mean? At the very least, we knew that everyone is a sinner, everyone wrestles with their spiritual and moral failings. We also knew that everyone is mortal. That our bodies are rarely and temporarily "perfect." That we age and die. And we also sensed that everyone carries

27. Williams, "Sacraments of the New Society," 96.
28. Williams, "Sacraments of the New Society," 101.
29. Stancliffe, "The Fraction," 98.

emotional and psychological wounds. No one is immune to the wear and tear of life.

The incarnation and the torn bread remind us that it is into this broken world that Christ came. And the Church constantly struggles to grasp the depth of this identification. I found myself being asked recently: "Do you think Jesus had dirty finger nails?" The answer is, of course, "Yes, much of the time." He lived in a country with limited access to water. (When most water is drawn from wells, it is used sparingly.) So of course his feet and his hands were often dirty. How often do we see pictures of a sweaty Jesus? Again, the new eucharistic prayers are making this important truth liturgically alive for us:

> Lord God, you are the most holy one,
> enthroned in splendour and light,
> yet in the coming of your Son Jesus Christ
> you reveal the power of your love
> made perfect in our human weakness.[30]

Jesus embraces our humanity. He does not glide above it.

This dose of reality is crucial for us, as we live so often with illusion. Jean Vanier, the founder of the L'Arche communities, writes frequently about the reality of human brokenness and about the liberation that comes with accepting our own brokenness.

> When you have been taught from an early age to be first, to win, and then suddenly you sense you are being called by Jesus to go down the ladder and to share your life with those who have little culture, who are poor and marginalized, a real struggle breaks out within oneself. As I began living with people like Raphael and Philip [persons with severe learning disabilities], I began to see all the hardness of my own heart . . . Raphael and the others were simply crying out for friendship and I

---

30. *Common Worship*, Eucharistic Prayer F, 198–99.

did not quite know how to respond because of the
other forces within me, pulling me to go up the
ladder.[31]

Vanier challenges us to go beyond the rhetoric of the God
of the poor and to live as if God really does love and live with
the poor. And that, in different ways, is all of us.

People may come to our communities because they
want to serve the poor; they will only stay once they
have discovered that they themselves are poor.[32]

Torn bread reminds us that Jesus is here with us, in our
brokenness.

Divine Habitation

But this is not simply a participation in our pain and brokenness, it is also a promise of hope. As Kenneth Stevenson
has made so abundantly clear, for Richard Hooker (Elizabeth
I's greatest theologian and a founding figure for Anglicans),
"participation" was the key theological term to describe the
relationship between Christ and humankind, and Hooker
used it as the framework within which to set his sacramental
theology. Stevenson cites one of the most beautiful sentences
written in English to describe the incarnation: "God has dei-
fied our nature, though not by turning it to himself, yet by
making it his *own inseparable habitation*."[33] Stevenson himself immediately comments:

This is a way of expressing the union of the human
and the divine in Christ, made available for all
people . . . which avoids excessive and negative
penitence, affirms the reality of the weakness of

---

31. Jean Vanier, *From Brokenness to Community* (Mahwah, NJ: Paulist Press,
1992), 18.

32. Vanier, *From Brokenness*, 20.

33. Kenneth Stevenson, *Covenant of Grace Renewed: A Vision of the Eucharist in
the Seventeenth Century* (London: DLT, 1994), 26, citing Richard Hooker, *The Laws
of Ecclesiastical Polity*, book 5, chapter 54, section 5. Italics mine.

human nature, but places it always and everywhere in the hands of a loving and eternal God.

This sentence could be taken as the theological foundation
upon which my own essay rests: real about the human condition but confident in the love of God and in the intimacy of
God's engagement with humankind. For Hooker, our participation in Christ meant that our future was assured. Our final
home is in the heavenly places with Christ the ever-incarnate.

Hooker related his christology to his sacramental theology
in a sophisticated way, trying both to incorporate aspects of
both Protestant and traditional Catholic theology, but also
to undermine the bitter divisions of the sixteenth century by
reminding his fellow Christians both of the magnitude of the
gift given in the sacraments and also of proper human response
of modesty in the face of such magnitude and mystery. In the
context of this essay, what is striking is that despite his modesty, Hooker was so convinced of the necessity of holy communion: those "who will live the life of God," he says, "must
eat the flesh and drink the blood of the Son of man, because
this is a part of that diet which if we want [lack] we cannot
live."[34] In other words, it is essential for our spiritual growth
that we continue to be fed by holy communion. And Hooker
was not frightened of traditional "realist" language, which
is not surprising because neither was the Book of Common
Prayer, despite Cranmer's alleged "Zwinglian" eucharistic
theology.[35] While its location was designed to remove any hint
of transubstantiation, that Cranmer preserved the "prayer
of humble access," such a traditional relic of Catholic eucharistic piety, was both sign and instrument of the distinctive
emerging Anglican theological identity. So we are cleansed as
we "eat the flesh of thy dear Son Jesus Christ," his body—
which in a strange and beautiful resonance is like eating the
crumbs from under the table. It is possible to sense the deep
eucharistic piety of Cranmer here—which was not under-
mined by Cranmer's instruction to the curate to take the

---

34. Stevenson, *Covenant of Grace*, 28, citing *Laws* 5.67.1.
35. See the fuller discussion in Bartlett, *A Passionate Balance*, 133–37.

spare consecrated bread home. This was both special bread and ordinary bread. It was its use and its effect that made it holy. It is a dynamic sense of sacramental presence.

Hooker shared this sense of the dynamic presence of Christ, and in a passage which many commentators have noted as being of especial significance for him (he is citing an older text which is written as if from Christ), Hooker writes:

> . . . this hallowed food, through concurrence of divine power, is in verity and truth unto faithful receivers, instrumentally a cause of that mystical participation, whereby as I make myself wholly theirs, so I give them in hand an actual possession of all such saving grace as my sacrificed body can yield, and as their souls do presently need, this is to them and in them my body . . .[36]

In other words, there is an intimate connection between eating the bread and receiving Christ's body. It is therefore only as Christ's body—the bread—is broken and shared and eaten, that the Christian is enabled to participate in Christ.

Caught Up in Christ's Life

This discussion takes us on to the third of our themes evoked by the action of breaking. In the liturgical practice of some presiders, the bread is broken and then held up—though Anglican consensus discourages it.[37] This gesture of lifting up can suggest the idea that as Christ participates in human life, so we too are caught up into his life. In particular we are caught up in Christ's self-offering to God. This can be a

36. *Laws* 5.67.12. Italics original. For detailed discussion, see Stevenson, *Covenant of Grace*, 30.

37. See the guidelines proposed by the "inter-Anglican" consultation published as David Holeton, *Our Thanks and Praise: The Eucharist in Anglicanism Today* (Toronto: Anglican Book Centre, 1998), 30: "Gestures by the presider during the eucharistic prayer should underscore the unity of the prayer. The traditional manual acts which draw attention to the institution narrative or other portions of the prayer serve to locate consecration within a narrow portion of the text and may contradict a more contemporary understanding of Eucharistic consecration."

doctrine which makes evangelical Anglicans uneasy, because it can resonate with the idea that we extract from God spiritual rights as we "re-offer" the offering of the death of Christ. That is not what I mean here and is not what I think is meant by historic or current Anglican liturgical theology.[38] The emphasis is always on the "once for all" sacrifice of the cross. And Cranmer was of course scrupulous in separating out our "offering" from the gift of Christ by placing it after communion. The offering we make is both one of "thanks and praise" and also one of prayer for a worthy life. We "offer" ourselves to be God's servants "formed in the likeness of Christ." But of course it is Christ at work in us as his body which enables this wider offering. This understanding of our association with and ultimately participation in the offering of Christ has been picked up strongly in the new ordination rites. Thus:

> The ministry of priests (who continue to exercise diaconal ministry) is focused in calling the Church to enter into Christ's self-offering to the Father, drawing God's people into a life transformed and sanctified.[39]

But in what sense is this offering to be one of brokenness, as with the torn bread?[40]

Liberative Purpose: Broken Open for Life

We began this essay with some caution about the way language of human brokenness and sacrifice can become abusive.

---

38. Even the phrase "we plead with confidence" in Eucharistic Prayers E and G is focused on the "once for all" sacrifice on the cross. *Common Worship: Ordination Services*, 197, 203.

39. *Common Worship: Ordination Services* (London: Church House Publishing, 2007), 4.

40. This is another reason for considering an earlier fraction, as part of a eucharistic prayer, because when we hold up the torn bread, it may remind us that we come to the Father through the damaged body of the Son. To elevate an unbroken wafer seems to me to present to ourselves a thin expression of the love and reality of the incarnation.

The distinction between being broken in the offering and being broken as the offering is crucial. The point is that the world is a broken place and to love in this world is costly. Ministry is always and predominantly passion-shaped, even if lived within the confidence in the future which the resurrection establishes. Michael Sadgrove, reflecting on his own ordination and striving to express the costliness of Christian ministry, goes back to Archbishop Michael Ramsey:

> In your service of others you will feel, you will care, you will be hurt, you will have your heart broken. And it is doubtful if any of us can do anything at all until we have been very much hurt, and until our hearts have been very much broken. And this is because God's gift to us is the glory of Christ *crucified* . . .[41]

Is this running the risk of sliding back into a form of spiritual masochism? If it is not breaking us, is it not real ministry? No. Because the point is not the breaking but rather the real cost of real loving. No. Because the purpose of this is not pain, but liberation.

Divine Longing

To make this clear, we will finish with two further quotations from Vanier. The first expresses Vanier's deep, tangible, and dangerous doctrine of the incarnation as an expression of divine longing:

> Since the day the Word became flesh
> and became one among us,
> each human being is intimately linked to Jesus.
> The Word became man [sic] in every way:
> a human vulnerable heart
> with the capacity to love
> and the capacity to weep and to suffer pain,

---

41. Michael Sadgrove, *Wisdom and Ministry* (London: SPCK, 2008), 113.

and so be able to forgive and be compassionate.
Jesus is one of us, one of our flesh . . .
. . . [and] he yearns for each one to live and
   celebrate life.
and he says so clearly that
he is the hungry and the thirsty,
he is the person in prison or sick in hospital,
he is the stranger, the person lying naked in the street.
Here lies the mystery.
The body of Christ is humanity.[42]

This beautiful passage both reflects Vanier's sense of Christ's participation in "human-being-ness" so as to bring life and also, amazingly, a sense that God too is changed by incarnation. For God in Christ, brokenness becomes (was always?) the only way to save this broken world. But the purpose is salvation, health, life in its fullness. Vanier finishes this particular book with this poetic reflection, picking up on the great insight of Irenaeus:

Jesus, the Lamb,
who comes to bring peace to the world
by taking away sin
and opening our hearts to the poor and the
   broken,
so that together we can celebrate our oneness
and grow to freedom.
For the glory of God
in the wholeness of his Body
is each human person fully alive.[43]

In other words, while we need the broken bread as a sign and instrument now, we will not need it for ever.

---

42. Jean Vanier, *The Broken Body: Journey to Wholeness* (London: DLT, 1988), 128. Italics mine. As always in Vanier, this poetic prose sits on top of profound biblical and theological reflection; here we find references to Hebrews and Matthew, as well as to sophisticated understandings of the theology of the incarnation.

43. Vanier, *Broken Body*, 141, referring to Irenaeus *Adversus Haeresis*, 4.20.7.

CHAPTER 8

Giving

John B. Thomson

For the Life of the World

THE BIGGEST SHOCK WAS MY first Sunday. As a new fresh-faced vicar eager to see the church grow and impact on the neighborhood, the sobering reality was to see what a small congregation we were. In total that morning we comprised about 65 adults and a handful of youngsters eyeing each other up across a sea of empty pews. After the full house of my induction the week before, this Sunday was a reality check. Visitors and well-wishers were gone. We were now the gang God had called together to share in his mission in this parish in one of the lowest churchgoing areas of England.

Many congregations in England today appear small, relatively marginal, and uncertain about their mission in contemporary society. According to the sociologist, Grace Davie, English society, like most of Europe, is characterized by a "take it for granted" view of public religion.[1] Like other public utilities, it is there to be used when wanted, but otherwise not participated in. Hence, as Lynda Barley has shown, while

---

1. Grace Davie, *Religion in Modern Europe: A Memory Mutates* (Oxford, UK: Oxford University Press, 2000), 55–61.

86 percent of the population visit churches each year and 72 percent claim to be Christians, only 8 percent attend regularly.[2] According to Davie, the committed core, therefore, act vicariously for those who believe but don't actively belong.

Such a casual popular approach to public faith combined with the fragility of many congregations and a sense of being on the edge of things, raises sharp questions about mission. The Church of England's *Mission Shaped Church* report seeks to engage with such questions.[3] What are these small gatherings of Christians to be and to do? What are they here for? Can sixty-five adults and a handful of youngsters make a difference amidst an apparently indifferent community?[4] In particular, if the Christian way or journey is fundamentally about embodying the grace of God and thereby underwriting the Christian conviction that everything to do with God is gift, how are we to be divine gifts in the diversity of contexts we find ourselves in?[5] How can such small and relatively impotent communities witness to the great mission of God to redeem, restore, and renew the world in the face of large-scale indifference?

The Gift of Being Church:
A Kind of Crater in the World

It was the American theologian Stanley Hauerwas who made the surprising assertion that the first task of the church in mission is to be itself since "the truthfulness of Jesus creates and is known by the kind of community his story should form."[6] What he meant by this was that the church is the community, which tangibly represents the effects of God's

2. Lynda Barley, *Churchgoing Today* (London: CHP, 2006), 2.

3. *Mission Shaped Church* (London: CHP, 2004).

4. John B. Thomson, *Church on Edge? Practising Ministry Today* (London: DLT, 2004).

5. John Milbank, *Being Reconciled: Ontology and Pardon* (London: Routledge, 2003), ix–xi.

6. Stanley M. Hauerwas, *A Community of Character: Toward a Constructive Christian Social Ethic*, 4th ed. (Notre Dame, IL: University of Notre Dame Press, 1986), 10, 37.

grace in lives open to that grace. Hence it represents a sign of
salvation, an expression of the living holiness of God active in
the world. The church does not therefore have to do anything
in the first instance to indicate the grace of God for the world.
Its very existence is evidence of that, even taking account
of its fragility and failures. Certainly the church is not the
kingdom of God and hence is not everything God is about.
Nevertheless, as an explicit witness to the grace of God, the
church, which Hauerwas regards as the worldwide and historical community of Christians, embodies and expresses the
gospel, which is for all. To play with Karl Barth's phrase, the
church is the crater left behind by the explosion of God's salvation in Christ. In consequence, as Christians gather and
allow God to transform them, they become able to see the
particular mission challenges before them. As gift and givers,
they are trained to see how they are to be cascades of grace
in diverse contexts.[7]

What this means for bread-and-butter congregations is
that anxiety about being relevant and effective can give way
to an assurance that as effects of God's grace, simply being
who they are is a major gift for the world. Their gift is to
be signs which, though not exhaustive or finished expressions of God's love, are still significant signs of that grace,
however small or fragile they may be. God is the principal
agent in mission rather than human beings. Focusing first
and foremost on what God is about rather than upon what
we can do for God does not imply passivity or complacency.
As will become apparent below, the transformation of sinful
Christians is a major enterprise of God, and discipleship is
about cooperating with God's grace. However, focusing upon
God gives hope that human fallibility and fragility do not
determine the effectiveness of grace. We are gifts of grace for
the world's blessing precisely as those who know ourselves
to be forgiven sinners. Tangibly being church, therefore, acts
as a sign of what God is bringing about through the slow
time of transformation. It is a form of exemplary politics as

---

7. Ann Morisy, *Journeying Out: A New Approach to Christian Mission* (London:
DLT, 2004), 30–31.

a new society emerges configured around the grace of God expressed in Christ. As such, what the church is becoming enables the mission of God to be provisionally seen and gives faith an empirical bite. A particular example of such a tangible sign of material grace is a congregation located on a rough Barnsley estate. Until recently the whole area had an air of dilapidation and depression, with most buildings boarded up and local teenagers looking bored. Yet this little community of twenty-five to thirty adults with a handful of youngsters has managed to renovate their building, maintain an active Christian presence in the area, and remained committed to serving that community despite the absence of a vicar. Just by being there they are like a clump of snowdrops on rough ground, a sign of hope and gift in a community forgotten by most of society. As part of the local Anglican church, the Diocese of Sheffield, they are a mission station, a gift webbed into the wider church under the oversight of the bishop. They therefore represent the commitment of that local church to this deprived area of Barnsley, and yet also enable that community and area to sense that the mission of God is about connecting them into a larger and more diverse Christian community, symbolized in the diocese. Simply by being there, they are a sign of salvation, a gift of hope for a neglected community.

The Gift of Worship: Meaningful Flesh

As mentioned above, although being the church is the first gift of mission, being the church involves being transformed so that we can cooperate more faithfully with the agenda of God. In eucharistic language, God takes, blesses, breaks, and gives. In order to be gifts which speak of salvation, we need to experience the blessing and breaking of transformation as God takes what we are and works to form us into witnesses of grace. While creation is gift and reflects the glory of God, the work of transformation mediated through eucharistic worship in particular is about intensifying this glory and gift by transforming lives so that they speak of salvation over-coming sin. It is therefore through ongoing transformation that we become gifts signifying saving grace for the world, effective on God's terms and within God's mission. Worship, particularly eucharistic worship, therefore, is about giving, because it forms Christians into gifts for the world as signs and agents of God's reign and mission in the world. It shows people what God does in lives openly offered to grace and regularly trained in the practices of discipleship.

Such transformation for Anglicans is rooted in the public worship of the gathered community. As we gather in worship, we imbibe the transforming grace of God eucharistically through word and sacrament in a way that affects who and what we are. Indeed, as Rowan Williams has pointed out, Anglican divines Richard Hooker and George Herbert believed that transubstantiation was fundamentally about human lives rather than arguments about the status of bread and wine post-consecration.[8] Transformation into an icon or window into God is not primarily about the condition of the bread and wine so much as about the condition of the community, which has received the gift of God into itself in order to embody that gift in the bread and wine of ordinary living.

Worship, therefore, is a missional gift since it forms people whose lives are marked by the effects of God so that they display the salvation of God available to all. They are thereby being made Christians since righteousness is not simply imputed to them but also imparted to them. In consequence, it begins to make sense to go to church regularly since through participating in the transforming effects of worship, we become revelations of God and God's love for the world. Our lives begin to display something of the world God is bringing about through Christ, in contrast to that given over to sin. Indeed, as Archbishop Michael Ramsey said, worship forms Christians into meaningful flesh, flesh that signifies what God is about and signifies God compassion for the world.[9] The gift of meaningful flesh offers the world a

---

8. Rowan Williams, *Anglican Identities* (London: DLT, 2004), 24–45.
9. Williams, *Anglican Identities*, 87–101.

challenge. The challenge is to make sense of this flesh, even when it can appear odd to common sense analysis. Indeed sometimes being odd in a sinful world is one of the gifts of the church to that world. It indicates that this gathering is on God's terms rather than being determined by human choice. As such it witnesses to God's effect upon the church. Worship, therefore, forms people into evidence for the saving impact of God in the world. Being made distinctive through worship is simply another way of becoming holy witnesses. It is how Christians continue as part of the ongoing revelation of God to the world.

Gathering to worship, therefore, is akin to participating in a training session. As we participate in the liturgy and its spiritual exercises such as praise, confession, attention to scripture, intercession, and taking the sacraments, we not only hear the word of God but are trained in the virtues of Christian practice and learn the habits of life which reflect and express the grace of God. In short we become Christians, or in Augustine and Aquinas's terms, people of charity. Such training or formation means that as we share in God's mission, we do not need to pull out a book of rules or a guidebook to know what to do. Instead, like competent athletes, we can improvise in the diverse situations we are part of, confident that our training has equipped us to make good judgments that will enable us to participate faithfully in God's mission.[10] Such improvisation means that new situations require fresh expressions of faithful Christian practice. In one examining village near Doncaster, a congregation has set up a cinema in part of the church as a way of re-engaging with its local community, most of whom find it too expensive to travel to Doncaster. In addition, local children help the vicar and members of the congregation prepare meals, which they share together. In both cases, entertainment and eating are signs of the hospitality of God which Jesus exhibited.

Worship therefore sharpens up our eyesight as we begin to see the world through the lens of God's love. Its practices

---

10. Samuel Wells, *Improvisation: The Drama of Christian Ethics* (London: SPCK, 2004), 78.

dispose us to reach out to the stranger, visit the sick, spend time with children and those marginalized, just as we see Christ doing in the gospels. Worship and mission therefore belong together since it is only as God transforms us that we can begin to see what God is asking of us in particular contexts. In addition such worship needs to be common or open to all the baptized if it is to be faithful to Jesus, the expression and invitation of God's love for the world. To participate in the mission of God therefore requires hospitable worship, if we are to discern the distinctive character of that mission where we find ourselves. Faithful mission requires that we listen to one another as we listen together to the Spirit. Indeed the gift of a catholic worshipping community representative of all sorts of human beings is the sign that God has space for all of us if we will accept it. This is partly why Anglicans as a rule have held to a generous and embracing understanding of catholicity and communion.

Worship as a transforming experience is vital if the church is to be both a gift to the world as it shares in the mission of God and a gift to the world as it reveals to that world the effect of worship. Worship forms witnesses. It sets before the world the hospitality yet holiness of God, the open yet refining fire of grace, the taste of God's goodness and the challenge of God's purity. Furthermore, the common character of worship, stressed particularly by Anglicans, means that all Christian communities and disciples have a distinctive part to play in the drama of God's activity in the world. Christ has won the victory over sin, evil, and death, but as the ongoing body of Christ in the world, Christians become bearers of that victory to the world. Indeed, unlike pagan ethics, which sought and in various ways today still seeks to advocate an ideal of heroic and powerful self-contained agents who can shape the world in their own image, Christians seek to be saints whose lives witness to what God can do, particularly in human weakness.

In consequence, worship enables very ordinary Christian communities to trust that in the offering of their life, God will transform or transubstantiate them into Christ-like communities that are able to give themselves in mission to the world on God's terms. Their understanding of what it means to serve the world, to reach out to that world in mission and to be hospitable to that world, will emerge as they become more like Christ through the effect of grace upon their own lives. Indeed, as John Booty says, for Anglicans "a praising community is an agent of evangelism."[11] Worship is good news for the life of the world since it speaks about the reality of divine transformation or, in older language divinization, the formation of human beings for life with and for God. Thus both by worshipping and by offering hospitality to the world, Anglicans believe that God's grace will work to effect change and response in ways that go beyond our immediate perceptions. Indeed, thinking back to my parish experience, it was actually the impact of congregational worship and its formative effects that primarily drew people to God. Other activities such as visitations, a generous approach to occasional offices, caring for the marginal and elderly in the parish and beyond, engaging with local schools and other institutions, drew their meaning and energy from the effect of God present in the weekly gathering to worship. This was the primary gift of the church, which, as I have mentioned above, by being and becoming itself, is the gift of the social life of Jesus in and to the world.

The Gift of a Language: Christian Description

If worship is about forming people through praise to become divine gifts for the world, able to see and thereby share in the mission of God, it is not only sign but speech that enables that mission to be executed. The church, though, is not simply a community speaking words, it is a language itself.[12] Its form of life tells a salvation story about God, the

---

11. Cited in Stephen W. Sykes, *Unashamed Anglicanism* (London: DLT, 1995), 205.

12. Stanley M. Hauerwas, "The Church as God's New Language," in *Christian Existence Today: Essays on Church, World and Living in Between* (Durham, NC: The Labyrinth Press, 1988), 47–65.

cosmos, humanity, and other creatures within this great epic, as will become apparent in the next section. As language, the church offers the world a way of understanding God's saving action and character in contemporary signs by seeing how this community lives with God in its bread and butter existence. As a language expressed in diverse dialects across time and space, the church describes the world in the light of Christ. This is its third gift to the world, emerging from its identity and the transforming impact of its worship.

In the past, as Christendom Western societies sought to express such a language or form life. The corruption of this experiment, however, meant that since the Reformation, the seventeenth-century wars of religion, and then the eighteenth-century Enlightenment, the mother tongue of Christendom has mutated into something called "secular speech." This, according to Jeffrey Stout, was historically an attempt to enable Christians who found it increasingly difficult to respect their diverse Christian dialects to find a way of living together in relative peace using second-order language for things such as politics, economics, and law.[13] However what was seen as a way of ensuring a peaceable discussion between various Christian dialects, such as Roman Catholicism, Presbyterianism, Methodism, Anglicanism, and Pentecostalism, has increasingly become an excuse for those who dissent from Christian believing to see the secular as the default language, or form of life, policing all other ways of describing the world and its significance. Consequently, to be faithful to God and to the vocation of the church, it is vital that Christians recover confidence in our mother tongue, even if the way we speak this language can often seem quite diverse.

To give back primacy to our Christian description of the world, though, is neither sectarian nor simply about rhetoric. Instead it is about recognizing that we are Christians before we are citizens or members of families, nations, or any other organizational identity. We cannot turn the historical clock back and imagine that we can speak as God's language free

13. See Jeffrey Stout, *Democracy and Tradition* (Princeton, NJ: Princeton University Press, Princeton University Press, 2004).

from our past. There are different dialects of Christianity. Indeed, in some ways the particularity of the incarnation suggests that we should expect this. Likewise, we will only be given a definitive grammar of God's language at the end of the age. Hence, in the interim we offer ourselves in worship, trusting that through this and in the light of the journey we and other Christian communities have made, we shall learn how to speak faithfully, if not perfectly, as God's language for today. The gift of the church to the world, therefore, is to live as Christians in the world so that the world may see and hear the story of God's love focused in the gospel and embodied by the church. We walk in order to become people whose walk talks and who through walking are given the words to talk.

As God's language, the character, plausibility, and nature of that language will therefore be seen in the way the language functions or enables Christians to live faithfully with God in that world. Living conscious that we are creatures rather than autonomous agents offers a liberating gift to people anxious that everything about their destiny is in their own hands. We are not simply independent, self-interested consumers out to maximize our own well-being at the expense of everyone else and hence in structural conflict with everyone else. Rather, recognizing that even our enemies are made in the image of God and befriending them as fellow neighbors in God's world offers a different sociology in a fractious and divided world. Forgiving those who have offended us and asking forgiveness of those we have offended, especially God, speaks of a redeemed creation in which peaceableness rather than violence is most fundamental. Undertaking lifelong vows such as those of celibacy, marriage, or ordination speaks of trust in the promise-keeping character of God, in and through the vicissitudes of life. All these gifts contrast with much in contemporary society where tabloid moralism, the therapy culture of self-preoccupation, and the destructiveness of serial relationships undermine human flourishing. However, the critical challenge for Christians, given the ambiguous history of the church, is to walk before we talk. Performance is crucial to plausibility, since otherwise the meaning of the Christian way is lost to charges of hypocrisy and double standards.

To be transformed into a language that speaks of the hope and challenge of the gospel is therefore a vital gift of the church for the life of the world. One way of enabling Christians to appreciate the significance of this gift is to help them to recognize the way the practices of worship represent a sort of language lab in which they can become fluent speakers of this language. To this end, in the Diocese of Sheffield we developed a discipleship course called "DOXA."[14] Rather than trying to teach the faith as a set of ideas or doctrines in the abstract, DOXA invites participants to see how worship forms them into a language that speaks of a distinctive testimony to the saving action of God. The template of holy communion maps the shape of Christian discipleship in a way that speaks of the story of grace. It reveals how each disciple represents a divine signature. Certainly the course also involves reflection on scripture, and there are sections devoted to in-depth studies on Christian practices. However, the most important exercise is to allow ordinary disciples to understand how they are becoming God's language for the world and as a language, how their lives and speech reveal God.

Involved in such Christian linguistics is the challenge to face the pain of where our language has broken down into incommensurable dialects or been abusive of others, for example in the history of the Crusades or the slave trade. It is also about recognizing that just as worship has to be common if it is to be truthful, so this language has to be learned with other Christians rather than independently of them. This means that when new or unexpected ways of speaking or performing the language emerge, such as over sexuality or usury, it is important to listen to all members of the community, particularly those we disagree with, if the language is to develop faithfully, and be able to speak to the world as an illuminating gift of God. Furthermore, such reflection upon practice helps

---

14. John B. Thomson, *DOXA: A Discipleship Course* (London: DLT, 2007). *Doxa* is the Greek word for glory.

participants appreciate the longevity of their language and the way it has developed through time. Meditating on the way this language has been spoken of in the rich heritage of scripture and in the history of the church helps to embolden and humble contemporary speakers, since it locates them in a broad community of fellow speakers rather than simply the community of the present or of a particular culture. In more fragile congregations this can be a great encouragement and enable people to take heart in the sharing of their faith. In larger congregations it can act as a check upon triumphalism and self-confidence.

The Gift of a Story: Sharing Our Testimony

The presence of a community being transformed through worship to be God's language in the world embodies a story about God and the cosmos which narrates life for that world. Evangelism is telling this story, the story of creation, reconciliation, and eternal friendship with God made possible by the action of God in Jesus Christ. It is also about sharing our testimony to the love and embrace of God in our own lives, as such little stories are set within this great cosmic epic. Indeed, as we share these stories, we become aware that other people's stories have equal place in this complex drama and that part of the gift of the church is to invite all people to locate their stories within God's great epic. One of the indicators of the divine quality of Jesus' story is that it can embrace all other human stories in a way that redeems and yet does not diminish them. Our stories are taken, blessed, and broken, and through this transformation, offered as narratives of grace. Another is that this story denotes creation as God's. The dignity of creation is therefore underwritten by this divine ownership with the implication that it should be inhabited with appropriate respect for its owner. Certainly the full telling of God's story awaits the finale or day of judgment when Christ will read the scroll. In the interim, that story is still being generated as new people participate in the drama and contribute their narratives to the whole.

Furthermore, since this story is about God, it is capable of offering space to all people without diminishing their diversity. This surely is what Jesus displayed as he actively engaged with the marginalized or poor of his society. The story, as we have learned it to date, speaks of hospitality for all who repent and in the process lifts up the lowly and puts down the mighty from their thrones. Monarchs and minions mix in the narrative God represents. Such a story, as liberation theologians and South American Pentecostal pastors have reminded the church, is not a consolation for the poor and powerless, but an energizing gift restoring dignity and giving hope in the struggle for justice in life. Equally, the truth of the story is tested by its capacity to challenge the comfortable to move beyond their comfort zones into service among those most different or disturbing to them. In such movement a counter story is told which contrasts with that most often heard in Western societies. If God gives us everything we need, as the gospel declares, then as gifts we can risk ourselves in the adventure of service to the world, aware that love for God's sake means love for our neighbor's sake. The offering of our lives at the eucharist is an offering for the sake of our neighbor and flows from the transforming practice of holy communion. We are sent out in the power of the Spirit to engage with that world in the light of the story we are a part of and as bearers of that story.

Aware that we are part of an ongoing story that is not yet complete ensures that as we serve the world, we do so with humility and aware of our limitations. Stories assume the reality of time and an ending. This reminds those who inhabit them that today's interpretation of the story is dependent to a large extent on the way the story has been told to date. It also implies that the story will be told somewhat differently in the future as context and perspective mutate. Furthermore, the "time-ful" character of the story points to a future finale when the story will be fully told on God's terms. Consequently, Christian service in the world must recognize that mission is not about imposing a fixed ideology so much as sharing a contingent though plausible interpretation of God's ways with the world. Otherwise the gift of the gospel becomes imprisoned in contemporary ideas. The mystery of God and human fallibility remind us that our deepest convictions cannot claim to represent the whole truth of the gospel. Certainly the truthfulness of the story of grace will be tested by its ongoing capacity to relate to all, dead and alive, across the diversities of human culture and pedigree. In this way it will continue to point to the peaceable destiny that God has for a redeemed creation and act as a hope for the life of the world. It will be part of what Timothy Gorringe calls "the long revolution of remaking by God."[15]

This long and often slow revolution helps us to realize that there is much of the story we do not yet know. In the light of this, a certain reserve will characterize the judgments we make about those who do not publicly share the Christian story. The hidden work of the Spirit spoken of in the story is a reminder that grace operates beyond the consciousness of the church. Relations with other faiths and with those professing no public faith will therefore begin from this awareness and will seek, conversationally, for what is capable of mutual affirmation rather than simply looking for conflict and contention. In so doing, Christians need not be ashamed of sharing their faith and their conviction of its truth, since plurality means that all should contribute and debate rather than one ideology policing all others. Indeed, given the proportionately greater historic and contemporary contribution of the Christian story to Western society, Christians should not be ashamed of articulating this, not as a way of dominating other faith traditions, but as a way of enabling society to be honest about its identity. Thus, while the claims of Christianity await the finale of God for their full display, it is possible to represent the Christian story robustly in a way that is for the life of the world.

The gift of this grand narrative of God's saving mercy and grace was something that impacted upon me when I grew up in Uganda, East Africa. There I discovered a remarkable thing happening. People who had little power or influence in

---

15. Timothy J. Gorringe, *Furthering Humanity: A Theology of Culture* (Aldershot, UK: Ashgate, 2004), 23.

society regarded themselves as monarchs. Just as Spaniards call each other lords and ladies, so these humble Africans recognized that in God's story, all—especially the disposed and disenfranchised—were monarchs, queens, kings, princes, and princesses (cf. 1 Peter 2:9: "You are a chosen race, a royal priesthood, a holy nation, God's own people, in order that you may proclaim the mighty acts of him who called you out of darkness into the marvelous light [of God]"). The story the world told them was swallowed up by the more important story that they learned of from scripture and particularly from the impact of the Balokole revival movement. Later when I spent time in South Africa during the latter years of the apartheid era, the passion for a non-racist society was equally resourced by the divine narrative.

Contemporary Western society is characterized by enormous pressures to be successful, glamorous, and wealthy. Hence I am continually surprised by the presence of ordinary Christian communities welcoming those beyond their midst to share in the story of grace which challenges these values. I have consequently become increasingly convinced that our core Christian story is critical for human flourishing, particularly in Western societies increasingly colonized by technology and bureaucracy. In these societies the significance of some human beings, such as the elderly, those with special needs, those who do not fit contemporary norms, is being diminished. The gift of the divine story embodied by Jesus and now re-coded in the life of the church acts as a check to these tendencies as a community committed to the well-being of such as these live out the story of God.

The Gift of the Gospel
for the Life of the World

Christianity is fundamentally a way rather than an idea, a form of life rather than a philosophy, a participation in the saving activity of God in the world rather than a package of beliefs. Hence mission is about walking in this way as witnesses whose lives together and dispersed embody the giving of grace.

The sixty-five adults and a handful of youngsters that formed the congregation on that first Sunday of my incumbency were therefore much more remarkable than I realized at the time, despite appearing to be on the edge of contemporary society. Located on this edge, their mission was first and foremost to be and become more profoundly the church as a sign of salvation since in God's mission the "who" takes precedence and indeed determines the "do." This meant that gathering for public worship assumed critical importance if that sign was to be formed. In addition, through such transformation or transubstantiation, they began to represent a language that described how God is involved in the world for its good and for its life. This form of life was shaped by the template and training of worship enabling their lives to speak, albeit tentatively and imperfectly, of the great story of God. Such speaking was not simply rhetoric but the practice of discipleship. It involved reaching out to those in the parish who had little time or inclination to be part of this community. It included patient visiting of those who had links with the church through the occasional offices. It entailed welcoming in strangers, such as drug addicts, prostitutes, the mentally ill, and folk from overseas, and seeking to express God's embrace of them. It recognized the importance of memory, symbol, and place in mission through its careful renovation of the buildings and its encouragement of local people to visit the church building and treasure it as theirs rather than simply the congregation's. It raised horizons by linking up with the overseas church as a way of ensuring that the catholicity of the church was not simply an idea but a practice of giving, loving, and learning from all Christian people. In particular, through generous corporate giving, it sought to signify the grace of God in an area of England struggling to recover from economic and social depression. To be a community which God is transforming to embody a language of hope and a story of salvation was and is the gift of the church for the life of the world. Like Jeremiah, the challenge of living in what can seem like an exilic situation is about seeking the well-being of the society we are a part of in a way that witnesses to the love of God for that society. Such congregational and diocesan gifts are fragile and often ignored, but they are all over England since the God Jesus embodied is always God-with-us, never God in isolation from his people. As a patient missional presence in an increasingly frantic world, they are a material gift witnessing to the grace of God focused in Christ and active in that world for its salvation.

Part Three

Seasons of Celebration

A T CHRISTMASTIME IN AUSTRALIA, WHERE I once lived, Santa has been seen to arrive at Bondi Beach on a surfboard. He joins so many of the population on the beach on Christmas Day, where an open-air barbeque is traditional festive fare, because in the already simmering heat, few wish to turn on the oven to cook a turkey. Carols—a better clue perhaps to "the real meaning of Christmas"—celebrate "Christmas in the bush" with animals—not the donkey and lambs on the shepherd's trail, but crawling lizards, squawking cockatoos, swimming platypuses, laughing kookaburras, wise bandicoots, among others—all playing their part in helping "the outback ring" for "the birth of God."[1] Not only is the menagerie different to northern hemisphere carols that imagine animals—the familiar donkey, cow, sheep (and dove) of "Jesus our brother strong and good,"[2]—but the images of the landscape are different too: droughts and floods, and midnight scrub. Significantly, for a song sung in the very heights of summer, the "baby in the straw" "outshines" everything else in the imagined scene.

Christmas cards may still sometimes evoke snowy scenes, but the weather outside is dazzlingly bright. Advent, building up to the height of summer at Christmas, is a season of glare, which brings new associations to some of its themes of judgment and harshness. So the snowy cards—where they

1. Leigh Newton, "Christmas in the Scrub," in *As One Voice, Volume 2: Uniting God's People in Song* (Manley Vale, NSW: Willow Connection, 1984 [1996]), no. 168.

2. Anonymous twelfth-century French carol, found, for example, in *New Century Hymnal* (Cleveland, OH: Pilgrim Press, 1995), no. 138.

remain—may function as a kind of "plea" for shelter from the glare,[3] a different scene, more merciful. At any rate, the experience of the local climate is largely at odds with the inherited imagery of Christmas, originating, as it does, in a context quite different from this particular part of the southern hemisphere.

Other seasons, too, are out of kilter. So Easter, rather than coinciding with a natural season of growth, falls in the autumn of the climatic cycle, as some things go to earth. In a temperate place, the seasons may be less marked in any case, so the greenery never turns bare, to suggest death—except, perhaps, in dreaded and terrifying bushfire, as much of the year may be warm, with no exposure to bitter cold—while the vastness of the country itself challenges any neat appropriation of seasons, and indigenous people have traditionally identified six seasons, each more nuanced than the four familiar in, say, the United States.

This cluster of examples suggests that while experience of the seasons is real enough in any particular place, matters of interpretation are part of their meaning, and that to some extent, "seasons" are constructed.[4] This is certainly true of the ways in which the cycles of the liturgical calendar have been fused with climatic patterns "local" to the north and strange, if not incomprehensible, in parts of the south.

From the beginning, Christians knew that they were constructing the seasons of their calendar, and they had their reasons for doing it. While some of the details of the origins of parts of the Christian year are really quite opaque— sometimes much contested in contemporary research into them—it is clear at least that, for example, the celebration of Christmas developed in relation to both pagan and Jewish religious practice, sometimes intentionally asserting Christian meanings directly in the face of surrounding

---

3. Anita Monro made this point in her address to the Societas Liturgica Conference, Sydney, August 2009.

4. For a cluster of reflections, see Stephen Burns and Anita Monro, eds., *Christian Worship in Australia: Inculturating the Liturgical Tradition* (Strathfield, NSW: St. Pauls, 2009).

(Jewish/pagan) understandings of time. So, as one well-known theory goes, Jesus' "birthday" may have come to be celebrated on December 25 in direct conflict with the winter solstice observed by pagans. The point Christians may have wished to make is that Jesus outshines any god that pagans worship. In the early Christians' imagination about this, nature itself seemed to respond to the birth of Christ, with the lengthening of days following the solstice as it were reflecting the light of Christ's presence. Or, in another theory, December 25 came to mark the birth of Jesus because it could be deduced (from some scavenging around in pieces of evidence and conjecture) from the gospels and the mapping of calendars that he died on Nissan 14, which corresponded to March 25. As Jewish tradition often claimed that "great" people were born and died on the same calendar date, the distinctively Christian twist to this in relation to Jesus was to claim his birthday in relation to his conception (March 25 is celebrated as the Annunciation). Their point was that Jesus was greater still than any hero of the Jewish people. Either way, nobody knows Jesus' actual birthday, that is, the birthday of "the historical Jesus," but that is not the point, for December 25 is clearly a construction of meaning intended to convey truth about Jesus to others in the cultures that "hosted" the early Christians. Indeed, in its judgments of relative pagan dimness and casting of Jewish heroes as second-best, the early Christian witness can hardly be regarded as other than somewhat hostile in its presentation of "good news" about Christ.

All this is to say that liturgical time draws its meanings from a complex interplay of nature, culture, and scripture. It may mediate meanings of Christ, but the liturgical calendar is not a "given," as becomes clear with awareness of global appropriation of the traditions of marking Christian time. What this means with the shift of gravity in global Christianity to the south—if not to Australia, sometimes said to be "the most godless place on earth,"[5] then to the massive Christian communities of Africa and Asia in all their

---

5. The saying can be traced to an early Presbyterian missionary, James Denney. It has entered into common discourse on the state of religion in Australia.

diversity and differences—with at least some of each of those continents, of course, being equatorial, raising another set of questions/problems about how imagery from the tradition about liturgical time can best be appropriated.

The four writers in Part Three all make sense of the liturgical seasons from locations in the northern hemisphere, although from different places and cultures within it. David Runcorn guides us through the "exhilarating journey" of the Christmas cycle, marking the moods—and marking out the challenges—of the seasons of the cycle: Advent, Christmas, and Epiphany. Advent, which begins of course toward the close of the secular year, is the beginning of each liturgical year, giving way to Christmas on Christmas Eve, which in turn yields to Epiphany on January 6 (when Orthodox Christians still now celebrate Christmas Day itself). The cycle is completed with the festival of Candlemas (February 2), recalling the presentation of Christ in the temple—somewhat confusingly following some of the key events marked by Epiphany, that is, the baptism of Jesus, the visit of the wise ones, and the ministry of Jesus at the wedding of Cana. Epiphany and Candlemas in one sense muddle any straightforward chronological sense of episodes from the nativity and public ministry of Jesus; but as Runcorn shows, these seasons have a logic of their own. He vividly introduces Advent to us as an experience of "coming up against" the confronting truth that "we are not the center of the story," and yet of Christmas as a celebration of "matter mattering," and in particular of "our body as something God desires." In turn, Epiphany makes these things "public." Throughout his reflections, there is strong emphasis on the liturgical celebration of the seasons, and the kind of spirituality that might flow from them,[6] with many ideas for practice that help to bring alive the meanings he describes.

---

6. See David Runcorn, *The Spirituality Workbook: A Guide for Explorers, Pilgrims and Seekers* (London: SPCK, 2006). For reflections on other foci in the calendar, see David Runcorn, *Touchwood: Meeting the Cross in the World Today* (London: DLT, 1992), and David Runcorn, *Rumours of Life: Reflections on the Resurrection Experiences* (London: DLT, 1996).

Following Runcorn's reflections on the first cycle of the liturgical year, the next chapter turns to the second major cycle: the sequence that runs for the ninety days of Lent and Easter. Beginning with Ash Wednesday, it leads to the Triduum/Three Days of Easter, and on into Pentecost, a season that incorporates the important festival of the Ascension of Jesus. Ruth Meyers guides us through the terrain of the Easter cycle, doing so by focusing, as an American, on the new Church of England rites. She draws our attention to liturgical texts, ancient precedents for contemporary practice, and the interconnectedness of the movements that transport us "from ashes to fire" (Ash Wednesday to Pentecost Sunday) through these seasons. Along the way she makes further connections with worship throughout the year, including the way that intercession is often shaped according to early practice on Good Friday, and the symbolic actions that feature in the liturgies of the Easter cycle but that enrich worship through the year.

If Runcorn and Meyers unfold the two key sequences of the Christian year for us, then the next two authors take two cycles in the annual pattern of worship that move at a somewhat different pace. Ellen Clark-King takes "ordinary time" as her focus. Some liturgical scholars resist the descriptor of "ordinary time" on the basis that "the English word 'ordinary' connotes the prosaic or humdrum, and no Sunday is prosaic or humdrum,"[7] given that Sunday is the day of resurrection. Clark-King shows that there is indeed much to animate us in these seasons. She draws out several themes for us to consider: as a season "not tied to any one particular theological mood," it is "open and hospitable," spacious, which is a mark of how it might grace us. With no dominating theme, it not only provides variety, but invites us to weave our own personal stories into a divine horizon. Clark-King further maps the season on to the secular year and stresses the color of the season, green in particular ways. In all of this, just as Clark-King's earlier fascinating study of the spirituality of "ordinary" women

---

7. Gail Ramshaw, *Treasures Old and New: Images in the Lectionary* (Minneapolis, MN: Fortress Press, 2002), 15.

heard their voices and took them seriously,[8] here we find a similar "listening" to the season.

Finally, the book comes to a close with a reflection by Mark Pryce. Describing liturgy as a "midwife to hopeful living" and in a way akin to his "companions" to the lectionary and festivals,[9] he clusters and comments upon several poems that open up the sanctorale, with a particular focus on the complimentary festivals of All Saints and All Souls (November 1 and 2). Attending to poems by Judith Wright, R. S. Thomas, and others, he juxtaposes the joy and sorrow, grief and hope they voice and that are found in the observance of the November holy days. He also shows how these particular days relate to other dynamics across the year, and especially its paschal heart in the Triduum's concentration on death and resurrection.

---

8. Ellen Clark-King, *Theology by Heart: Women, the Church and God* (Peterborough, ON: Epworth Press, 2004).

9. Mark Pryce, *Literary Companion to the Lectionary* (London: SPCK, 2001); Mark Pryce, *Literary Companion to the Festivals* (London: SPCK, 2003).

CHAPTER 9

The Christmas Cycle

David Runcorn

Introduction: Not Less Than Everything

PICTURE A CITY PARK ON a warm summer afternoon. A couple have enjoyed a picnic and are dozing contentedly on the grass. They are unaware a camera hovers just above them. It begins to pull away steadily into the sky. The couple, the park, the neighborhood, the city all rapidly shrink in size. Before long we have left planet Earth altogether and are travelling deeper and deeper into space. Planets, stars, and galaxies pour past as the camera continues to the farthest reaches of the cosmos.

There in the inky darkness the camera pauses for a moment and then goes into reverse—sliding back through the vast, silent tracts of the universe, back to earth and down, in ever increasing detail, toward a park, a sleeping couple, and the remains of a picnic, where it all began.

But the camera doesn't stop. A journey that revealed to us the unimaginable vastness of the universe now travels into earthly life in ever smaller detail. The camera continues through the skin and into the body of the sleeping man, through the arteries, blood vessels, and cells in ever smaller detail—into the most minute molecules and atoms that lie at the source of life as we know it.

The "Christmas cycle"—that is, the seasons of Advent, Christmas, and Epiphany—takes us on a similarly exhilarating journey. Something is beginning that will ultimately include not less than everything. The farthest uncharted reaches of the cosmos to the tiniest particle of created life are all caught up it.

In these few hectic weeks, our imaginations must be stretched to embrace the final destiny of the whole cosmos as the stars shake and the sun darkens before the glorious majesty of God at the end of time. And yet to contemplate God at this time of year, we must also picture a baby in its mother's womb, bumping along in the dark on the back of a donkey. Someone has spoken of this as worshipping with bifocals.

Not surprisingly, the biblical and liturgical themes in these seasons swing between uncompromising judgment and immense tenderness, tough wisdom and merciful comfort, hope beyond and present challenge.

Back in the park the couple is completely unaware of their intimate place within a journey that has left watchers alive with wonder. They slept through it. Being asleep when we should be awake is a familiar way the ancient spiritual traditions speak of the human condition. It was a feature of the first disciple's behavior even in the presence of Jesus (Luke 9:32 and 22:45–46). In fairy stories and folk tales, it is a sleep of death, of drugged enchantment, of fundamental unawareness. And all our instincts tell us that only a love that is true can awaken us.

Advent: The Awakening Word

"It is now the moment
for you to wake from sleep. . . ."
(Romans 13:11)

The first call of Advent, the start of a new Christian year, is clear from the sentence of scripture read on that Advent Sunday[1]: "Wake up!"

It is not a gentle shake on the shoulder with a morning cup of tea. It is more like a shout in the ear or the fire alarm going off. It is an abrupt wake-up call. It shocks into new awareness. The mood is urgent, active, excited, and uncompromising. But in contrast to the compulsive and driven behaviors we find so hard to resist at this time of year, Advent's summons is purposeful and focused. We are called to prioritize—to be prepared, take stock, keep watch, proclaim. The energy is outward. Look up, wake up, shout aloud, rejoice!

Advent, we say, means "coming." It is a season of antici-pation. But Advent means more than coming. *Venio* means "come." *Ad* means "against." In an *Ad*vent, we "come up against it."[2] We are up against it in the first instance because, more than any other time in the Christian year, our season of faith struggles to resist the competition of a huge cultural commercial festival that starts to build momentum from early September. Christian it may be at its roots, but to find ways of living with Christian distinctiveness during this period is desperately hard. Our experience can be that we ritually lament the superficiality and consumerism and then live with quantities of guilt.

But more vitally, this season breaks upon our world to bring us up against the living God. The liturgy and the scriptures in these weeks confront us with the news that we, with our compulsions and drives, are not the center of the story. And in the light of this, our most basic assumptions about life and priorities are exposed, shaken, and called to change. This "coming" is not to meet *our* needs or fulfill *our* longings. In fact, the scriptures warn us to beware of

---

1. Romans 13:11–14 is the New Testament reading on Advent Sunday in Year A of the lectionary cycle.
2. Jim Cotter, *Prayer at Night* (Sheffield, UK: Cairns Publications, 1988), 73.

complacently assuming this coming will be the good news we expect.[3]

The gospel reading for the First Sunday in Advent (Year A) is Matthew 24:36–44. Jesus is teaching about the signs of the times, the end of the age, and the coming reign of God. He says that his final coming will be "as the days of Noah were" (v. 37). We might then expect a list of the notorious sins and transgressions of the Noah story—for "the earth was corrupt in God's sight, and the earth was filled with violence" (Genesis 6:11)—but no sins are mentioned at all. The parallel Jesus offers with Noah is quite unexpected: the days of Noah were marked by people "eating and drinking, marrying and giving in marriage. . ." (v. 38). There is nothing evil or sinful about that. But crucially, theirs was a world living completely oblivious to the real crisis, urgency, and priority of the times: "and they knew nothing" (v. 39) is the judgment of Jesus on that time.

The cycles of bible readings in this season are as exciting as they are disturbing. The readings over these weeks are often very vivid and may especially lend themselves to dramatic reading. Or congregations not accustomed to gospel processions may consider using one to accent the vivid gospel readings with earlier scriptures and the judgments and other strange and stunning teachings Jesus offers. The season can be highlighted visually too: with the shorter winter days, there are many creative possibilities for using light and darkness to good effect—for darkness and light are core Advent themes, appearing not least in the gospel readings.[4] In sound or symbol, somehow the liturgical "cries" of Advent need to be heard strongly. Thankfully, creative resources for this

---

3. Familiar to many from the carol "O Come, O Come Emmanuel," the "Seven 'O's" were originally antiphons sung before and after the *Magnificat* during the seven days leading up to Christmas Eve. In the carol and in other ways, they have been adapted for carol services of vigils in this season. See *Common Worship: Times and Seasons* (London: CHP, 2006), and David Kennedy, *Using Common Worship: Times and Seasons 1: All Saints to Candlemas* (London: CHP, 2005). For a very creative liturgical and theological reflection on the seasons covered in this chapter, see also Robert E. Webber, *Ancient and Future Time: Forming Spirituality Through the Christian Year* (Grand Rapids, MI: Baker Books, 2006).

4. For example, Year B, First and Third Sundays of Advent.

season have developed strongly in recent years and are well represented in *Common Worship* and new liturgical resources emerging around the Anglican Communion.[5]

In fact, at eucharist in this season, local customs for celebrating and sharing communion vary a great deal, stressing different aspects of its meaning and gift as they do so. But one very practical factor needs to be borne in mind. That is that this—Advent—is one of the most stressful times of the year in our society. The community that gathers for worship may well be tired and preoccupied. So there always needs to be place in our worship for drawing breath and centering down.

The old word for these extended periods of the Christian year is "tides"—as in Christmas*tide*. I think that this is a more helpful way to think of the way worship works than the somewhat mechanical sounding image of "cycles." Even the language of "season" has lost its moorings in the subtle rhythms of creation and now refers to something more fixed and programmed. (Think: football season!) But these Advent weeks, building to a climax, make their way with an ebb and flow— with what is, in fact, a wise pastoral mixture of intensity and rest. There are times for loud proclamation and contemplative vigil, for urgent activity and deep listening. In the shape and expectancy of our worship, we do well to seek the same.

A core focus for communion is hospitality and table companionship, spilling over into coffee after the service. I return to this theme later in the chapter, but Advent may be a time to consider something closer to the original Passover meal on which Christian communion is based. At the first Passover there was not time for preparing a "proper" meal. Passover recalls a meal that was food for the journey, sustenance for demanding faith, refreshment on the move. Hence, the word for Advent may be that spoken to Elijah in the wilderness— "Get up and eat, otherwise the journey will be too much for you" (1 Kings 19:7). Advent may be a time to vary how

---

5. See especially *Times and Seasons* (London: Church House Publishing, 2006).

communion is distributed so as shared to capture something of special urgency of the season's drama.[6]

These Advent weeks hold together the vision of the weight of the glory of Christ's final coming and the fragility of his gracious arrival in human flesh in a stable in Bethlehem. And this bifocal vision comes up against the life of Christian communities—and the many occasional worshipers who are their guests at this time of year—as they read the word; tell the simple, complex "bifocal" story; and seek to live lives of service—to their guests and others—in the power of the Spirit. The vision holds us in the promise of what is to come and as yet scarcely glimpsed.

I was once on a train going through one of those very long tunnels under the Alps. I was comfortably settled with food for the journey and a book to read. I knew where I was going and what time I would arrive. Then I happened to look up just as the train passed an unexpected break in the tunnel. Suddenly my enclosed world of order and provision was breached, for a fleeting moment, by a glimpse of another reality: from the drabness of the tunnel, I found myself looking out on a world of brilliant light, vivid colors, alpine meadows, snow-capped peaks, mountain villages, and fields.

Then it was gone and we were thundering through the dark again. But the glimpses of another reality burned into my imagination. The brief sighting awakened something in me. In that moment I saw where I wanted to be—something I was seeking though I hardly knew it. What I saw was what I was travelling for! I could no longer be patient within the comforts—food, books—of my chosen journey and the limits of what was literally tunnel vision. I have, ever since, wished to glimpse that scene—light, space, beauty—again. . . .

Advent kindles again the fierce longing, hopeful restlessness, and heightened vigilance of a people who must wait for the dawn. So throughout this season we pray, "Come, Lord Jesus!" (Revelation 22:20).

6. For different methods of communion, e.g., see Richard Giles, *Creating Uncommon Worship: Transforming the Liturgy of the Eucharist* (Collegeville, MN: Liturgical Press, 2004), 199–200.

Christmas: The Word Made Flesh

With all the hectic activity that surrounds this time of the year, it comes as a surprise to be reminded there are just twelve days in the Christmastide, the Christmas season (which does not include Christmas Eve—though this has become a very important day in itself for most churches today). If the twelve days of Christmas feel much longer than they are, it is perhaps not just because the shops started stocking up from early autumn, but because the round of carol services and seasonal events start several weeks before!

A very practical consideration in planning and offering worship through this time is that a high percentage of services are "all age" or child friendly in style, and their content is often heavily shaped by the presence of the occasional worshiper—as it should be among Christian communities with good news to share. The challenge of these opportunities is to be both simple and profound. We—occasional worshiper and long-time, faithful stalwart together—are reflecting upon, celebrating, and proclaiming the extraordinary mystery we call "Incarnation"—the mystery of a God who embraces our humanity as God's own reality and "lives among us" (cf. John 1:18).

There is no question that the consumer pressures upon this season are huge, distracting, and need in some way to be confronted. But care is needed as to how this is done (not least because people know very well when they are being told off and therefore, not unreasonably, stop listening). It is customary to lament how materialistic Christmas has become and how the "spiritual" meaning of it has been lost. But if the incarnation means "word made flesh," God become truly human, then the real challenge is that we can never be materialistic enough! The Christmas message is of a God who is radically and physically down to earth. The wisdom and word of God becomes one of us. Hence, Christian living in the fullness of this wide word is radically this-worldly. The sheer physicality of the Christian message was a shock to the first generations of Christian people and their neighbors, and it should shock us still. One early Christian wrote of this word: "We declare to you . . . what we have heard, what we have

seen with our eyes, what we have looked at and touched . . ."
(1 John 1:1).

It is significant that the first doctrinal disputes in the
Church centered on the denial that in Christ, God really had
taken human flesh. The claim was he only *appeared* to be
human but remained pure spirit. (At least one of the most
popular carols comes perilously close to endorsing this view
with the dreadful line, "veiled in flesh the Godhead see"!
"Hark the Herald Angels Sing" would have been a popular
carol among the first-century followers of Docetism.)[7] So one
of the earliest tests of orthodox faith was precisely the willingness to affirm the full, physical humanity of Jesus. One
New Testament affirmation of this is: "every spirit that con-
fesses that Jesus Christ has come in the flesh is from God"
(1 John 4:2). Other early Christians were very clear on this:
"What God has not assumed, God has not saved."[8]

The incarnation, the heart of Christmas, is the radical center of Christian faith. The coming of Christ in our
humanity is so much more than a drastic, tragic, but passing,
rescue mission. The earliest Christian teachers insisted that
although human sin transformed the coming of Christ into a
tragic redemption, the Incarnation remains above all the fulfillment of God's original plan, the great synthesis, in Christ,
of the human, the divine, and the cosmic. Everything in effect
exists in an immense movement of incarnation which tends
toward Christ and is fulfilled in him.[9]

What we meet in the Christmas story is not a way of faith
that demands the despising or rejecting of our embodied,

---

7. "Docetism" comes from the Greek *dokew*—"to seem." This teaching was
clearly present in churches through the time the New Testament was compiled, and
theologians were already attacking it by the end of the first century. In his letter to
the Smyrneans (110 CE), Ignatius of Antioch draws out both practical and spiritual
consequence of this teaching: "They [the docetists] abstain from the eucharist and
from prayer, because they confess not the eucharist to be the flesh of our Savior Jesus
Christ, which suffered for our sins, and which the Father, of His goodness, raised up
again" (7.1).

8. This saying is attributed to Gregory of Nyssa—a hugely influential theologian
and teacher who died in 394 CE.

9. Olivier Clément, *The Roots of Christian Mysticism* (New York: New City, 1993),
38–39.

material existence. To meet Christ is to meet Christ in our flesh and hence to be invited to look upon our own fleshly existence with new and unexpected reverence. So we are never to despise or diminish what Christ delights to embrace. That truth still comes as a surprise to many; hence Christmas, for all its apparent familiarity, may take a lifetime to learn.

For sure, both a practical and theological tendency to split the "spiritual" from "physical" world, and to treat the spiritual as separate and more superior, has been one of the most persistent and damaging confusions in the life of the Church. The confusion is still around today, and the present popularity of "spirituality" is prone to the same distortion of dishonoring the physical, the flesh, the body of Christ, and the bodies of all his human companions across the world in which God became incarnate.

The incarnation teaches us that Christian discipleship is a call to a new embodiment—an embodiment to a this-worldly faith. Matter *matters* to God. Christ brings this world, is at home in our flesh, and this world and our flesh are hence the site of a new consecration. In short, life is sacrament. Ruben Alves puts it like this: "God's desire is revealed in our body . . . Have you thought about this? That at Christmas what is celebrated is our body as something God desires." But he goes on to observe how hard this historic faith has found it to celebrate this truth:

> Something strange happened . . . we thought to find God where the body ends: and we made it suffer and transformed it into a beast of burden. We became cruel, violent, we permitted exploitation and war. For if God is found beyond the body, anything can be done to the body.[10]

Unless the incarnation forms the foundation of human living, a number of damaging distortions follow. First, there will be a tendency to a pessimistic, negative view of the

10. Ruben Alves, *I Believe in the Resurrection of the Body* (Seattle, WA: Wipf and Stock, 2003), 8–9.

material world, and to locate sin with physical acts and things. In this distortion, the "spiritual" is seen as separate from and superior to the body, and we should be warned that traces of this thinking are present in aspects of Christmas liturgy. The carol "O Come All Ye Faithful" includes a line that is traceable to early Christian worship—"Lo, he abhors not the virgin's womb."[11] But wherever did we learn that God might find a woman's womb abhorrent? What unhealed distortions lie behind such thinking? How would it change our worship if we sang, "Lo he *delights* in the virgin's womb"? It is as unloving to thoughtlessly indulge the body as it is to despise it. Our culture desperately needs a vision for embodied life that heals and redeems. The Christmas message offers precisely that.

Second, I fear that an over-spiritual, under-materialistic faith will tend to be focused inward and to be individualistic. It will lack a vision for shared life, for the very point at which Christ identifies himself with us—our common flesh—is denied. Finally, a neglect of the physical and material at the heart of Christian faith results in the sacraments being treated as irrelevant or meaningless. The sacraments (especially in this context, the eucharist) are built upon a wholehearted biblically funded theology of creation and incarnation. An observable feature of otherwise creative and adventurous "mission-shaped" activity in today's church is the absence of any place for the sacraments.[12] The witness of mission-shaped activists may too often, too easily seem to be non-sacramental, or at best to marginalize the sacraments. But this is a loss that means that a key point of connection and meeting with Jesus that he gives to us—the meal "in remembrance of [him]"—is absent or underplayed, and this is a loss to both worship and mission.

---

11. New translations/versions of this hymn therefore make amends—e.g., *New Century Hymnal* (Cleveland, OH: Pilgrim Press, 1995) has "born of the Virgin's womb in human form" (no. 135).

12. For further discussion, see Philip Seddon, *Gospel and Sacrament: Reclaiming a Holistic Evangelical Spirituality* (Cambridge, UK: Grove Books, 2006); and Chapter 8, "In the Breaking the Bread—Communion, Sacrament, and the Spiritual Life," in David Runcorn, *Spirituality Workbook* (London: SPCK, 2005).

The Christmas season is the place where the first shock of divine physicality—revealed in our flesh—can best be felt again and embraced for the gift it is. And the eucharist—a sure sign of the word we see, touch, and taste—is at the heart of this proclamation. For in the eucharist, perhaps beyond all expectation, the world may discover itself to be a sacrament in which divine presence is waiting to be revealed.

Epiphany: Word for the World

Perhaps there was a knock on the door one evening. "Are we expecting anyone?"

The door is opened. Strangers enter (three by tradition, although scripture mentions three gifts but not necessarily three people—Matthew 2:1–12). The strangers are from a far land, from a culture that seems strange to "us," and they may well speak with heavily accented tongue. They come with a story of compelling call, overwhelming joy, long journeying, and a star that shines nearby. They bring treasure for the little one they have come to honor and worship.

Barely have the decorations been packed away than Christmas becomes Epiphany. In the early churches, Epiphany *was* Christmas (and it still is in the Eastern churches, when Christmas Day is celebrated on January 6). The Church in the West, however, moved the feast of Christmas to December 25 (replacing a pagan festival celebrating the birth of the sun with a festival to celebrate God's Son), and in turn the liturgical focus of Epiphany shifted to celebrating not the birth of Christ, but the appearing (*"epiphaneias"*) of Christ to the wider, gentile world. Epiphany is a season that has seen welcome restoration in recent liturgical revisions. One crucial factor is what was a one-off festival (on January 6) now runs from that day through to Candlemas ("The Naming of Christ," celebrated on February 2).

Epiphany ensures there is no time for, or tolerance of, any domestication of Christmas into some private religious world. In this sense, it has strong continuity with Christmas. Epiphany insists the doors to the world must be left open.

Despite restorations and revisions of earlier traditions, hospitality is still a neglected theme of the Christmas and Epiphany seasons. Yet the welcome of outsiders and strangers on God's initiative alone is a common strand through the biblical readings. And it is one that continues, with growing controversy, throughout the ministry and parables of Jesus. A key message of Epiphany is that there is simply no telling who will be coming and going when Jesus incarnate is around!

The weeks of Epiphany help us begin to reflect on what the coming of Christ means in the midst of the realities of our—that is, God's—world. In the Sunday pattern of scripture readings at the eucharist, it does this especially by focusing around four stories.

In each of the three years of the lectionary cycle, Epiphany Sunday focuses on the coming of the magi, telling their story of a divine revelation and initiative that breaks the bounds of race, nation, culture, and orthodox religion (Matthew 2:1–12). That Matthew alone records this story is the more startling, as his gospel is very carefully aimed at conservative Jewish readers. An account about favored outsiders with, what is more, astrological overtones was not one to invent for such a readership. On the second Sunday of the season, the focus is on the baptism of Jesus, the revelation of God's Beloved in human flesh, and the beginning of his earthly ministry— in the lectionary, Matthew's, Mark's, and Luke's accounts of the baptism are used in turn over three years. On the third Sunday, the gospel readings present Jesus calling his disciples and relate memories of some of their early responses to him. Another key reading of the season is the story of the wedding at Cana (John 2:1–11). John's gospel offers this story as the entry point of Jesus into public ministry. "Jesus did this, the first of his signs . . . and revealed his glory; and his disciples believed in him" (v. 11). The weighted Greek here suggests that the "miracle" (as some translations say) was an "arch-sign"—that is, not simply the first of many but, as it were, "The Sign" that provides the key for understanding all the wonders that follow.

Throughout this season, gospel readings reveal a God found in unexpected places, proclaiming unexpected welcome. At the heart of Epiphany is divine hospitality. And what all the stories illustrate is that this hospitality is God's initiative and God's delight, embodied in and by Christ Jesus. At the wedding in Cana, the hospitality, as traditionally organized, runs out and is powerless to renew itself. The celebration, having barely begun, grinds to a halt. Only Christ, who is present unrecognized, can renew it. And he does so with overwhelming and, frankly, irresponsible generosity.[13] This, says John, is the key to all that follows.

As the ministry of Jesus unfolds, it becomes clear that the hospitality of God subverts all socially and spiritually respectable patterns of belonging. The scandal of the ministry and parables of Jesus is seen in who ends up welcomed to the banquets he speaks about and the meals he hosts. By any expected measure the invitations kept falling into the wrong hands—and falling *out* of the hands of those who expected to be on the "invited" list.

In the weeks of Epiphany, the eucharist—the meal with Christ—is the place to reflect on what kind of community we are participating in, hoping for, and building. Christ's community is to be a community of open doors. His vision is both unsettling and exciting. It calls for generosity and demands an open heart. For who knows who is receiving invitations and how far those invited are traveling in order to be present? To express this sense more effectively, a well-known church in America moved its communion table to be near the main entrance as a way of symbolizing that it wanted to express a welcome and hospitality before anything else.[14]

But there is a tension to be acknowledged that runs through eucharistic hospitality. In placing emphasis on welcome rather than placing conditions upon people wishing to receive communion, it may be we neglect Paul's concern about the peril

13. The six stone water jars would have produced a combined total of nearly 800 liters of wine—"after the guests have become drunk" (John 2:10)!

14. St. Gregory of Nyssa Episcopal Church, San Francisco. See www.saintgregorys. org for photographs of the liturgical space.

of handling holy things lightly or without understanding (1 Corinthians 11:26–32). If this is a place of extravagant welcome, it is also the meeting place with the living God.

It might be important here to consider patterns of eucharistic discipline (and the reasons for it) in previous eras of the church:

> The early church had a secret discipline that prevented pagans and even candidates for baptism from taking part in the Eucharistic meal itself. Full initiation into the relationship of informed faith was necessary if the church was not to endanger people by bringing them prematurely into the field of force that is communion in the body and blood of Christ.[15]

Henri Nouwen insists that true hospitality involves both receptivity and confrontation. Confrontation without receptivity oppresses and excludes. But receptivity without confrontation is little more than bland niceness. Hospitality means offering ourselves as a real presence. And "real presence" is precisely the gift of Christ in the eucharist.[16]

A Personal Ending

It was five o'clock in the morning. I was kneeling, still sleepy, at the back of the darkened monastery chapel. It was bitterly cold. A recently installed wood-burning stove beside me was leaking more smoke than heat. My eyes were starting to water. I was trying not to cough. I was about to lose my way forever in the thick liturgy folder a monk had given me, but not before a line from one of the innumerable psalms caught my itching eyes—my life is dried up "like a wineskin in the

---

15. Martin L. Smith, *Fruits of the Season* (Cambridge, MA: Cowley, 1997), 52.

16. See Henri Nouwen, *Reaching Out: The Three Movements of the Spiritual Life* (Colorado Springs, CO: Zondervan, 1998), especially Section 2: "Hostility to Hospitality." See also David Runcorn, "Hospitality and Community," in C. Edmondson and E. Ineson, eds., *Celebrating God's Gift of Community* (London: Hodder & Stoughton, 2006).

smoke" (Psalm 119.83). It was the feast of the Epiphany, January 6, and the service had several hours to run. It was full of processions, chanting, rituals, silence, bible readings, incense, more incense, and then at last, with utmost solemnity and devotion, the breaking and sharing of bread.

I had nothing in my upbringing or church experience to prepare me for what I found myself participating in. It was like entering another world with its own distinct culture. My "Christian world" at that point would have looked with deep suspicion or dismissive amusement at what was going on. I sat, knelt, bowed, listened, and watched, and processed, and tried to keep up—as best I could. But something happened that morning when I came forward to share communion. Profoundly and unexpectedly, something in my depths stirred and awakened in recognition—deeper than words or feelings. As I returned to the back of the chapel, I felt as if I had received communion for the first time. It was a moment of Epiphany. God is with us.

CHAPTER 10

The Easter Cycle

Ruth A. Meyers

Pascha

THE LITURGIES OF THE EASTER, or "paschal," cycle of the church year invite worshipers to remember and celebrate the heart of Christian faith: the paschal mystery of Jesus' death and resurrection. Maundy Thursday, Good Friday, and Easter Sunday, which focus on the events of Jesus' suffering, death, and resurrection, are the high point of the cycle. Beginning with the ashes of Ash Wednesday, Lenten repentance and renewal build to their culmination in these services, and the Great Fifty Days of Easter flow from them as a time of joyous celebration that concludes with the fiery gift of the Holy Spirit on the day of Pentecost.

Christian communities began commemorating Jesus' death and resurrection in an annual feast as early as the second century. The *Pascha*, the Greek term for the Hebrew *pesach* ("Passover"), was an evening vigil that concluded with the celebration of the eucharist in the middle of the night. That single celebration encapsulated the totality of redemption through Christ: his incarnation, suffering, death, resurrection, ascension, and glorification. The gospels tell us that Jesus was crucified at the time of the annual Passover feast, and the themes of the Jewish Passover helped shape the Christian celebration of the Pascha: the sacrifice of the lamb, passage through the waters of the Red Sea, freedom from slavery, hope of deliverance. Moreover, Christians rejoiced in their participation in Christ's suffering and their passage from death to new life.

In the fourth and fifth centuries, the single annual celebration became a series of liturgies commemorating Jesus' suffering, death, and resurrection. Today, while each of these services—Maundy Thursday, Good Friday, and the Easter liturgy—focuses on one aspect of the redemptive event, together they are one great feast of redemption, celebrating Jesus' victory on the cross and in the resurrection, as well as our new life in Christ. The distinctive features of these liturgies and of the full paschal cycle, from Ash Wednesday through the day of Pentecost, arise from worship practices that developed over the course of several centuries.

Contemporary liturgies for the paschal cycle, including the resources in *Times and Seasons*, give new emphasis to baptism. By the end of the second century, some Christians viewed the Pascha, the annual celebration of Jesus' death and resurrection, as an especially fitting occasion for baptism, the sacrament in which Christians are initiated into Jesus' death and resurrection. During the fourth century, it became common for adult candidates for baptism to undergo their final intensive preparation during the weeks leading up to Easter and, as newly baptized Christians, to receive further instruction in the weeks that followed. The entire Christian community was encouraged to join the candidates in prayer and fasting as they prepared for their Christian initiation. These ancient practices have been a primary source of inspiration for today's liturgies.

Lent

In the Lenten journey of renewal, Christians recall the paschal mystery into which they were baptized as they prepare for their annual celebration of that mystery. Far more than an extended reflection on Jesus' passion and death, Lent invites Christians to renew their minds and hearts, expressing repentance and deepening their commitment to love and service in the world. Liturgical texts and music, as well as vestments and the decoration of the church, set a tone that is more somber and austere than in other liturgical seasons. Yet Lent is also characterized by joyful celebration of God's abundant mercy, as the extended preface for the eucharistic prayer proclaims: "as we prepare to celebrate the Easter feast with joyful hearts and minds, we bless you for your mercy."[1]

In addition to its emergence in the fourth century as the time of final preparation for baptism, Lent became the time for public penance by those who had committed serious sins. At the beginning of Lent, repentant sinners would be received into the order of penitents in a formal ritual that included prayer and laying-on of hands. They were then relegated to a designated place in the liturgical assembly and excluded from receiving communion. Throughout this period, they also engaged in penitential practices such as prayer, fasting, and wearing sackcloth and ashes. The prayers of the community and blessings by the bishop sustained the penitents in their journey to reconciliation. Lenten public penance concluded with a ritual of reconciliation on Maundy Thursday, restoring the community to wholeness in preparation for the annual paschal celebration.

While these public rites of penance and reconciliation were gradually replaced by private confession during the early Middle Ages, Lent continued to be a penitential season, now a season of penitence for the entire Christian community. With the rise of infant baptism, Easter ceased to be a principal baptismal day, and the penitential dimension of Lent became foremost.

This penitential emphasis is often expressed in Anglican liturgical materials, complemented by references to God's mercy and compassion. A reminder that Lent is also a season of preparation for baptism appears in the first form of

---

1. *Common Worship: Times and Seasons* (London: Church House Publishing, 2006), 218 (hereafter, referred to as *TS*). See also *Common Worship: Services and Prayers for the Church of England* (London: Church House Publishing, 2000), 309 (hereafter, referred to as *CW*). Both are foci of the following reflections.

intercession, which includes a petition for those who are preparing for baptism and confirmation.[2] Even if there are no candidates in the congregation, the petition serves to remind worshipers that Lent is a season of preparation for baptism in the wider Church. A similar petition could be added to the prayers for the Church in the second form of intercession.

Ash Wednesday

Lent begins on a particularly solemn note. From the presider's introduction, explaining the meaning of Lent, through the dismissal, the liturgy again and again calls the assembly to repentance and assures them of God's abundant mercy. On this day, confession of sin comes as a response to the proclamation of the word, not as preparation for it, and the confession replaces the creed and the intercessions, making it a central focus of the liturgy. The confession takes the form of a litany, providing an extended meditation on human sin and divine mercy. The first form emphasizes the many dimensions of sin, while the second (an adaptation of the 1662 BCP litany) stresses redemption through Jesus' incarnation, life, death, resurrection, and glorification.

In addition to self-examination and repentance, the liturgy calls the community to fasting. "I invite you . . . to the observance of a holy Lent . . . by prayer, fasting, and self denial," the presider declares at the beginning of the service.[3] The readings from Isaiah and Joel attest to the antiquity of the practice and its significance as a sign of repentance. But fasting must be accompanied by a change of heart. "Return to me with all your heart, with fasting . . . rend your hearts and not your clothing," Joel proclaims (2:12–13). Isaiah calls for a change in behavior: "Is not this the fast that I choose: to loose the bonds of injustice, to undo the thongs of the yoke, to let the oppressed go free, and to break every yoke?" (Isaiah 58:6). Leo the Great, fifth-century Bishop of Rome, issued a similar call:

---

2. *TS*, 215.
3. *TS*, 223.

Let us forgive, that we might be forgiven; let us grant the pardon which we ask, and let us not be anxious to be avenged since we ourselves wish to be forgiven. Let us not pass over the groans of the poor with a deaf ear, but let us offer mercy to the needy with unhesitating kindness, that we may deserve to find mercy at the judgment. Those who direct their energy to this perfection with the help of God's grace will go through the holy fast faithfully . . . they will come to the blessed Passover . . . In newness of life they will worthily rejoice in the mystery of the regeneration of humanity.[4]

As Leo reminds us, the inner repentance and renewal of Lent must be manifest in our behavior toward others. "In your mercy forgive what we have been, help us to amend what we are, and direct what we shall be; that we may do justly, love mercy, and walk humbly with you, our God,"[5] the congregation prays in the Ash Wednesday confession, alluding to the prophet Micah (6:8).

As a tangible sign of repentance, imposition of ashes may follow the verbal confession of sin. The ritual creates some tension with the appointed gospel, in which Jesus decries the hypocrites who "disfigure their faces so as to show others that they are fasting" and urges his followers, "when you fast, put oil on your head and wash your face, so that your fasting may be seen not by others but by your Father who is in secret" (Matthew 6:16–18). This gospel had been appointed for the first day of Lent for several centuries before the liturgy began to include imposition of ashes on all participants. It continues to remind worshipers of the danger of engaging in spiritual disciplines in order to be noticed, rather than to deepen one's relationship with God.

---

4. Leo the Great, Sermon 39.6, in *St. Leo the Great: Sermons*, trans. Jane Patricia Freeland and Agnes Josephine Conway, Fathers of the Church 93 (Washington, DC: Catholic University of America Press, 1996), 171.

5. *TS*, 227.

Sundays of Lent

The call to a season of fasting and the penitential focus of Ash Wednesday continue on the First Sunday of Lent, when the gospel tells of Jesus' forty-day fast in the wilderness and his temptation by the devil. Knowing that Jesus faced and withstood temptation, we are strengthened in our own battles with temptation. "We give you thanks because he was tempted in every way as we are, yet did not sin. By his grace we are able to triumph over every evil, and to live no longer for ourselves alone, but for him who died for us and rose again."[6]

On the Second through Fifth Sundays of Lent, the lectionary introduces different emphases in each year of the three-year liturgical cycle. The Year A readings, all from the Gospel of John, present strong baptismal images and narratives: rebirth by water and spirit is a key teaching in Jesus' dialogue with Nicodemus (John 3:1–17); Jesus' encounter with the Samaritan woman at the well centers on living water (John 4:5–42); the healing of the man born blind introduces the theme of enlightenment (John 9:1–41); and the raising of Lazarus is a story of death and resurrection (John 11:1–45). In this year of the liturgical cycle, baptism rather than penitence comes to the fore, especially if preaching, hymnody, and other liturgical texts complement the readings.

In Year B, the appointed gospels point toward Jesus' victory on the cross and the gift of new life through his self-offering. Covenant is a prominent motif in the Old Testament readings: God's covenant with Noah made after the flood (Genesis 9:8–17; First Sunday of Lent); God's covenant with Abraham (Genesis 17:1–7,15–16; Second Sunday of Lent); God's covenant with Moses, given in the Decalogue (Exodus 20:1–17; Third Sunday of Lent); and the new covenant promised to Jeremiah (Jeremiah 31:31–34; Fifth Sunday of Lent). The Year C gospels strike notes of repentance and divine forgiveness.

---

6. Preface (for the eucharistic prayer) L2, *TS*, 218.

Palm Sunday

The gathering of the community takes the form of a commemoration of Jesus' entry into Jerusalem. Assembling in a place apart from the primary worship space allows worshipers to participate in a procession. This is not a dramatic reenactment of the triumphal entry in order to reproduce the gospel narrative in as much detail as possible, but rather an invitation for the congregation to participate in Jesus' journey to the cross. We are the crowds, acclaiming Christ as our ruler.

The tone of the liturgy shifts markedly after the procession, as the collect of the day recalls Jesus' suffering on the cross. Now, at the beginning of Holy Week, we join Christ in his passion and death, that we may also share in his resurrection. The prayers of intercession on this day echo elements of the passion narrative. The Creed and penitential prayers are omitted; the other texts of the liturgy adequately summarize the essential teachings of the faith and call the assembly to repentance.

Three Holy Days:
The Heart of the Paschal Cycle

The liturgies of Lent culminate in the celebration of the three holy days, sometimes referred to as the *Triduum* (a Latin word meaning "three days"), extending from the evening of Maundy Thursday through Easter Day. Together, these services celebrate the paschal victory of Jesus' death and resurrection and the significance of that victory for Christians today.

Maundy Thursday

The liturgy on this day is both somber, as the remembrance of Jesus' passion begins, and joyful, as the assembly celebrates their redemption: "We know that it was not only our ancestors, but we who were redeemed and brought forth from bondage to freedom, from mourning to feasting."[7] The gospel

---

7. Preparation of the Table, *TS*, 300.

appointed is the account of Jesus washing his disciples' feet, and it is this narrative that gives the feast its title. "Maundy" is derived from the Latin word *mandatum*, meaning "commandment," a reference to Jesus' "new commandment, that you love one another" (John 13.34).

The liturgy may start with a reference to baptism, as oils are received from a diocesan celebration earlier in Holy Week. The introduction reminds worshipers that the service on this night is the beginning "of the celebration of our Lord's paschal victory, his death and resurrection,"[8] and if there are candidates for Easter baptism, that the celebration will conclude with those candidates being initiated into the paschal mystery.

The service moves quickly from this introduction to its primary emphases: Jesus' act of humble service in washing his disciples' feet and the institution of the eucharist. These two primary themes are interwoven throughout the service. The gospel narrative of the footwashing is complemented by Paul's account of the last supper (1 Corinthians 11:23–26). The Old Testament reading, the institution of the Passover feast (Exodus 12:1–14), sets the context for the events of Jesus' suffering, death, and resurrection. As Christians begin the annual celebration of Christ "our paschal lamb" (1 Corinthians 5:7), we hear the biblical story of the first feast of the Passover lamb and recall its significance: delivery from slavery, the promise of a new life in freedom.

The ceremony of footwashing, a vivid expression of Christian love, may confront the congregation with the reality that washing feet is at the same time intimate and a tad messy, an act that may feel awkward or embarrassing. Individuals may identify with Peter in his reluctance to have his feet washed. The presider and others who may be invited also to wash feet recall Jesus' willingness to step into the role of a servant and so remind us all of the loving service that is to characterize Christian life.

The intercessions at this feast draw upon Jesus' teaching in his "farewell discourse," according to John's gospel his

---

8. *TS*, 292.

words to the disciples at the last supper (John 13:31–17:26). The full text may be read as part of a watch at the conclusion of the liturgy.

The liturgy of the sacrament on this night takes on heightened meaning as the assembly remembers Jesus' final meal with his disciples and his promise that "every time we eat this bread and drink this cup, we proclaim the Lord's death until he comes."[9] For congregations that will include giving of communion in the Good Friday liturgy, consecrated bread and wine are set aside at this Maundy Thursday communion, since by ancient custom there is no celebration of the eucharist on Good Friday.

The final emphasis of the Maundy Thursday liturgy comes to the fore at the conclusion. With the stripping of the holy table and the sanctuary, the mood turns especially sober. The barren space evokes the desolation of Jesus' passion, given voice in the accompanying recitation of Psalm 88 or verses from Lamentations. The final words of the liturgy take worshipers to the garden of Gethsemane and Jesus' prayer that the cup of suffering might pass from him. The ministers and people depart without the customary "thanks be to God" in response to a dismissal; the paschal liturgy will continue tomorrow.

Good Friday

The solemnity of Maundy Thursday continues with the Good Friday remembrance of Jesus' crucifixion. Paradoxically, this seeming defeat is also a victory, and John's gospel, traditionally read on this day, gives particular emphasis to this interpretation: Jesus, speaking of his impending passion, said to his disciples, "The hour has come for the Son of Man to be glorified . . . I, when I am lifted up from the earth, will draw all people to myself" (John 12:23,32). The Old Testament and New Testament readings that precede the passion gospel underscore Jesus' sacrificial self-offering. The "servant song"

---

9. Anthem at the Breaking of the Bread, *TS*, 301; a reference to 1 Corinthians 11:26.

of Isaiah 52–53 tells of the servant who was "despised and rejected" yet "bore the sin of many, and made intercession for the transgressors" (Isaiah 53:3,12). The selections from Hebrews (10:16–25 or 4:14–16; 5:7–9) present Jesus as the high priest offering sacrifice for the sake of the world.

Though Jesus is victorious on the cross, the Good Friday liturgy is nonetheless somber as the congregation recalls the harsh reality of Jesus' torture and death at the hands of the state. The Proclamation of the Cross underscores the suffering Jesus underwent. A large wooden cross carried into the midst of the assembly makes his agony an especially vivid reality. Several of the anthems remind us that on the cross, Jesus redeemed the world, and even that "by virtue of your cross joy has come into our world."[10]

The redemptive work of the cross is emphasized in the prayers of intercession, among the most comprehensive in the church year. In praying these extensive prayers, the assembly joins in Jesus' priestly offering of himself on behalf of the world and so participates in his sacrifice.

Sadly, in the course of Christian history, Good Friday has been the occasion of Christian anti-Semitism, as Christians have attacked or persecuted Jews in response to the narrative of the passion. English translations of John's gospel typically render the Greek word *Iudaioi* (literally, "Judeans," perhaps referring to inhabitants of Judea) as "Jews," and Christians have blamed their Jewish contemporaries for Jesus' crucifixion, sometimes with acts of great violence. Christians who keep Good Friday today are heirs of this history, and those who shape the community's celebrations must consider how best to present the gospel and the adoration of the cross in ways that do not perpetuate Christian anti-Semitism. *Times and Seasons* provides two contemporary alternatives to the traditional reproaches. These new texts emphasize that Jesus' words are to be understood in reference to the Church today, not to Jesus' Jewish contemporaries. The intercessions no longer ask God to "have mercy upon all Jews, Turks, infidels, and heretics, and take from them all ignorance, hardness

---

10. Anthem 4, *TS*, 315.

of heart, and contempt of thy Word,"[11] and instead ask for "greater understanding between Christian and Jews" and that the God of Abraham "bless the children of your covenant, both Jew and Christian."[12]

Holy Saturday

Holy Saturday comes as an interlude in the series of *Triduum* liturgies. Although the *Common Worship* lectionary includes readings for Easter Eve, by ancient custom there is no celebration of the eucharist on this day.[13] A service of the word, perhaps gathering those preparing the church building for the Easter celebrations, could provide opportunity for quiet reflection on Christ's descent among the dead.

The Easter Liturgy

The three holy days culminate in the joy and splendor of the Easter Liturgy, a nighttime service rich in symbol: light, word, water, bread, and wine. In this feast, the assembly remembers God's saving acts, rejoices in Christ's victory over death, and celebrates their participation in the new life of grace.

The Easter Liturgy traditionally begins in darkness, a time of watching and waiting. The image of Christ as light vanquishing the darkness, a powerful theme of the paschal celebration, is symbolized by the Easter candle and the accompanying prayers and ceremonies as it is lit. The Exsultet, an ancient paschal song of praise that immediately follows the candle lighting, gathers the assembly in exuberant rejoicing in Christ's victory over sin and death. Again and again the minister proclaims, "*This* is the night. . . ."[14] The fruits of Christ's triumph are ours, happening now, in this paschal feast.

The service of light may come before or after the vigil readings. When the Easter Liturgy begins with the service

---

11. BCP 1662.
12. *TS*, 317.
13. *TS*, 323; *CW*, 556.
14. Exsultet, *TS*, 337, 359, 411, 413, 414, 416. Emphasis added.

of light, the Old Testament readings are heard in the context of the proclamation of Jesus' saving work. The assembly remains in semi-darkness, the readings and responses illuminated by the Easter candle and the smaller candles held by each person. Alternatively, the service of light may follow the Old Testament readings. While some light is needed so that readers are able to see the scriptures they are proclaiming, this is not the strong Easter symbol of Christ, the light of the world. With this pattern, the vigil emphasizes waiting: Christ in the tomb awaiting his vindication, the people of God throughout history awaiting their redemption.

In the Vigil, the assembly recalls the history of salvation. Central to this proclamation is the Exodus narrative of the Israelites crossing the Red Sea, which is always included in the sequence of readings.[15] The Israelites' deliverance from slavery and safe passage through the Red Sea parallels Jesus' passage through death into new life and our passage through the waters of baptism into the risen life of Christ. The vigil may include any number of additional readings from the Old Testament. Ordinarily, the story of creation (Genesis 1:1–2:4a) is the first reading, as the beginning of scripture and the beginning of salvation history. *Times and Seasons* suggests several motifs that might guide the selection of readings, but there are multiple and overlapping themes, and any group of readings will open several dimensions of God's saving grace. The proclamation of scripture and the assembly's response— through silence, prayer, song, or other action—builds anticipation for the announcement of the Easter gospel.

Whichever pattern is selected—light followed by Old Testament readings; or readings, then light—the assembly then joins in the Easter acclamation and enthusiastic rejoicing sounded with organ fanfare, bells, cymbals, or other instruments. The *Gloria in excelsis* follows, a song of praise heard

---

15. The lectionary in *Common Worship* lists this reading as Exodus 14:10–31; 15:20,21 (*CW*, 557), which concludes with Miriam leading the women in joyous dancing, celebrating God's victory. *Times and Seasons* alters the final verses, assigning instead Exodus 15:1a (*TS*, 375, 382), which identifies "Moses and the Israelites" as the celebrants. This alternative is used even for the cluster of readings with the theme "Women in Salvation" (*TS*, 373).

only once (on Maundy Thursday) since Ash Wednesday. The New Testament reading, always Romans 6:3–11, reminds us of our baptismal participation in Christ's death and resurrection. Then the Easter gospel, a story of the women discovering the empty tomb, is proclaimed. "Alleluia" echoes again and again, from the Easter acclamation to the gospel announcement, and continues to resound until the dismissal.

The liturgy of initiation is a fitting response to the announcement of Christ's resurrection. Through the paschal mystery, we have been buried with Christ in baptism, so that we might also walk in newness of life (Romans 6:4). Ideally, there will be candidates for baptism every year at this liturgy, because the celebration reminds each Christian of their baptism.[16] But even if there are no candidates for baptism and/or confirmation, the Easter Liturgy will include elements of the baptismal rite. The decision, in which adult candidates and parents, godparents, and sponsors of infants renounce evil and accept Christ, serves as the verbal renewal of baptismal vows for those already baptized, and if there are candidates for baptism, the congregation joins them in their responses. The prayer over the water, used whether or not there is to be baptism, recalls the waters of the Red Sea and the waters of death. The people then reaffirm their faith; the interrogatory creed is an ancient baptismal practice, sometimes recited as the candidates were immersed in the baptismal pool. Those who are already baptized may receive a tangible reminder of their baptism, either by a minister sprinkling the congregation with the water or by each person touching the water, then making the sign of the cross on their forehead.

Intercession is an appropriate element of the Easter Liturgy. In ancient baptismal rites, the newly baptized joined the assembly's prayers for the first time. While unbaptized persons are not excluded from prayers of intercession in today's

16. The first English prayer books (1549, 1552, 1559) called for public baptism to be administered on Sundays and holy days, "when the most number of people come together," in part because this would remind everyone present of their own baptism (http://justus.anglican.org/resources/bcp/1559/Baptism_1559.htm; http://justus.anglican.org/resources/bcp/1552/Baptism_1552.htm; http://justus.anglican.org/resources/bcp/1549/Baptism_1549.htm).

worship, participation in intercessory prayer is an important sign of the new life of baptism, as the presider explains in the seasonal introduction to the intercessions at baptism: "You now share, with all the members of the Church, the privilege of praying to our Father, through his Son Jesus Christ, in the power of the Holy Spirit." In our intercessions, Christians join with Christ in his self-offering for the world and so enact our participation in the priesthood of believers. Following the pattern of *Initiation Services*, intercessions can be included immediately before or after the Welcome and Peace.[17]

The Easter Liturgy culminates with the liturgy of the table. The seasonal texts underscore the themes of resurrection and new life. But this part of the service unfolds according to the same pattern as every celebration of eucharist, for every eucharist is a celebration of the paschal mystery of Jesus' death and resurrection.

Easter: The Great Fifty Days

With the Easter Liturgy, the Great Fifty Days of Easter begin. The rejoicing of the Easter Liturgy continues throughout the season, as Lenten fasting yields to the paschal feast: "alleluia" echoes in speech and song; the *Gloria in excelsis* is sung once again; the lit Easter candle is prominent at all services; vestments and decorations underscore the festivity of the season.

Sundays of Easter

The identification of the Sundays in this season emphasizes the unity of the fifty days. While the Book of Common Prayer and *Alternative Service Book* numbered Sundays "after Easter" and then the "Sunday after Ascension Day (Sixth Sunday after Easter)," *Common Worship* considers Easter Day to be the first Sunday of the season, and each successive Sunday is a Sunday "of Easter," from the second

---

17. *CI*, 74.

through the seventh Sundays. The Great Fifty Days conclude on the Day of Pentecost.

As Lent emphasizes repentance as an essential element of preparation for the annual paschal celebration, Easter celebrates the deliverance from slavery to sin that results from Christ's victory over death. An "Act of Penitence" may be used at the Sunday Eucharist during this festive season,[18] and it is a fitting alternative to the confession and absolution. Water, signifying the washing away of our sins and the gift of eternal life in baptism, is blessed, then sprinkled on the congregation. Like the sprinkling during the Easter Liturgy, the water is a tangible reminder of the baptismal water through which Christians participate in Christ's death and resurrection. A hymn, song, or anthem during the sprinkling can amplify the meaning of this action.

During Easter, following ancient custom, the lectionary appoints readings from the Acts of the Apostles for the first reading, rather than a selection from the Old Testament. Acts tells of the formation and growth of the post-resurrection community of Christians, and hence these narratives serve to remind contemporary Christians of the implications of the resurrection for Christian life and mission. The second reading offers a theological commentary on the inner life of the Christian community.[19] In Year A, these readings are from 1 Peter, in which baptismal images abound. Year B brings a semi-continuous series from 1 John, and Year C provides selections from Revelation.

Throughout the season, the gospel each Sunday presents a distinctive theme or motif of the resurrection. On the Second Sunday of Easter, the gospel is always the Johannine story of Jesus' appearance to the disciples who are huddled behind locked doors (John 20:19–31). The reference to Jesus' appearance to Thomas a week after appearing to the other disciples (John 20:26) makes this an apt gospel on this Sunday. On the third Sunday, the readings turn to resurrection meals.

---

18. *TS*, 430.

19. Consultation on Common Texts, *The Revised Common Lectionary* (Nashville, TN: Abingdon Press, 1992), 13–14.

Texts that speak of Jesus' presence in the breaking of the bread will echo the gospel, particularly in Year A, when Jesus' appearance on the road to Emmaus is the appointed gospel. The Fourth Sunday of Easter focuses on Jesus as the Good Shepherd; the presentation of this image in John 10 is divided among the three years of the lectionary. On the fifth and sixth Sundays, the gospels are selected from the farewell discourse in John's gospel, as the energy of the season shifts from the immediacy of the resurrection to Jesus' teaching about the commandment of love and the promise of the Holy Spirit. Then, on the Seventh Sunday of Easter, the lectionary assigns a portion of Jesus' high priestly prayer (John 17), an intercession to the Father for the unity of his followers.

Several of the gospel images are woven into the second form of intercession for the season.[20] Those in the third form (which is also appointed for Ascension Day) emphasize Jesus' glorification.

Ascension Day

The chronology in the first chapter of the Acts of the Apostles (Acts 1:3) places this feast on the fortieth day after Easter. It celebrates Jesus' continuing presence and reign with God, and his commission of the disciples to be his witnesses to the ends of the earth (Acts 1:8). A principal feast of the Church, it is appropriately celebrated with the eucharist, texts, and music continuing to resound with Easter joy. The focus of the fifty days shifts to anticipation of the bestowal of the Spirit on the feast of Pentecost and our commission as disciples.

The Feast of Pentecost

On this day, the Church celebrates the fiery descent of the Holy Spirit on the first disciples and the gift of the Spirit to the Church, to us. In the early centuries of the Church, Pentecost was considered to be a baptismal feast, second only

---

20. Intercessions H2, *TS*, 433.

to the Easter Vigil.[21] While not providing for baptism, the liturgy in *Times and Seasons* stresses the renewal and commissioning of the congregation. Oil, either the fragrant chrism used at baptism or oil blessed for this occasion, signifies the gift of the Spirit, molding Christians in the likeness of Christ ("Christ" means literally "the anointed one") and empowering them to be witnesses to Christ's love. Texts throughout the liturgy rejoice in the gift of the Spirit and pray for the renewal of that gift. Finally, with candles lit from the Easter candle, the people renew their commitment to live as Christ's people in the world, and they are sent forth "filled with the Spirit's power."[22]

The Great Fifty Days, and the entire paschal cycle, come to a glorious conclusion on this day. Journeying from ashes to fire, with prayer and song, symbol and movement, the congregation has celebrated the paschal mystery and renewed their faith and commitment to Jesus, the crucified and risen one.

---

21. The first English Book of Common Prayer (1549) acknowledged that in ancient times baptism was administered only on Easter and Pentecost ("Whitsunday"). Since it did not appear possible to restore this custom, the drafters of the prayer book settled for public baptism on Sundays and holy days (http://justus.anglican.org/resources/bcp/1549/Baptism_1549.htm).

22. *TS*, 502.

CHAPTER 11

Ordinary Time

Ellen Clark-King

O RDINARY TIME IS OFTEN THE period of the year when busy clergy and congregations may either breathe a sigh of relief or a sigh of boredom according to their respective natures. There is a brief burst of Ordinary Time between Epiphany and Lent, but its longest period covers the many Sundays between Trinity and Advent—the time in the church year when "nothing happens" and we use our green vestments almost every week. There are no major festivals for people to get excited about, nor periods of penitence and preparation to help them focus their thoughts on spiritual matters. It can be seen as an empty space, dotted here and there with more minor celebrations, but lacking the heights and depths of Advent through to Pentecost. In this chapter we will look at some of the hidden blessings of Ordinary Time: the gifts it has to offer us in our spiritual and church life if we take the trouble to look a little deeper.

The title of this period of the church year does not come from the fact that it is ordinary in the everyday sense of "not special," but because the Sundays are known by their ordinal number rather than by name. "Ordinal" Sundays giving rise to the term "Ordinary Time." However, it is its "ordinariness" rather than its numerical nature that will provide the focus for this current exploration, mainly because it is its "ordinariness" that, counter-intuitively, marks it out as different from the rest of the church year.

In many cultures, winter was the time for telling tales. It was the season when early dark brought an early return to home with long evenings gathered round the fire, full of indoor chores enlivened by the sharing of stories. It's entirely congruent with this way of being that the heart of the Christian story is told, at least in the northern hemisphere, in the darkest months of the year—new light and life in December starting our journey through the high points of Jesus' life story to its climax in death, resurrection, and ascension, ending with the descent of the Spirit to open the next page in the tale. So what does this leave us with for the summer and autumn months? Actually, quite a lot. Not only is there the teaching and mission of Jesus which provides the context, and some of the theological content, for the events of Holy Week and Easter; there is also the continuation of the story of Israel's encounter with God as recorded for us in the Hebrew Scriptures, and the story of the Spirit's continuing work in the world as recorded by the writers of the Epistles. But there is also the space to interweave our own stories with that of God's people so that the winter's tale of Advent and Lent through to the springtime of Easter and Pentecost becomes a living part of our own continuing stories.

Ordinary Time allows us space to tell our own Christian stories. In the rest of the Christian Year, we hear the story of God's love and redemption sung out loud and strong as we live and travel and die and rise again with Jesus. In Ordinary Time the story has not changed—it is still God's love and redemption that we celebrate in our worship—but now there is a quieter note as we see how the rest of creation, and the lives of everyday Christians—our own included—can sing this same tale in their own more limited way. So again the more usual meaning of "ordinary" comes into play in our understanding of this season—it is a time when our ordinary lives can be put into the context of the extraordinary story of God's relationship with humankind.

Ordinary Time reminds us of the fact that God is actively at work in the mundane ordinariness of our lives, as well as in the exalted story of Jesus Christ and in the lives of the angels and saints. Christianity, after all, is not a spectator sport—and neither is Christian worship. One of the things that we should expect to happen as we come to worship together is that we should be changed—both as individuals and as communities. This change ought both to bring us closer to God and to bring the reign of God a little closer to the world. We, as Church and Christians, should *become* sacraments as well as take part in sacraments—in other words we should become outward and visible signs of the grace of God at work in our hearts and in our world. All worship, after all, stands at the intersection of the ordinary and the extraordinary: the place where our everyday reality and time opens up to the transformative touch of the transcendent and eternal reality of God.

That this is a true possibility, rather than merely a pious hope, is shown by the stories that "ordinary Christians" are able to tell of their relationship with God, and of the love and courage that God has gifted them with in their own lives. This is a truth that all those of us who are lucky enough to spend time listening to "ordinary Christians" through our pastoral work can attest to. One conversation I had yesterday springs to mind. It was with a woman in her 60s who had been flooded out of her apartment. Rather than bemoaning her lot and her lost possessions, she celebrated the chance to be closer to the church in her temporary home at the YWCA and enthused that she was getting to share a kitchen with a whole host of fascinating characters. Or there is the woman in her 80s whose faith is as fresh and questioning as the day she was confirmed many years ago. Or the young man who speaks with great clarity about his surprise at finding himself called to be baptized as an adult in response to his encounter with the truth and passion of God. And there are of course, and everywhere, thousands more ordinary Christians whose lives are a source of God's love and hope to those among whom they live.

Ordinary Time and Ordinary People

The Jesuit poet Gerard Manley Hopkins says something crucial to the role of Ordinary Time in the closing lines of his poem "As Kingfishers Catch Fire": that Christ "plays" before God in thousands of places, "lovely in limbs," "lovely in eyes not his," through "the features of [others'] faces."[1]

In Ordinary Time we are reminded that the story which began with Jesus Christ has not yet come to an end but is continuing, however imperfectly and haltingly, in the life of the Church and of each individual Christian. It's as if we catch the spark of Christ-like living in the high seasons of the year and then learn how to keep it alive and burning within us in the more measured rhythm of this slightly less exalted period. Our liturgical year, whether in festal, penitential, or ordinary mode, has one main purpose: to enable us to encounter God in our worship and in our lives. From Advent through to Pentecost, it does this by telling again the story of God's creative and redemptive action in the world. In the Sundays after Pentecost, it does this by drawing our own stories into God's story or, to put it another way, by showing us how God's story might be lived out in our own lives. This purpose is, in my opinion, better served by the title of Sundays after Pentecost rather than Sundays in Trinity—it being the continued work of the Spirit among us that is being recognized and validated in this season.

One of the things that strikes me constantly in my work as a priest is the depth of the way that "ordinary" women and men in the Church experience their vocation to be Christ-like. The prayer ascribed to Teresa of Avila is being lived out in churches throughout the world with little drama and often even less reward:

---

1. Gerard Manley Hopkins (1882), "As Kingfishers Catch Fire," in Alexander W. Allison et al., eds., *The Norton Anthology of Poetry* (New York: W. W. Norton & Company, 1983), 858.

Christ has no body now but yours
No hands, no feet on earth but yours
Yours are the eyes through which He looks
compassion on this world
Christ has no body now on earth but yours.[2]

Before I explore this further in more theological and liturgical ways, let me show what I mean by introducing you to two of my companions in my current congregation.

The first, let us call her Grace, is ninety-five years old and has been a member of the Anglican Church for all of those ninety-five years. She still drives to church nearly every Sunday, though when she arrives she has a special chair with arms to enable her to stand and sit more easily. Like most lives that have lasted so long, Grace has seen her fair share of loss and bereavement, having lost a child as well as her husband. However, when you meet Grace, one of the first words that springs to your mind is joy. Here is a woman whose faith is vibrant and shines out in her humor as well as in her loving approach to everyone around her. I don't imagine that she has ever felt sorry for herself: she is far too busy noticing and helping to meet the needs of others, and taking delight in the company of old friends and new young companions. Grace would insist on her own ordinariness, turning away compliments with an unfeigned humility, while her life is in actuality a speaking icon of the love of Christ.

The second is a younger man in his 50s whom we shall call Victor. He isn't someone you would point to as a traditional saint, having a wicked sense of humor and a certain impatience with some of the less competent members of the congregation. But he is someone I turn to first whenever I am in need of help. Victor can be relied on both to say "yes" if it is at all possible and to do so without giving the impression that he is conferring a great favor and will expect your constant gratitude in exchange. His work and his volunteer time are both focused on being there for other people, and he lives out on a daily basis

---

2. This prayer is widely anthologized as being Teresa's, though this is in fact uncertain.

the injunction to go the extra mile. Victor is far from pious and far from perfect, but you can see the reflection of Jesus' commitment to meet the needs of those he encountered in his willingness and availability. Victor, like Grace, would call himself ordinary, but again his presence among people allows something of God's love to be seen, and his actions bring the kingdom of God that much closer to this world.

These are the ordinary people whose ordinary stories find a liturgical home within Ordinary Time, in the particular way that these Sundays facilitate an encounter with God that is both sacramental and incarnational. They allow us to focus on the transformation of the ordinary into the extraordinary, and on the action of God in drawing close through the material reality that shapes our human lives. This is, of course, what God does throughout the liturgical year, and Advent through to Ascension tells the story of the Incarnation in a unique and irreplaceable way. But the energy of the incarnation is not consumed in that story; it overspills into God's encounter with humanity more generally, and Ordinary Time helps us to remember that we are the continuation of the story. We are the ones anointed with the Spirit to bring God's love to God's aching world.

Ordinary Time teaches us that our automatic reaction to the high calling to become sacraments—"I'm not special/wise/holy enough"—is not a sufficient excuse to sit out of God's dance. God works in and through the ordinary, as a quick glance at the earliest disciples will illustrate. Ordinary people as well as ordinary time are capable of being transfigured and transformed by the immanent presence of the Holy Spirit. The calling of Christ is not to the special, but to those who are open to offering their ordinariness for transformation. Fishermen, tax collectors, insurance agents, cafeteria staff, lawyers, call center workers, and you and I are the ordinary material of God's work of transformation; as St. Paul says: "not many of you were wise by human standards, not many were powerful, not many were of noble birth" (1 Corinthians 1:26). God is capable of transfiguring us, the ordinary folk of the human race, and drawing us into the story of redemption which is told in both extraordinary times and lives and in ordinary ones too.

The Blessings of Ordinary Time

Three particular blessings of Ordinary Time help us toward the grace of that transfiguring: space, variety, and freedom. These all spring from the fact that Ordinary Time is not tied to any one particular theological mood—it neither has the penitential and preparatory atmosphere of Lent and Advent, nor the celebratory focus of Christmas, Epiphany, and Easter—or to any one aspect of the Church's foundational story. Ordinary Time is open and hospitable to many different emotional tones of worship and to exploring many different treasures within our scripture and tradition.

The blessing of space is one that can be experienced in many different ways. For me it is known in the freedom of spirit that comes with looking at a wide expanse of sky, whether it is seen over the ocean in my current home on the west coast of Canada or over the fens in East Anglia where my family has roots. Such openness can grace us with an experience of expansion: a sense that we can breathe freely and deeply, that we are not being crowded out by all the millions of people that share our earth, that all our worries and concerns are not occupying all our available space. Ordinary time graces us with a spacious openness by its very length. It need not be either seen as blessedly empty or frustratingly boring, but as a joyous spaciousness that allows us to relax into a gentler rhythm as we explore some of the byways as well as the highways of our faith.

Along with space comes a blessing of variety. Although all the Sundays are "ordinary," they are by no means all the same. Each year the lectionary follows the story of Jesus' life as told by one of the gospels, gifting us with a great diversity of material: the parables, the stories of healing, the controversies and conflicts with authority, the teaching on how we should relate to God and to one another—and these are only examples. We are also led through some of the great stories of the Hebrew Scriptures which provide an ongoing narrative of hope and faith and the struggle of human beings to understand themselves and God. As do indeed the Epistle readings, which allow us to hear the voices of early Christians as they work out the theological truths that their new faith is calling forth. The variety of Ordinary Time is a good reminder that all aspects of human life can and should be brought into our relationship with God in order to be transformed.

This space and variety adds up to an experience of freedom. Ordinary Time gives those planning and leading liturgy more scope to shape the mood and focus of each Sunday's worship. It is possible to allow local needs and concerns to weave in to the over-arching pattern provided by the lectionary, so that the Church remains both catholic and also, in the best sense of the word, parochial: responsive to its calling to be both universal and local. In a way that is not always so straightforward during seasons specifically dedicated to celebration or penitence, it is possible for the Church to celebrate and mourn along with the wider society: harvest festivals and the celebration of the earth's bounty find a home in ordinary time, as does Remembrance Day with its yearly reminder of the cost of war and violence. In a way that is characteristic of Christianity as a whole, ordinary time allows us the opportunity to weave our own personal stories into the story of our creation, redemption, and ongoing befriending by God. Ordinary Time offers a special way for our worship to be grounded and incarnate, tied into our lives as we experience them outside the church walls.

The Green Church

One way in which most people identify that we are in Ordinary Time is by the church being dressed in green. Green is the color of growth, and so of life and of hope. These resonances make it a very appropriate color to fill the church for such a large percentage of the year. The Christian story is full of our calling to grow into our full humanity, which we do as we become more richly and completely the image of Christ.

Such growth is the result of the grace of God at work within us, what Hildegard of Bingen referred to as "*veriditas*" or the "greening power" of God. Such growth is what the Orthodox churches refer to as "divinization" and the Reformed churches as "sanctification": the maturation within ourselves of the image of God that we are created and called to bear. In this greening, growth, and maturation, we not only become more open to God ourselves, but also, and as a direct result, we become more ready to bear fruit for all of creation.

The green of Ordinary Time also ties in quite clearly with Christ's teaching about himself and his mission to the world: "I came that they may have life, and have it abundantly" (John 10:10). The green hangings and vestments remind us of our calling to abundant life and our mission to ensure abundant life for all others who share our fragile planet with us. At this time when environmental issues are so pressing, and when our contemporary Christian spirituality is emphasizing our need to include ecological concerns within the remit of our care, it is more than ever significant that we should worship surrounded by the green of life. Which is also the green of hope: symbolized by the new growth that comes to the temperate countries of the world with spring and to the warmer climates with the rains. So in Ordinary Time we are reminded to be a people of hope, a people who do not rely on their own energies to make the world right, but who know that they are fellow workers with the Spirit of God. Growth, life, and hope are truly ordinary as they are to be found everywhere within our world, but they are also truly Spirit-filled and divine because their origin is in the creative and loving power of God: the extraordinary within the ordinary—the great mystery of the incarnation itself.

And in our current ecological crisis, green has another resonance for us. It is a reminder that we as a Church need to commit ourselves to working for the well-being of all God's creation, not to mention working for the very survival of the earth's ecosystem that our consumer and industrial lifestyle is threatening with cataclysmic change. Ordinary time's green livery can serve to remind us that we human beings are called to be the adults of the created order: those who work with God for the care and flourishing of the whole. To be green is a sacred calling to limit our own consumption for the good of the whole planet with which we have been gifted by God.

The Spiritual Journey

The experience of ordinary and extraordinary times is not only true of our liturgical year, it is for many of us also true of the experience of our spiritual pilgrimage throughout life. The fortunate among us have times when we are sure through the wonder of our experience that God is real, that God is present, and that God loves us. There may even be a very few for whom this assurance is more than fleeting and is a reality in which they are able to rest for much of the time. I wish I was one of them! For I, like most of us, have only very fleeting moments of such sublime assurance, and these are scattered among far longer times when my belief in God's reality, presence, and love is an act of faith rather than an act of experience. Indeed it sometimes seems to be counter to the evidence of my life and the lives of those I live among rather than merely absent from it.

One of the psalms seems to express the seesaw motion of the spiritual life with great truth: Psalm 42. The psalmist goes back and forth from the assurance of hope in:

> Why are you cast down, O my soul,
> And why are you disquieted within me?
> Hope in God: for I shall again praise him,
> My help and my God.

to

> My tears have been my food day and night,
> While people say to me continually,
> "Where is your God?"

and

> I say to God, my rock,
> "Why have you forgotten me?
> Why must I walk about mournfully
> Because the enemy oppresses me?"

This speaks to many of us of our inability to stay on the spiritual heights surrounded by that "peace which the world cannot give." Even if we would not all lay claim to something as mystic-sounding and dramatic as a dark night of the soul, many of us can attest to the dreariness of what might be called a "gray afternoon of the soul" when the reality of God seems very far from the reality of our lives and of the world we inhabit. It's appropriate that the Sunday after Easter should traditionally be known as "Low Sunday," not just because numbers attending church tend to be small that week, but also because plateau experiences often follow on from our spiritual highs.

One of my tasks as a spiritual director is to help people find God in the everyday as well as in the moments of intensity. And, of course, one of my tasks as a Christian is to do this for myself as well. And in this it helps to be able to point to a time of the church's year that addresses this reality. Ordinary Time can be seen as the liturgical equivalent of the plateau experiences of our spiritual journey—the times when the spiritual highs are just a mere memory and we have to get by with the habit of prayer rather than finding it a particularly rewarding practice . . . in the same way that sometimes we have to rely on the habit of worship rather than feeling uplifted by every service we have ever attended.

These times can be hard to live through and may make some people feel that they are failing in their Christian pilgrimage because they no longer experience the consoling sense of God's presence with them. But they are most often times of inner growth when, like fallow fields, we are restoring our ability to grow and being made ready for our next step along the journey. The Christian pilgrimage, after all, is a life-long marathon rather than a quick sprint to the finish line, and it needs times when we slow down somewhat and take a breath for the next hill.

This is not to say that people cannot feel spiritual highs during ordinary time—whether that is the ordinary everyday-ness of their lives or the ordinary season of the church year. Sometimes it is the high festivals that leave us feeling flat, as if we expect too much of them and are disappointed, whereas it can be a particular verse from the gospel, or from a hymn, that strikes our hearts in a new way on the most everyday of Sundays. It can be at the times when we feel least expected to be part of a collective spiritual high that we are able to relax into our own deepest sense of God's presence with us.

Ordinary Time and the "Secular" Year

In our church in Canada, we run a teaching series twice a year known as "Anglican 101." Its purpose is to introduce new church members to some of the practices of Anglicanism that long-time members take for granted. One area where there are always a lot of questions is around worship: why we do what we do, what words like "Lent" and "sacrament" mean, why the colors change at different times of year. In a country where the separation of Church and state is even fur-ther advanced than in the United Kingdom—"spring break," for example, being the spring school holiday that happens in March regardless of the date of Easter—there is little knowl-edge of the highs and lows of the liturgical seasons. Christmas greetings have been largely replaced with "Happy Holidays!" and the Easter Bunny is a far more recognized figure than the risen Christ.

This is not a state of affairs that I am personally happy about, but it is a reality with which the church has to deal. And one of its consequences is to allow Ordinary Time the role of providing an opportunity for the church to reflect God's interest in the world outside the church's walls by making room for secular concerns in its planning and celebrations. The church can show that, even if the secular world does not have room for the church's priorities, the church is not, in fact, separate and cut off from people's secular experiences.

How a church does this will depend on its own understanding of its secular context and the concerns of its particular neighborhood. The most traditional example would have to be the Harvest Festival: a secular celebration of plenty, baptized as a celebration of God's bounty and care for us. This is still a major highpoint for many rural churches and one of the times when people who do not regularly attend church come because they feel that their concerns are being taken seriously and recognized as having spiritual resonance. It's one of those moments when the secular and sacred years are allowed to touch to the enrichment of both. Although, it must be said, in some urban areas it may be more an exercise in nostalgia than a recognition of what is truly important in the community's lived experience.

But even where Harvest is a relevant festival, it should not be the only occasion when the world outside the church finds its way inside. Ordinary Time allows the freedom to show the church's interest in and care for the environment by dedicating a Sunday to ecological issues or, in a more homely fashion, to celebrate the gifts of God's creation through a service of the blessing of animals. It may be important in some communities to recognize the rhythms of the school year, blessing teachers and students as they return to their classrooms, or to focus on local issues of justice and social outreach. The exact occasion is not of primary importance; the crucial thing is to let people know that the life journey of their community is not ignored or considered irrelevant by the church in its midst.

So Ordinary Time can be characterized by a spirit of hospitality to the world outside the church: inviting the community as well as individuals to entwine their life story with that of God's activity in Jesus Christ and the Holy Spirit. This needs to be done with thought and discretion, as well as with openness and generosity: we don't want the story of God's love which shines through Ordinary Time as through all the church year to be obscured by secular stories, but to be illuminated and illustrated by the interaction. This means that every Sunday should not become a Sunday devoted to a particular cause or movement so that that story hides the Christian one, but that occasional such Sundays can enrich both our church life and that of our local community. Ordinary Time can become a space for encounter, with the church's walls lowered to allow easy entry from the world outside.

Conclusion

Ordinary Time should not be seen as the Ugly Sister of the church calendar. It provides us with a great opportunity to tie our own multifaceted stories into the great Story of God's redemptive relationship with God's creation. Its very ordinariness reminds us of the role that we ever so ordinary women, men, and children have to play within God's purposes. We too can be transformed by God's grace into people worthy to "stand in God's presence and serve" God. In the same way that Ordinary Time sanctifies our ordinariness, it also sanctifies the ordinary times of our spiritual lives—the periods when we are not caught up into heaven's dance but are plodding wearily along our own dull way. We need not doubt God walks with us in the valleys as much as in the heights. Nor should we doubt that God is found at work in the world as well as in the church, and Ordinary Time allows us the opportunity to make connections between the two spheres that the liturgically "busier" seasons less often permit.

So, do not sigh when the church puts on its green raiment, but use it as a time to celebrate, and commit ourselves to protect the abundance of life God has graced us with. Make the most of the spaciousness, variety, and the freedom it gives us to tie in the life of the world around us with the life of the church at prayer. Most of all reflect on the glorious ability of God to transform the ordinary into the extraordinary and to catch up your life into the ongoing song of redemption and hope.

CHAPTER 12

Celebrating the Saints

Mark Pryce

I N THIS CHAPTER I OFFER poems and reflections inspired by them which may help to emphasize something of the character of the feast of All Saints and the Commemoration of the Faithful Departed (All Souls) which immediately follows it. I begin by outlining the pastoral context of the celebration, paying attention to the lived experience of individuals and communities who are rejoicing in the triumphs of the saints, and at the same time mourning the loss of loved ones. I go on to suggest that the paschal theology at the core of our faith offers Christians a spirituality which holds together the joy and sorrow of the season, opening up a space in which grief (with all its complex processes of emotions and adjustments) can find a place with thanksgiving and inspiration, an interplay which fosters hopeful living.

Liturgy and poetry are midwives for this hopeful living. They do not create it, but they may assist in its birth, in finding form and expression. Both liturgy and poetry offer an occasion, a space, a forum, in which the sacred things of the human heart and of the communal consciousness can come out to play, make connections, forge allegiances which give insight, courage, and resolve. I suggest that appropriate liturgy, as a nuanced language for expression and enactment, becomes a place in which diverse or conflicting emotional feelings and spiritual searchings can find a space before God that is both intimate and communal, at once looking back to the past and forward to a future of promise and fulfillment. Poetry, with its capacity to pay profound attention to complex human experience, and to hold ambiguities and contradictions of feeling and perception together in a rich ecology of meaning, offers Christians a form of expression in which bliss and brokenness can both find a voice in a God-ward song that offers a transforming spiritual freedom to those who participate.

The Radical Power of Remembering

Ben Okri's poem "An African Elegy" is a wonderful expression of the renewal and reorientation this honoring of the dead imparts to the living through remembering. He recalls those who have gone before—his African ancestors known and unknown, how they were appreciative of the earth's goodness even though some were weighed down with terrible suffering. In this remembering the dead take the living to the heart of what it is to be fully alive, digging deep down to the roots of existence. In this way the poet celebrates memory, how it unleashes a spiritual power in the present for those who will take time to appreciate forebears: they tell him that "life is good," to "live it gently," yet "with fire" and "always with hope."[1] To meditate on the dignity of those who have gone before, on their capacity to "sing and dream sweet things" and to live life to the full in a defiant, faithful hope for a better future, is a radical act which transforms the present.

This process of celebrating those who have gone before in a way that transforms the present is an experience familiar to Christians. The transforming remembering—*anamnesis*—which is at the heart of the eucharist, is a recalling of the crucifixion and resurrection of Jesus in such a way that we are

---

1. Ben Okri, "An African Elegy," from *Africa Elegy* (London: Jonathan Cape, 1992). The full text of the poem may also be found in Mark Pryce, *Literary Companion to the Lectionary* (London: SPCK, 2001), 24-25.

drawn anew into the saving power of this dying and rising. What is memory reorientates our lives in the present toward God and toward one another afresh; we are re-focused upon and within the eternal present-ness of God. Out of this remembering the central self-giving act of God in Christ flows our recalling of all those, past and present, who have been transformed in Christ, as we look to the completion of God's future. As the faithful give thanks for what God has done for them in Christ, so they give thanks for what God has done in those who have gone before, and who rest in God still. As the Prayer of Intercession in the Book of Common Prayer (1662) puts it:

> And we also bless thy holy Name for all thy servants departed this life in thy faith and fear; beseeching thee to give us grace so to follow their good examples, that with them we may be partakers of thy heavenly kingdom . . .

Or as the Collect for All Saints' Day prays:

> O Almighty God, who hast knit together thine elect in one communion and fellowship, in the mystical body of thy Son Christ our Lord: Grant us grace so to follow thy blessed Saints in all virtuous and godly living, that we may come to those unspeakable joys, which thou hast prepared for them that unfeignedly love thee . . .

To remember the way of life of faithful people who have gone before is an encouragement for those who will follow "their good examples"; with the power of God's grace, it is a way of sharing in the fullness of God's rule.

A more catholic appreciation, such as the Eucharistic Prefaces in *Common Worship* (2000), goes beyond the departed as exemplars in faithful living, to celebrate them as ongoing spiritual companions:

> And now we give you thanks for the glorious pledge of the hope of our calling which you have given us in your saints; that, following their good example

and strengthened by their fellowship, we may run
with perseverance the race that is set before us,
and with them receive the unfading crown of glory.

In remembering the saints before God, the pilgrim church
finds the mundane world transformed with a sense of their
spiritual company—what Ben Okri describes from his African
perspective as "surprise/In everything the unseen moves." For
those who will remember with thanksgiving, the nature of
what is real is caught up in a spiritual economy where those
who have gone before do not cease to pray, but continue to
support the faithful on earth through their continuing prayer.

The Pastoral Context

In some churches the two festivals of All Saints and All
Souls are celebrated in immediate succession, on the first and
second days of November. The two are connected, but distinct. In other communities the two are brought together in
one celebration—sometimes called All Saints Sunday, which
gives a dual emphasis to a single celebration of those disciples
who have "run the race before us," celebrating those acknowledged Saints who are renowned as "heroes of the faith" along
with the faithful men and women who have a personal significance for individual Christians and local communities—
family, friends, fellow worshipers, and co-disciples perhaps.
We rejoice in the saints who have triumphed in their faithful
discipleship, even as we remember those souls whom we love
but see no longer.

In places where the Commemoration of All Souls is kept as
a distinctive time for a memorial service or requiem, participants who are mourning family, neighbors, and friends may
well be remembering those who have recently died. These
occasions are often intensely personal and immediate in character; there will be gatherings of people mourning partners
and parents, children and siblings, neighbors and colleagues.
For some, death will have come as a relief to them; others will
have had no expectation of what was to happen. Some will
have been ready to relinquish the one they have lost; others

will feel that a loved one has been cruelly wrenched away from them. There will be a powerhouse of different circumstances and experiences and emotional responses around death, a pastoral situation that deserves care and consideration on the part of ministers and church communities—an opportunity for sincere prayer and for service to those who come.

In countries where wartime commemorations are observed in November, such as Remembrance Sunday in the United Kingdom, this gives a further nuance to the celebrations of All Saints-tide. Public acts of remembrance that incorporate thanksgiving and gratitude together with an appropriate sorrow at the destruction of war are also the focus of private expressions of grief for the loss of comrades and loved ones. Contemporary conflicts give this remembrance period a renewed poignancy—and in communities closely connected with the military, a loss that is raw.

To celebrate the saints and to remember the departed draws us into joy and sorrow all at once. To remember the dead may inspire thanksgiving and at the same time invite those who remember to touch their grief and loss. To remember the dead can release feelings of utter loneliness and abandonment, and yet recalling the blessings of former companionship—laughter, love, shared experiences, joint achievements—these can offer comfort in a solitary present. Remembering may trigger hopelessness, and yet it may open up a sense of resolution, nurturing the spiritual expectation for ultimate fulfillment, the anticipation of the gathering together of all things in Christ (Ephesians 1:10). The remembrance season of All Saints-All Souls is a dangerous celebration in so far as it touches on the painful places where those who grieve may be hurting. It is a healing celebration in so far as this touch may bring insights that offer reassurance and spiritual strength.

The widower R. S. Thomas' exquisite elegy for his late wife Mildred describes with such clarity the vulnerability of those who grieve, and yet the strength they receive from reflecting on the past. He recalls her grace and fragility with great fondness—she was like a snowflake, a feather—and in the end her beautiful life is nothing more than ashes which he holds, cremated remains, and the weight of his grief is as heavy as an anchor. The memory of her holds him down; there is no moving on. Yet her memory sustains him in place through tempests of emotion.

Comparisons

To all light things
I compared her; to
a snowflake, a feather.

I remember she rested
at the dance on my
arm, as a bird

on its nest lest
the eggs break, lest
she lean too heavily

on our love. Snow
melts, feathers
are blown away;

I have let
her ashes down
in me like an anchor.

—R. S. Thomas, 1913–2000[2]

Though they may not be so eloquently expressed, such sentiments gather in every church at All Saints-All Souls tide.

---

2. R. S. Thomas, "Comparisons," from *Residues* (Newcastle-Upon-Tyne, UK: Bloodaxe, 2002).

Liturgical Remembering as the Spiritual Place of Exchange

Bearing in mind the nuanced character of this Remembrance season of All Saints-All Souls, worshiping Christians need to draw on a rich theology for discerning how as the faithful, as saints who remember the Saints, we may be authentic in our eucharistic offering. Our awareness of suffering need not detract from joy, and acute consciousness of personal grief or communal hurt need not dilute the joy of a gospel that in and through Christ crucified, risen, and ascended, all human beings find God's forgiveness and their fulfillment in his eternal will. Our remembering in this season offers us joy as we recall the triumphs of the Holy Spirit at work in the lives of the individuals and communities called saints, and we celebrate their profound witness, their share in Christ's sacrifice, in his self-emptying servanthood, rejoicing in a faithfulness that follows even to death. Within the Communion of Saints, this is a celebration *in their company*, with angels and archangels and the whole company of heaven, as we renew our sense of all that God has done for us as a holy people in the birth, death, and resurrection of Jesus Christ whom we recall.

Yet this joyful season may also be when eucharistic thanks is to be offered out of acute loss and deep pain, in places of grief or hurt which yield no spiritual consolation, where time is not counted in days or years but in the ebbs and flows of bereavement's bleak tides. It is a season in which resurrection-faith becomes a practical spirituality—not in well-meant abstractions about the hope of eternal life, but in attentiveness to what was good and beautiful in the dead, in finding out what grounds there is for thanksgiving in the lives of the faithful departed. It is a season for foraging for that which is of God in God's beloved, a time for eulogy—literally, for speaking good words about what God has in and through his people. In this fostering of gratitude is the unfolding of a gospel of love and of costly redemption and of the sustaining of all things; there is a participation in the economy of a God who creates and sets free, who loves and forgives, the Origin and End of life who holds all souls in life, eternally, as he is eternal with the eternal Father and the ever-renewing Spirit. To dare to celebrate the saints in the company of the grieving is to insist that Christianity is a way of life that is life affirming in its generosity, and that the vision of God-in-Christ which inspired the saints has transformed our own lives too.

This conjunction of human hurt and of healing in the experience of remembering the dead draws us back to the paschal mystery of Christ's dying and rising again.

The Mystery of Christ's Cross and Resurrection: God's Transforming Presence in Our Mortality

To remember the dead is to realize our own mortality—the vulnerability of our human life, and the certainty of our human death. To be fully alive is to value the relationships and connections that enrich our life as persons, and also to know the potential for death from which no possessions or affections can ultimately shield us. To be human is to die.

Judith Wright's poem reflecting on motherhood rejoices in the creation of the child within her womb, and rejoices also in the diverse universe of living things which is somehow summed up within her own process of nurturing life. It is a poem celebrating connectedness and interdependence, not only between mother and child, but also between human beings and the world into which they are born and which the gift of human senses and faculties enable them to appreciate and to safeguard. Yet this miraculous growth from nothing into life through connectedness between mother and child is also a process that leads to death, for the mother who nurtures human life is also the link to inevitable mortal decay.

Woman to Child

You who were darkness warmed my flesh
where out of darkness rose the seed.

Then all the world I made in me;
all the world you hear and see
hung upon my dreaming blood.

There moved the multitudinous stars,
and coloured birds and fishes moved.
There swam the sliding continents.
All time lay rolled in me, and sense,
and love that knew not its beloved.

O node and focus of the world;
I hold you deep within that well
you shall escape and not escape—
that mirrors still your sleeping shape;
that nurtures still your crescent cell.

I wither and you break from me;
yet though you dance in living light
I am the earth, I am the root,
I am the stem that fed the fruit,
the link that joins you to the night.

     —Judith Wright, 1915–2000[3]

In facing this mortality with which we are confronted by remembering the dead, some will deny the reality of death. Anyone who attends funerals will recognize this tendency toward denial: the ameliorating "Death is nothing at all . . . Do not stand at my grave and weep . . . I am only in the next room" approach to the cruel and shocking separation and wrenching apart which is the experience of bereavement. The Christian doctrine of the Incarnation embraces death as the inevitable end of human life: Jesus is born of a woman (in Judith Wright's words, "I am the stem that fed the fruit"), lives a life in all its fullness, and this life is fully extinguished in death, an extinction emphasized not only by the manner of his dying but also by the story that he is buried, entombed, consigned to oblivion ("I am . . . the link that joins you to

---

3. Judith Wright, "Woman to Child," from *A Human Pattern: Selected Poems* (Sydney, Australia: ETT Imprint, 1992).

the night"). The Christian story is not to adjust the difficult
and harsh reality of our mortality by diminishing death, any
more than scientific theories of genetic inheritance in children
and grandchildren lessen the pain of losing loved ones. The
Christian narrative recognizes our vulnerability as human
beings, and sets alongside this stark realism the strange story
of God's presence with human beings in Jesus of Nazareth,
a story which suggests that the mortal scheme of birth and
death is transformed by love.

Fully acknowledging our earth-boundness as human
beings, as Judith Wright does in addressing her own child,
Henry Vaughan ponders this mystery of God taking flesh in
Jesus Christ, exchanging "robes of glory" to become "a woeful
story." He finds the doctrine profoundly affirming of human
existence, as God embraces death within a profound love for
creation.

The Incarnation, and Passion

Lord! When thou didst thy self undress
Laying by thy robes of glory,
To make us more, thou wouldst be less,
And becamest a woeful story.

To put on clouds instead of light,
And clothe the morning-star with dust,
Was a translation of such height
As, but in thee, was ne'er expressed;

Brave worms, and Earth! That thus could have
A God enclosed within your cell,
Your maker pent up in a grave,
Life locked in death, heaven in a shell;

Ah, my dear Lord! What couldst thou spy
In this impure, rebellious clay,
That made thee thus resolve to die
For those that kill thee every day?

O what strange wonders could thee move
To slight thy precious blood, and breath!
Sure it was *Love*, my Lord; for *Love*
Is only stronger far than death.

> —*Henry Vaughan, 1622–1695*[4]

The logic of such an exchange is not obvious. For Vaughan, a person of faith, the incarnation story does not negate mortality, but enfolds death in a divine love whose dynamic is stronger than the ebb and flow of human nature, even as that nature is newly dignified by the presence of God who can "spy/ In this impure, rebellious clay" a worth which God values at not less than everything.

In their unfolding of the story of Jesus, none of the four gospels hides the bewildering nature of his ministry and teaching, and particularly the obscurity—perversity, even— of Jesus' passion, death, and resurrection for his disciples as they struggled to understand him. They were witnesses to these things, but the disciples made no simple, straightforward, or immediate connections between God's purposes and the experience of the cross. The gospels are emphatic in recounting the "memories of failure" on the part of the disciples as they misunderstood, or only faintly glimpsed, the meanings that lay at the heart of Gethsemane and Golgotha. This strong gospel theme that Jesus was largely abandoned by his followers as he died on the cross, and that he was feared and doubted at his resurrection, guards us against any glibness about the nature of death: it is not a place to which many of us are eager to draw near, nor does death yield up any easy analysis or interpretation. The New Testament texts do not hide the ambiguous nature of the cross as the expression of who God is as God relates to the creation in and through Christ crucified: the death of Jesus seems like an obstacle and a folly until one receives in faith its hidden power (1 Corinthians 1:18–25). Even then, the implications of what it means for living are difficult to comprehend and

---

4. Henry Vaughan, "The Incarnation, and Passion," from *The Poetry and Selected Prose of Henry Vaughan* (Oxford, UK: Oxford University Press, 1963).

costly to implement! To invoke the cross in the bleak experience of death is not to negate the grief or pain associated with it—humans continue to experience fear and terror, loss and fury in encountering death, Christians as much as any other people—nor does the cross abolish the very real break with embodied, pulsating life that we cherish and long to hold on to. The very ambiguousness of the cross, its hidden power, asserts God's presence and full participation in the terrible place of death. What seems like disfigurement, God's participation in death in and through Christ-crucified, an abandonment of divinity in dying alone and discarded, is the presence of divine love and compassion at the point of human experience farthest from what is lovely and compelling: the hour of death.

God-with-us in death is good news, and the mystery of the cross enables us as Christians to approach the complexities of remembrance with humility and compassion. For the Christian story is that God-in-Christ is present in the experiences of death and of grief, to be encountered there as a fellow traveler and fellow sufferer. Encompassing the reality of death in the scope of God's love, the paschal mystery offers a place for grieving and for hope in the midst of grief. It is a place in which death is fully acknowledged and held. The poet Charles Causley made a poem of words found on a Normandy crucifix of 1632, a meditation on the crucified Christ which tells of the glory and the suffering of God's love in Christ, and of divine presence, deep affinity, and involvement, within human suffering and grief.

I Am the Great Sun

I am the great sun, but you do not see me,
I am your husband, but you turn away.
I am the captive, but you do not free me,
I am the captain you will not obey.

I am the truth, but you will not believe me,
I am the city where you will not stay,
I am your wife, your child, but you will leave me,
I am the God to whom you will not pray.

I am your counsel, but you do not hear me,
I am the lover whom you will betray.
I am the victor, but you do not cheer me,
I am the holy dove whom you will slay.

I am your life, but if you will not name me,
Seal up your soul with tears and never blame me.

—Charles Causley, 1917–2003[5]

Celebrating the Saints: Celebrating That Which Is of God in Others

This spiritual vision of Christ crucified, present in our bewildering mortality, is vital and compelling; yet we know that he draws us to himself to turn us toward others. On the cross he gives to his mother Mary a new son; and to his beloved disciple John a new mother (John 19:25–27). What he lays down in his death is not only a physical body, but also a body of relationships, an emotional life of friends and relatives, loves and longings. These he sacrifices along with his physical self. These God raises up; not only the resurrection of a corporeal body, but also the raising of a transformed body of relationships. It is among the gatherings of his friends that the risen Christ appears and gives his greetings of peace, breathes the Spirit, unfolds his insights of truth and blinding presence. It is in community that the risen Christ is known. Where he attends to individuals—to Mary Magdalene, to Peter, to Paul—his message is to turn them toward others with gospel proclamation and gospel care. As we encounter Christ crucified and risen in the eucharist, we encounter him in his people gathered as his body—the mystical body—the company of saints who are in Christ, within time and beyond time. To look toward others, both to the living and to the departed, is a Christ-ward perspective. To celebrate the saints, and to commemorate the departed, is to

---

5. Charles Causley, "I am the Great Sun," from *Collected Poems 1951–1997* (Basingstoke, UK: Macmillan, 1997).

see Christ *easter in others,* God's power made perfect in our human weakness.

For the Welsh poet Waldo Williams, true patriotism is to be conscious of others. He writes as a pacifist, as a socialist, and as a Welsh nationalist; for him, remembering neighbors and forbears is what makes a nation and at the same time a truly human society. He writes also as a Christian; and the answer he gives to the ancient question "What is man?" is that the compassionate act of remembering is what makes us truly human.

What Is Man?

To live, what is it? It's having
A great hall between cramped walls.
To know another, what's that? Having
The same root under the branches.

To believe, what is it? Guarding a town
Until acceptance comes.
Forgiveness, what's that? A way through thorns
To an old enemy's side.

Singing, what is it? The ancient
Genius of the creation.
What's work but making a song
Of the trees and the wheat?

To rule a kingdom, what's that? A craft
That is crawling still.
And to arm it? You put a knife
In a baby's hand.

Being a nation, what is it? A gift
In the depths of the heart.
Patriotism, what's that? Keeping house
In a cloud of witnesses.

What's the world to the strong?
Hoop a-rolling.
To the children of earth, what is it?
A cradle rocking.

—Waldo Williams, 1904–1971,
translated from Welsh by Tony Conran[6]

Writing more intimately, as a daughter, mother, and grandmother, Anne Ridler's poem, "Nothing Is Lost," asserts that
the presence of those who have gone before is always with us
and around us, if only we have the insight for it. Like many
bereaved people who are suddenly reminded of the loved one
they have lost by some object or occurrence, she mourns her
late father as she reads a Latin poem he had written for her in
his own hand. It is not that such souvenirs make the departed
person suddenly present; for her, as a Christian, they are spiritually present always in the Communion of Saints. The act
of remembering, stimulated by such objects, makes this spiritual reality apparent to us who are generally insensitive to it.
Physical resemblances in families and ethnic groups that pass
down generations link us with original Adam, and with many
others between. In touching her sleeping child, the mother
touches many babies long since dead—for in our humanness,
our mortality, in Adam, we are all one and shall all die. Yet
this very sharing, one with another, genetically, historically, is
a manifestation that we are all one in Christ, through whom
all things were made, and in whom all things shall be made
alive. For the poet, a grieving daughter who is also a tender
mother, this is a matter of profound solace: *"Nothing is lost,*
for all in love survive."

Nothing is lost

Nothing is lost.
We are too sad to know that, or too blind;
Only in visited moments do we understand:
It is not that the dead return—
They are about us always, though unguessed.

6. Waldo Williams, "What Is Man?" from *The Peacemakers: Selected Poems by*
Waldo Williams, translated by Tony Conran (London: Gomer, 1997).

This pencilled Latin verse
You dying wrote me, ten years past and more,
Brings you as much alive to me as the self you wrote it for,
    Dear father, as I read your words
    With no word but Alas.

    Lines in a letter, lines in a face
Are faithful currents of life: the boy has written
His parents across his forehead, and as we burn
    Our bodies up each seven years,
    His own past has left no plainer trace.

    Nothing dies.
The cells pass on their secrets, we betray them
Unknowingly: in a freckle, in the way
    We walk, recall some ancestor,
    And Adam in the colour of our eyes.

    Yes, on the face of the new born,
Before the soul has taken full possession,
There pass, as over a screen, in succession
    The images of other beings:
    Face after face looks out, and then is gone.

    Nothing is lost, for all in love survive.
I lay my cheek against his sleeping limbs
To feel if he is warm, and touch him
    Those children whom no shawl could warm,
    No arms, no grief, no longing could revive.

    Thus what we see, or know,
Is only a tiny portion, at the best,
Of the life in which we share; an iceberg's crest
    Our sunlit present, our partial sense,
    With deep supporting multitudes below.
                          —Anne Ridler, 1912–2001[7]

7. Anne Ridler, "Nothing Is Lost," from *Collected Poems* (London: Carcanet, 1994).

Acknowledgments

The authors, editor and publisher are grateful for permissions to include copyright material from the following sources:

Material quoted from The Book of Common Prayer, 1979, according to the use of The Episcopal Church is published by The Church Publishing Inc., and is in the public domain.

Material quoted from *Common Worship: Services and Prayers for the Church of England* (2000) and *Common Worship: Daily Prayer* (2005) is copyright The Archbishops' Council. Used by permission.

Material from *Enriching Our Worship 1* (1997), supplemental liturgical material for use in The Episcopal Church is published by Church Publishing Inc., New York.

Charles Causley, "I am the Great Sun," from *Collected Poems 1951–1997* (Basingstoke, UK: Macmillan, 1997). Used by permission.

Anne Ridler, "Nothing Is Lost," from *Collected Poems* (London: Carcanet, 1994). Used by permission.

R. S. Thomas, "Comparisons," from *Residues* (Newcastle-Upon-Tyne, UK: Bloodaxe, 2002). Used by permission.

Henry Vaughan, "The Incarnation, and Passion," from *The Poetry and Selected Prose of Henry Vaughan* (Oxford, UK: Oxford University Press, 1963). Used by permission.

Waldo Williams, "What Is Man?" from *The Peacemakers: Selected Poems by Waldo Williams*, translated by Tony Conran (London: Gomer, 1997). Used by permission.

Judith Wright, "Woman to Child," from *A Human Pattern: Selected Poems* (Sydney, New South Wales: ETT Imprint, 1992). Used by permission.

CPSIA information can be obtained
at www.ICGtesting.com
Printed in the USA
LVHW080506251019
635329LV00010B/101/P